The Development of Language and Literacy in Young Children

Third Edition

Susanna W. Pflaum
Queens College, City University
of New York

Merrill, an imprint of
Macmillan Publishing Company
New York

Maxwell Macmillan Canada
Toronto

Maxwell Macmillan International
New York Oxford Singapore Sydney

Maxwell Macmillan Canada, Inc.
1200 Eglinton Avenue East
Suite 200
Don Mills, Ontario M3C 3N1

Production Editor and Text Designer: Susan King
Cover Design Coordinator: Cathy Watterson
This book was set in Palatino.

Photo Credits: cover, p. 169, Bruce Johnson; pp. 1, 3, Celia Drake; pp. 25, 105, Ben Chandler; p. 51, Constance Brown; p. 73, Janet Cagnon; pp. 103, 143, Lloyd Lemmerman; p. 201, Jean Greenwald.

This book was published previously under the title, *The Development of Language and Reading in Young Children*.

Library of Congress Catalog Card Number: 85-43231
International Standard Book Number: 0-675-20447-X
Printed in the United States of America

Print 5 6 7 8 9   Year 1 2 3 4 5

Preface

Readers familiar with previous editions of this book will find the third edition of *The Development of Language and Literacy in Young Children* quite changed. During the interim between 1978 and now, exciting and important work in literacy and language has changed the entire face of these fields. The most important change probably began with the work on the role of communication in language development. Scholars interested in emerging literacy found considerable value in the concepts and methods developed from findings in the study of language acquisition. The integration of these fields has enabled us to better understand both language and literacy development. In writing this third edition, it was my intention to extend the integrated fields as a metaphor for informal and formal learning and to bring this viewpoint to the readers of this book.

As educators search for greater understanding of how oral language, writing, and reading interact during the developing stages, it is important to recognize how families influence preparedness for formal learning. Preschool and primary grade instruction ought to include basic literacy experiences for all children and especially for those children who have less home preparation. Attention to these concerns represents the most substantive change in this new edition of the book.

Another important change is reflected in the book's changed title. Instead of "reading," the new title uses the word "literacy." We are very much indebted to those educators who have broadened our views to include writing development as integral to early learning.

All fields profit from lively controversies, and ours is no exception. I have tried to be fair-minded about literary issues regarding the education of young children. On one issue, however, my comments may appear to be one-sided: the use of basal reading programs. My comments are meant to heighten awareness of teacher development needs. As teachers take greater control over decisions about materials, directions, and the substance of their talk in class, their pupils benefit considerably. I believe teacher ability to make independent decisions about instruction is very important, and I have tried to represent this position in the new edition.

I am grateful to several people for their advice. Elizabeth Sulzby reviewed Chapter 3 for me when I really needed it; Victoria Hare read and commented on nearly all of the chapters. University of Illinois at Chicago graduate students in my Winter 1985 course read and commented on many chapters; Melanie Pflaum served as my undergraduate critic, and Joseph Grannis helped me through several difficult points, particularly the development of my "accordian metaphor" (Chapter 5). I also appreciate the comments of those unknown critics who read the entire manuscript. I profited by the criticism of all. And yet another group helped me enormously: the children of my friends and colleagues; James and Camille Blachowicz, Elizabeth Sulzby and Mitchell Rousie, Victoria and Russell Hare, and William and Ann Schubert. Moreover, without the understanding and interest of many colleagues at the University of Illinois at Chicago, I do not think I could have completed this task. Finally, my thanks also go to the people at Charles E. Merrill who kept this project moving smoothly, especially Beverly Kolz and Susan King. Throughout this process, I fear I neglected family and friends; I particularly want to thank Joe for his support and to thank my children, Melanie and William, for their help throughout.

Susanna W. Pflaum

Contents

PART I

Language Growth During the Preschool Years

1 Language Beginnings: Different Viewpoints

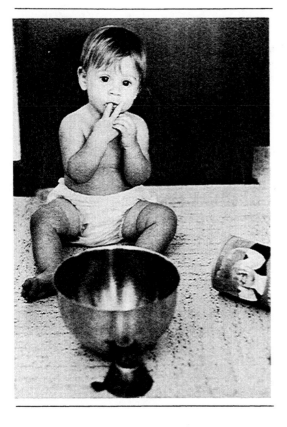

Three of us, all professors interested in reading and language, are preparing to eat dinner. The hostess has let one of us hold her two-month-old daughter. The baby coos in sequence with her temporary caretaker as he entices her with soft sounds and lots of smiles. Her coos appear after his vocalizations; the reciprocal exchanges seem like a dialogue, and we agree, it is like she is talking. Yet, of course, it will be many months before she uses real words to refer to real things. But we want to believe the process of language has started.[1]

Among different people, there are different views about where language starts. For example, the Kaluli people of Papua, New Guinea, according to Schiefflin and Ochs (1983), do not think a baby can talk until he or she uses the words for "mother" and "breast." Kaluli adults would not make our inferences that nonverbal exchanges are like talking. Apparently, the adults talk to their babies only after the emergence of the two critical words, and then in a three- or four-way conversation rather than in our common two-way exchanges.

The language skills of small children are amazing. A little girl who I recently had dinner with, and *who will not be three for four months*, asked me, "Will you get a carrot stick for me?" and, when I did, said, "Thank you." Her request is not only amazingly well-constructed and quite complex for her age, but it also exhibits understanding of the social functions of language which included such directly taught social comments as "Thank you."

And early language is creative. Children puzzle in interesting ways through language items they do not understand. My daughter, at age three, when guests she admired were leaving for Miami, asked, "Can I go to my ami, too?" And, when her parents were busily preparing for an oncoming hurricane, she asked in a worried voice, "Is a hurricane big and hairy?"

INTRODUCTION

The process of language learning is a challenge for us to understand, a challenge that has attracted the interest of scholars for years. Children move very quickly from that first cooing stage to competent three-year-olds with advanced social skills. The "errors" children make, like my daughter's, cause us to ask about the learning process and about our role in it. One goal of this book is to find answers to these questions. How do these language skills develop so rapidly? What is the role of the family in the process? Language is so complicated; does learning it quickly suggest anything about learning to read and to write?

An amazingly swift and creative process, nearly all children learn to understand language and to react through talk in just a few years (except for some severely disabled children). Children in nonliterate Papua, New Guinea; in the underclass of rich, industrial nations; in tiny Eskimo communities; and in affluent American suburbs all acquire substantial language skills by the age of four. Among the different explanations of child language growth, one explanation by

---

[1] The children whose language examples I refer to are friends, most of whom are the children of professors. My thanks to each of them and to their parents who all have been consulted about the inclusion of the children's utterances.

scholars of child language (e.g., McNeil 1970) states that human infants are naturally and genetically prepared to learn language; little specific direction is needed beyond the existence of language in the environment for its appearance in toddlers. Others believe that the context of adult and baby interchange provides a special environment requisite to language learning (i.e., Bruner 1983; Garvey 1984; Golinkoff and Gordon 1983). Varied observations and theories about language occupy the discussion of this first chapter; in later chapters, similar concerns about literacy are addressed. Another important goal for this book is to examine these issues for their educational implications; thus, I have drawn on theory to indicate specific directions for instruction.

A fundamental tenet of the discussions to follow is that professionals need to acquire knowledge to construct a workable model from which to design their practice. Experts serve us well when they demonstrate the knowledge supports of theory. When scholars make a new observation or uncover some new fact, they point out how it fits with their theory. If new facts do not fit, the theory must be modified or abandoned. Similarly, we need to learn the theoretical and empirical supports for instruction in order to build a model for instruction that has direction and consistency. Teachers working from a sound theoretical base make informed decisions about new ideas and practices, design instructional activities that meet the needs of their students, and continue to develop good instruction. Such a base comes from knowledge of the theories developed by scholars. Knowing the strengths and weaknesses of different explanations for the same phenomena enables us to more wisely select among educational alternatives. An important part of this book is the inclusion of instructional suggestions. I hope these suggestions will help this book's readers develop a workable model that will serve their teaching well.

To learn about language is to learn a fascinating story. We adults love to watch babies progress from crawling to walking and, finally, to skillful activities such as running and skipping. But we only can *watch* motor development. With language, the growth from early cooing through babbling, first words, primitive sentences, and real sentences is even more intriguing because as children acquire new language skills, they communicate with others. Thus, we not only are able to watch, but we also are able to *participate* in the communication. The communicative content of language learning is a major clue to understanding the processes of early literacy and language. Interactive communication forms the basis of the instructional suggestions in this book.

A set of suggested activities for readers appears at the conclusion of this and subsequent chapters. Some activities involve actual observation; some entail the rethinking of issues raised, and some require further exploration. The activities enable interested readers to assimilate the material in new, less didactic ways and to apply it to new situations. These sections are an integral part of each chapter; they provide for communication between the reader and author.

This first chapter presents different explanations for language learning and cognitive development. While much of the material presents alternative viewpoints, the purpose is to provide information so that we can construct a workable model to understand the process of language learning. The first section describes language learning within a cognitive development framework as we focus on the work of Piaget and of Vygotsky. The second section focuses on different explanations for language growth. In the final section, we sift through the ideas of the scholars in an attempt to produce an amalgam of theory and observation about language growth that will serve as a model for both informal and formal instruction.

LANGUAGE AND COGNITIVE DEVELOPMENT

An issue of interest to scholars and teachers alike is whether children's cognitive development depends on the emergence of language or whether children learn to think and thus are enabled to learn language. If cognitive development motivates language learning, then schooling would respond by putting greater emphasis on thinking rather than on reading and writing skills. However, if language learning enhances cognitive development, then educating would emphasize advanced literacy. But it is difficult to consider the separateness of these processes because language is inexorably intertwined with thought.

Most examples of complex thinking are verbal in Western society; indeed, our society prizes verbal ability as a mark of education and success. Our strong verbal orientation makes it difficult to recognize nonverbal characteristics, which, as we will see in the following discussion, probably mark many children's early cognitive activities. Our question revolves around the role of language in the ability to reason, to solve problems, to plan.

We will start our study of this question with a brief introduction to the work of two important thinkers. Jean Piaget and Lev Vygotsky were two developmentalists whose works have been—and continue to be—strong influences on our thinking about how language and thinking grow and intersect. Piaget's and Vygotsky's theories provide bases for a beginning understanding of growth and the adult (parent, teacher) role in learning. These elements are critical to our understanding of the role of education. While we will find differences in Piaget's and Vygotsky's interpretations of how much language growth influences cognitive growth, there are commonalities in the scholars' interpretations. Both Piaget and Vygotsky described the learner, including the language learner, as engaged in actively structuring a system through which to understand the world.

Piaget

Although there are varied interpretations of his work and there is evidence that some of his concepts are incomplete, much of the thinking about how children construct a system for interpreting their world comes from the work of the famous Swiss scholar, Jean Piaget. Piaget's major study involved how infants, children, and adolescents build logical thought. However, he also was interested in language, at least in early publications ([1926] 1955). Close colleagues of Piaget, such as Sinclair-deZwart (1973), have worked more directly with developmental language within the Piaget framework of logical, cognitive development.

We will review a few major Piagetian concepts of children's cognitive development before analyzing his position on language. For Piaget, cognitive development, from the very beginnings of life through adolescence, is marked by individuals' active and unconscious structuring of the input they perceive in the environment. That is, children deal only with those aspects of their world out of which they can make sense. In Piaget's terminology, children *assimilate* environmental input into their present cognitive structure. If the input is new and adds a new dimension to their thinking, their thought patterns are modified or changed by *accommodation*. Assimilation and accommodation are the basic processes by which individuals learn.

During the first year of life, even before language is acquired (the *sensori-motor stage*), children begin to figure out their own reality for themselves. Infants' thoughts during this stage are tied to actions or specific sensory qualities of stimuli. Children's first words also are tied to the actions they perform or observe. By the end of the period, at about eighteen months, children have arrived at a point where they think of themselves as separate objects in a world made up of permanent objects and can perform simple problem-solving tasks. By this age, children begin to view objects as separate from themselves (Furth 1970).

After the start of the *preoperational period*, which begins at about eighteen months and continues to about age seven, a number of important changes occur in children's cognitive development. The new *cognitive* abilities acquired during this period are determined largely by children's ability to symbolize. Children in the sensori-motor stage learn that objects have permanence; at the beginning of the preoperational stage, children master the use of objects to represent other objects and situations in play and thinking. When children pretend that blocks of various sizes "stand" for a family, their symbolic play demonstrates their representation of familiar family groups in another medium. Children at this stage of development also begin to make drawings, which help to organize their thinking. Although the drawings may not appear to be realistic to the adult observer, they are intended to be. Drawings help children develop mental images of objects. Finally, during the early part of this stage, children develop the ability to form real mental images of objects not present. Once they have formed mental images and once they have labels for these images, children comment on and describe absent objects and past events (Piaget and Inhelder 1969).

Piaget was concerned with the role of language in the development of thought for many years. In 1926, he published a book entitled *The Language and Thought of the Child* ([1926] 1955), which examined the function of the speech of children at play with other children. He found a great preponderance of *egocentric speech* among preschool children, with a greater amount of *socialized speech* emerging in children over the age of seven. Egocentric speech is centered essentially on one's own actions; children talk aloud to and about themselves even when in the presence of other children. Socialized speech involves real dialogue; information and questions are provided in an interactive situation. Piaget's later studies (Piaget and Inhelder 1969) have shown that the amount of egocentric speech in preschool children diminishes under certain circumstances; for example, when children converse with adults. And Shatz and Gelman (1973) confirmed that children adapt their speech in this way. Four-year-old participants in the Shatz and Gelman study used more complex structures when talking with adults than with their two-year-old siblings.

Generally, though, children appear to talk for and to themselves about their play and activities. It is important to note that, according to Piaget (1926), the egocentric speech of young children does not determine their behavior; it is a *verbal accompaniment to behavior.* Piaget's work suggests that language in its functional use is limited to a level of sophistication that already has been achieved in cognitive development. In his theory, cognitive development determines the course of language growth.

Sinclair-deZwart (1973) states that human infants acquire language out of the cognitive structures already learned during the sensori-motor stage. Early language is described as one way to represent events and objects in the world. According to Sinclair-deZwart, children at one-and-a-half have a stable understanding of action on objects and object permanence, including notions of anticipation. Brown (1973) found that there were several basic understandings expressed in the early language of children at this stage. These included naming, making references to recurring events, commenting on the nonexistence of objects and actions, describing doer-action ideas, describing action-object notions, and identifying possessor and possessed, for example. The early "sentences" produced by young children reflect the level and kind of cognitive understandings that Piaget and his colleagues noted in children's cognitive structures.

According to Piaget, language ability generally is determined by the level achieved in cognitive development; however, there are points where language does stimulate cognitive growth to a certain extent. For example, language enables children to detach thought from action at the start of the preoperational stage. Thus, thought becomes symbolic, and because language too is inherently symbolic, it becomes the natural medium for representing absent objects and past events. This ability to represent is a hallmark of the beginning of the preoperational stage, and language is one important source used by children as they move into this stage.

Although language does not contribute to the development of logical behavior, it is recognized as a tool of instruction in cognitive development for children who are in transition to the *concrete-operational period* of development. In a study conducted by four of Piaget's colleagues in Geneva (Inhelder et al. 1966), the effect of language training on success in conservation tasks was examined. Experiments examining the influence of language and other factors on the achievement of conservation by children between ages four and eight showed that:

> First, language training, among other types of training, operates to direct the child's interactions with the environment and thus to "focus" on relevant dimensions of task situations. Second, the observed changes in the

justifications given (by the subjects) for answers in the conservation task suggest that language does aid in the storage and retrieval of relevant information. However, our evidence offers little, if any, support for the contention that language training per se contributes to the *integration and coordination* of "informational units" necessary for the achievement of the conservation concepts. Language learning does not provide, in our opinion, a ready-made "lattice" or lens which organizes the child's perceptual world.[2]

Piaget's developmental theories explain how individuals construct mental systems with which they can make sense of the world. Language acquisition reflects the stage of thinking that a child has reached. Generally, those who interpret Piaget's theories for their educative implications stress the need to provide children with appropriate objects and events that will provide strong experiences on which to build systems of understanding (Kamii and DeVries 1977; Furth 1970). Similarly, Piagetians think the best pedagogical strategies engage children in activity appropriate to the youngsters' current level of thinking (Kamii and DeVries 1977). Teachers should question children so that the youngsters focus upon the point of conflict between current thinking and evidence that current thinking is not sufficient to explain the data before them. The teacher's role is to support the growth of thinking rather than to try to cause a change in thinking for which children are not prepared.

An Example from Literacy Acquisition

Ferreiro has observed young preschoolers' early experiences with literacy within a Piagetian framework (1984; Ferreiro and Teberosky 1982). In a recent paper (forthcoming), she describes one boy's adherence to an interpretation he made about letters. From information supplied by his parents, the boy interpreted that "S," for example, was *his* letter since his name had "S" at the start (Santiago), just as other name initial letters *belonged* to other people, his friends, and family. That idea, one he structured on his own, served him well as he learned about some letters; ultimately, the idea came to constrict his acquisition of the concept that letters are used regularly in different contexts to represent sounds. Although confronted with a lot more information, Santiago held to this notion because he had built an entire system upon it. Only after he experienced supportive learnings and new deductions about letters was he able to adjust his idea that letters "belonged" to people and to learn that letters were used to represent linguistic information rather than actual people. The many questions he had been asked by adults did not appear to alter his thinking. Ferreiro explained that only Santiago could shift this thinking, and he would do so only when prepared and after figuring out many other things about letters and words. Yet, we might wonder about the effect of many adult questions that Santiago received about

---

[2]B. Inhelder, et al., "On Cognitive Development," *American Psychologist* 21 (1966): 160–64.

words and letters, questions that included no explanation. Ferreiro implies that such questioning has no critical influence on thinking. As we turn to Vygotsky, however, we find a theory that characterizes the adult role in cognitive and language development as much more important.

Vygotsky

Until 1962, scholars outside of the Soviet Union were not aware of Vygotsky's work in psychology and education. Although he died in 1934 as a young man, he already had produced a great deal of work that still is having an impact on our thinking today. Moreover, he left behind a cohort of Soviet scholars who have continued in his tradition. His two major translated works are *Thought and Language* (U.S. publication, 1962) and *Mind in Society* (U.S. publication, 1978).

According to Vygotsky, children learn through maturation and the stimulation of social interactions. Like the Marxist concept of the dialectic, Vygotsky believed that development occurs as innate, biological maturation meets with the experiences of social interactions. Vygotsky describes two kinds of symbol systems in interaction. One symbol system, called *signs*, consists of internalized representations. The other, *tools*, deals with the external world of observables: objects and language. First, the use of tools by language learners mediates the organization, categorization, and integration of experiences. As children interact with objects and as they acquire labels for objects and actions through adult labelling, they learn the tools of the world. These tools gradually are internalized into categorical patterns of thinking, *concept clusters*. When these patterns are internalized in thinking, they become signs and are used to represent world knowledge through the system, which filters further actions upon the world. This differentiation between tools and signs is clear when comparing the communications of humans and of primates in the wild. Primates have the ability to signal (to warn of danger, for example), and they use tools. (Van Lawick-Goodall [1971] described chimps' use of narrow sticks to get ants to eat.) Their inability to integrate tools into signs and to generate signs for new situations marks the difference between them and humans and explains their inability to acquire language naturally. (But see the following to discover what occurs when primates are taught forms of human communication.)

As Piaget uses the concept of *egocentric speech* to characterize the monologuing of language-learning children, Vygotsky refers to *external speech* (1962). For Vygotsky, though, external speech is the child's mechanism for planning and conceptualizing, the means through which thinking develops rather than simply a representation of the child's focus upon self. Through external speech, children organize, plan, and find solutions. As children gain conceptual sophistication and as they manipulate signs, external speech becomes internalized. Vygotsky (1978) reported that external speech was more evident as children experienced greater difficulty in solving tasks and when adult help was removed. Thus, children revert to earlier mechanisms to help them think through difficult problems.

Vygotsky's Zone of Proximal Development

Vygotsky views communication with others as an important ingredient in the young child's expanding capabilities. Adults provide the names; they give directions and suggestions, and they gradually reduce the extent of their language help as children become more competent. Vygotsky describes a *zone of proximal development* (1978) to operationalize the role of the teacher. The zone " . . . is the distance between the actual development level as determined by independent problem solving and the level of potential development as determined through problem solving under adult guidance or in collaboration with more capable peers" (p. 86). According to Vygotsky, instruction should occur in the zone between the child's independent level and the level at which he or she can operate with adult help. In application to the language-learning child, learning probably takes place somewhere between where the child operates when speaking in monologue and the more advanced level he or she uses when in dialogue with adults. The zone of proximal development provides us with a strong explanation for the adult role in language acquisition.

Vygotsky's position is clear. Language is a major stimulant for conceptual growth, and conceptual growth is also dependent on interaction with objects in the environment. Moreover, adults (and older children) have a role in stimulating language growth through a variety of means. Finally, the zone of proximal development is the locus where that help should occur. For example, in the lengthy and difficult process of learning relative terms such as *more* and *less* (described in Donaldson and Balfour 1968), Vygotsky's theory suggests that adults not only name the terms in context, but that the adults also use explanation and comparison to specify—in words and actions—the relationships between terms.

This clear instructional role that adults play in children's learning is, of course, in contrast with Piaget's position. Another point of contrast concerns the interpretations of children's monologues. For Vygotsky, external speech represents the first step toward internalizing thinking. As described previously, for Piaget, monologues represent the current thinking level and do not stimulate further growth, which only comes through the action upon objects taking place as monologuing may occur.

Using the zone of proximal development notion, we may imagine the teacher as stimulating the child to expand a step beyond current functioning and to extend language levels within the zone. As we examine the descriptions of adult-child dialogue by language acquisition scholars in the following sections, we can see that adults apparently "up the ante" as they make it clear that children are expected to supply more advanced input during exchanges. (Snow 1983)

While the differences between Piaget and Vygotsky are fairly clear, it should be noted that the similarities are strong, too, and it is important to understand them. Both scholars posit a developmental trend in cognitive functioning characterized first by unstable responses to present objects and events, later by a perspective on objects and events that allows for more stable responses, then by invariant responses to objects and events, and finally, by the ability to abstract.

In the writings of both, cognitive growth is described as emanating from within a system constructed by the learner based on the learner's interpretation of his or her experiences.

Our understanding of learning is enriched enormously by the theories of development; curricula in the schools today reflect these contributions. For example, in Chapter 5, the preschool programs based on Piaget's theory are described as promoting children's independence in thinking and social responsibility. Teachers do not attempt to insert new learnings into children's behaviors; instead, educators build an environment that encourages the emergence of new modes of thought. Vygotsky's influence in education is changing how we interpret children's reading and writing (Johnson 1984). We are being encouraged to examine children's productions for evidence of how they understand the world and the academic tasks rather than for correctness. Traces of these theories also exist in the explanations for language by scholars of language acquisition.

EXPLANATIONS FOR LANGUAGE: CONTRASTING VIEWS

Although the task of explaining language acquisition is formidable, it fascinates scholars from a variety of fields. Perhaps they are attracted by the complexity. Certainly, they are dealing with a fundamental characteristic of humankind. What intrigues these linguists, psychologists, and educators is that within a brief part of the preschool period, most children learn hundreds of words. These youngsters acquire the word order and ending rules (syntactic structures) of the language and they communicate with a variety of people. They adjust their level of talk to their audience, and many have sufficient experience with written language to begin to experience the excitement of literacy.

It is not easy to explain the phenomenon of language acquisition. Such an explanation requires a broad account for both the creativity of the early structures and their consistency of use. It requires that word acquisition and that the role of interpersonal communication be explained. Furthermore, any explanation must be concerned with both natural maturation and the role of adult teaching. At this point, no theory that meets these criteria has been developed, at least as far as this writer knows. But by comparing different explanations, we can begin to understand the fundamental dimensions of meeting these criteria, and we can begin to gain insights about language learning that are likely to remain a part of any encompassing theory.

The part of language learning that is explained by the different scholars depends, in some measure, on which part of the language is initially deemed most important. Thus, those with a strong *behaviorist* background focus upon a rather limited field: the aspects of observable language that can be explained by imitative responses. Those who hold a *nativist* position (often those influenced by more modern linguistic and psychological theory) identify aspects of children's language that demonstrate an innate propensity for language with no apparent origin in the environment. And the third—and newest—group we study, those with a *communication* focus, look to the features of the communicative dialogue for clues to language learning. Out of these differences, we hope to gain an understanding of language growth consistent with the cognitive development theories of Piaget and Vygotsky.

The Behaviorist Position

Until twenty-five years ago, behaviorism was the common explanation for language learning. Today, the influence of behaviorism still can be seen in American schools (in systems of instruction that identify and have children attain a series of skills to reach competence, for example). During its heyday, the behaviorist theory was the basis for understanding language. Like other forms of human (and animal) knowledge, behavior was described as composed of discrete items. Behaviorists only deal with what can be observed. They examined language behavior for its patterns, and they used the patterns to reveal the steps to be met in learning. Inferred principles that appeared to regulate patterns of behavior were summarized as laws of behavior and learning.

Skinner (1957) defined verbal behavior as the observed, produced speech that occurs during the interaction of speaker and listener. He saw thinking as the internalized manifestation of speaking and listening. In this explanation, both overt language and thought appeared to originate in environmental interactions, including those that occur between parent and child.

Thus far, the behaviorist explanation for language learning parallels that of Vygotsky. (And, for that matter, so does the communicative theory that is described later in this chapter.) However, the characteristics of the personal interactions described by the behaviorists differ significantly from those of other explanations (DeCecco 1967). The behaviorist school's position states, roughly, that the adult role is to provide the model (such as words and phrases), which the child acquires through imitation. The process involves reinforcement by the adult, which encourages the child to try again and again and to attempt closer approximations of the model. Continued reinforcement of the "word" or other response in similar settings (in the presence of similar persons or objects) results in habitual responses. The conditions in which the reinforcers operate influence the extent of habituation of the response. Thus, Skinner thought responses were "conditioned." For example, long before other sentences appeared, one child of 1.2 (1 year, two months) said, *"Let's go bye-bye,"* probably an imitated item.

Applied to a specific language learning situation, one may imagine an infant making a series of babbling sounds (syllable repetitions) in the presence of a parent ("dada" at .9, or 9 months). When the sequence resembles "dada," enthusiastic response shapes the vocalization and its association with the condition of the parent's presence to not only resemble, but also to mean, "daddy."

It is more difficult to use the behaviorist theory (theories) to explain the acquisition of children's sentences. According to Braine (1963), for example, learning to place words in appropriate sentence slots requires that children learn simple sentence word order rules from adult language. Through imitation of simple and repeatedly ordered sentences, children learn the expected sequence of words. Previously acquired words then may be placed in the proper positions as the sequences are learned. For example, the child who says, on the same day, "Where's Daddy? Where's Judy? Where's Jocelyn's doll?" is effectively applying new words to a learned routine. To accept this statement is to accept the notion that the sentences children hear conform to precise patterns; we will see this notion is of dubious verity.

The behaviorist position stresses the importance of the environment in language learning. The environment, composed of object and people stimuli, also includes the specific conditions under which responses occur. Thus, the environment includes both models upon which language growth depends and feedback to child utterances, which shapes and encourages growth. While we find that much of the behaviorist thinking has been severely criticized, the theory contains several important notions that we will discuss. Today, these features of the environment—the provision of the model and the structure of the feedback— are considered to be important to language and literacy learning, although they now are defined somewhat differently. Moreover, the emphasis by behaviorists on the environment of learning has led educators to examine closely the context of the learning materials in schools. The concept that school curricular topics are best established through a new kind of task analysis came out of the work of the behaviorist school. This concept underlies much of the curricular reform since the 1960s.

Criticism of the Behaviorist Explanation

Many features of the behaviorist approach have been criticized. Chomsky (1959) found that Skinner's work failed because it offered explanation for only a small part of language, because it relied on research conducted on animals, because it provided essentially vague descriptions of essential terms (for example, "reinforcer" has been used quite broadly), because it depended upon the quality of the language input (adult language is not a perfect model), and because part of the explanation required belief that the learning of language is motivated by the child's need. The atomistic nature of the behaviors studied has bothered many critics.

If language, like other behaviors, were simply the accumulation of habituated responses and imitations that become words through reinforcement, then perhaps higher primates such as chimpanzees could learn language in the appropriate environment. Study of chimps in the wild indicates that their only natural "speech" consists of a set of signs that are always the same and applied to similar situations (Van Lawick-Goodall 1971). This "speech" does not resemble the generative, creative character of even very young humans' language. There have been attempts, of course, to train chimps in laboratories (see Nelson 1980), and these attempts have provided a good test of the assumptions of behaviorism.

Several chimps have learned to communicate through sign language, both initiating signs and responding to them. Another chimp has learned to combine tokens representing simple concepts and to do so spontaneously (Brown 1973). And at least one case exists of a gorilla whose sign language is quite impressive

(Patterson 1980). These primate training programs have bypassed the vocal organs in the learning of primitive language. To date, this learning has resulted from intensive, direct instruction, in contrast to the apparent informal contexts in which young humans acquire language. In contrasting chimp and human "language," Brown (1973) points out that human language is also unique in its power to transmit knowledge and culture, in its astounding variety of structures, and in its independence of situation (we can describe a different place and time to another person). In spite of the chimps' impressive learning, the human language learning capacity is significantly different.

We can test the behaviorist theory in another way by examining the question of children's imitations: the quantity and quality of their spontaneous imitations of adult language. A study by Ervin (1964) examined children's spontaneous imitations. It suggested that they are never more advanced in syntactic structure than are other nominative sentences. Further, she found that there are relatively few direct imitations and therefore concluded that there must be other methods for children to acquire their language. Brown and Hanlon (1970) found that parents do not even react to the "correctness" of their children's utterances; the parents are interested in the content, not the form, of the statements. The explanation that the parent is a reinforcer is weakened by this finding and others.

However, Kuczaj (1983) recently has found that children do imitate some of the single words spoken to them. Imitation is one source for language learning within children's current levels. But other scholars generally do not adhere to imitation as a strong explanation for language learning due to the extent of children's invented sentences (see Chapter 2). Invention simply would not be characteristic of one acquiring language through imitation.

While much of the essential character of the behaviorist theory is no longer supported in current thinking, certain aspects of the theory should influence our answers to some important questions. How, for example, can we explain the fact that children learn the words that are used in their environment? What is the role of adult models and other environmental factors in language acquisition; does the behaviorist explanation help? We turn now to a very different explanation for language, one that negates the prominence of environmental factors and emphasizes native ability. This theory first began with Chomsky (1965) and ultimately was called the "nativist" position when developed further by others.

The Nativist Theory

The linguist Chomsky presented a very different view of language (1965), one based on the idea that language is creative and develops innately. He described language as generated from underlying concepts; his generative grammar (a systematic description of language) caused a revolution among linguists, and it even influenced psychology. Partly because of his work and partly because of a natural shift of the pendulum that occurs in scholarly work, much current psychology is focused upon cognitive processes. Cognitive psychologists infer complex thinking processes from a variety of data and thus go beneath the surface behaviors. These scholars' interest in language, for example, includes questions about comprehension and interpretation in addition to speech production.

In his rejection of the Skinner paper, Chomsky (1959) described adult language input and the patterns of interaction between adult and child as devoid of much (not all) value to the language learning child. He speculated that children have an innate ability to acquire language as maturation triggers points of growth. The innateness may be seen in children's propensity to create language items that have not been heard before and that are unique (such as one child's "Cracker butter" and another's "Pour little cup drink Heidi" and "Froggy shut the mouth"). Chomsky (1965) and McNeil (1970) expanded this notion and suggested that children, simply by being human, acquire language inductively from the language in the environment rather than from the particular speech events of individual persons. Chomsky and McNeil explain that this inductive acquisition occurs through something similar to a *Language Acquisition Device* (LAD). This "device" is really a hypothesis, and McNeil stated that what happens in the description of LAD is similar to what happens with children (1966). According to this idea, LAD receives input from the language in the environment and analyzes it. The makeup of LAD enables the induction of rules based on the data. These rules then are the basis for the language that is produced, a means for expressing ideas. The rules are implicit, not like those of a game; they are principles of organization (for example, something like an unconscious knowledge that, *"When you have a proper noun followed by a common noun, it means possession, with the first the possessor"*).

Nativists believe children do what LAD does. Dependent on the youngsters' level of maturation, language features of the environment are selected and unconsciously structured to form a generating rule system for language output. The rule system is generative as maturation continues and as children can handle greater complexity; previously constructed rules are modified and new ones are formed to generate more complex language output. Each child's rule system is being modified constantly by his or her interpretation of the language of the environment; as a result, the increasingly complex set of rules forms the basis of increasingly complex language output.

Lenneberg (1967) extended this theory into biological terms. According to his argument, if language were considered specific to the species, then, logically, one might expect all children to learn to talk. And, indeed, nearly all children do learn language and do so without any overt adult training, as Lenneberg defines training. There are, of course, a very few children who do not learn much language because of severe neglect and some others who do not develop much language because of a physical disorder or a severe nervous disability. However, these children are in a distinct minority when compared with the number of children who learn language normally. Even in the case of disabled children, it often is surprising how much language is acquired; except for severe cases, handicapped and retarded children do learn some language. Studies indicate that comprehension and oral ability do not need to go hand in hand. Lenneberg (1967) reported a case of a nonverbal boy studied from age four to age nine. At four, he could not babble; he was totally inarticulate. At nine, after intensive training, he could say a word with great difficulty and then only if an adult said it with him. However, tests of language understanding indicated that he had near normal passive comprehension of language and its structure. Apparently, language comprehension develops even under most difficult situations, and speech is not necessary for its growth.

Another piece of evidence for the nativist position is that language, defined here as the time when words are combined into first sentences, begins within a consistent time range across cultural and social groups. From age 18 to 24 months, all children begin to combine words and start sentences (Brown 1973; Lenneberg 1967; McNeil 1966). Lenneberg (1967) also reported instances of hearing children born to deaf parents, who cannot reinforce the speech they do not hear, begin to speak at about the same time as children growing up in a normal family. Lenneberg's studies also indicate that position in the family does not appear to affect the time when language begins; the findings show that second and third children begin to speak at the same age as do the first children, in spite of the fact that parents often show more interest in the language beginnings of first children. Once they begin, first children may learn more language, but, according to Lenneberg, all normal children appear to begin to acquire language at approximately the same time.

Nativist proponents point to children's apparent ease of learning language. According to Lenneberg (and in contrast with later scholars), it is impossible to find factors in the environment of young children that will account for language change. The home does not provide situations that specifically propel children into new language forms (Lenneberg 1967). Children's readiness and the provision of language models around them appear to be enough to precipitate language acquisition. In Lenneberg's view, the motivator for language acquisition is inside children; it is their natural language learning ability.

The language scholars who worked within the nativist framework examined children's language quite apart from the adult language that surrounds children's language. These scholars proposed rules that appeared to account for the children's language. For example, Brown and his colleagues (Bloom 1970; Brown 1973; Brown and Bellugi 1964; Brown and Fraser 1964; Brown, Cazden, and Bellugi-Klima 1968) analyzed early sentence combinations that involved two- and three-word sentences to try to characterize the linguistic rules that account for the constructions; these scholars thereby operated with the assumption that an identifiable grammatical structure existed. And, indeed, as we will see in Chapter 2, there are commonalities in the syntax (grammatical structure) of children's language; nativists present the commonalities as universal rules that are indicative of a natural phenomenon.

Criticism of the Nativist Explanation

When Bloom (1970) discussed the now famous (among child language scholars) child remark, "Mommy sock," a difficulty with the nativist position appeared. It became clear that context of use ought to be considered in the study of language learning. The child in question could have meant in one instance that Mommy was putting on the child's sock; in this case, the child had generated a simple subject-predicate sentence. In another context, the remark could have meant the sock that belonged to mommy, a possessor-possessed production. Clearly, a full explanation of child language had to accurately reflect consideration of meaning intention, and the nativists had studied syntactic growth rather exclusively.

Nativists produced a too narrow view of language, according to some child language scholars (Golinkoff and Gordon 1983). Difficulties arose with the nativist position when the adult role was considered. After an extensive review of the studies that had attempted to explore the adult role in language acquisition and to search among the cognitive theories, Brown (1973) concluded that little was known yet about how adults might influence child language. But shortly, the first of many studies of dialogue between adult and child were to add to the beginning explorations. A series of studies by Cazden (1966) and others reported by McNeil (1970) produced inconclusive evidence that adult *expansions,* deliberate adult repetitions of child remarks with increased complexity, advanced children's language. Moreover, the influence of adult prompts, thought to be potential helps to the language learning child, had not been examined.

As a result of new questions and observations, many scholars broadened their search for language growth explanations; the new work, which studied the communicative context for language learning, forms the substance of the next section. Even though the nativists seem to have neglected part of the child language acquisition story, they have made significant contributions to our understanding, and their description of children's early grammar has not been seriously questioned. Because nativists drew attention to language as a representation of internally generated rules, language was correctly viewed as something beyond the superficial appearance of utterances. The focus on the child's natural propensity to learn language emphasized that language acquisition was a complex process worthy of further inquiry. The study of child language in the last ten years has involved a broad look into the environment in which language is learned.

A Communicative Focus

A Review of Material Thus Far

Let us review the ideas presented thus far, ideas which have led to the work described in this section. Piaget and Vygotsky outlined stages in cognitive development that were remarkably alike given the scholars' geographical and theoretical distance from one another. Piaget's characterization of the mental structures that children build for themselves through interactions with objects and events is a strong reminder to educators that children fit new experiences into existing systems. With the example of Ferreiro's Santiago, we saw how invariant those systems can be. Vygotsky concluded that learning was more susceptible to adult direction than did Piaget. According to Vygotsky, adults partly lead children into language; yet, the extent of growth is also determined by existing structures. The zone of proximal development is hypothesized as the locus for adult influence.

Specific explanations for language growth each make sound contributions to our understanding, too. The behaviorist theory, with its historical and contrastive value, was found to be weak because of its overemphasis on the surface features of language. Moreover, it is not compatible with either developmentalist; indeed, it is antithetical to their views. Nevertheless, the behaviorists did attempt to clarify the teaching/learning features of the environment. The nativists, on the other hand, largely ignored such factors, at least initially. These scholars focused instead on the apparently self-generating structures of children's language. Ultimately, this position too was found to be inadequate to fully explain language growth.

Communication in Child Language Acquisition

Such lively shifts and debates are marks of an active and important field of study. The problems with the nativist position caused a new shift in the pendulum. As with every theoretical shift, scholars looked specifically at the weakest point in the nativist theory. They looked at the question of the adult role in the teaching-learning of language. According to observations by Bruner (1975), an important scholar in developmental theory and language acquisition, parent-child exchanges are the locus for the start of learning; they provide the roots of emergent language. Further, these parent-child exchanges begin in the first weeks of life, and even at the beginning, they carry some essential features of conversation. Parents use exaggerated speech and gestures during caretaking that emphasize each part or turn the infant is to take. Even before the child forms real words, such turns occur (as in the example at the start of this chapter). These interactions also are marked by gaze-holding between infant and adult (Bruner 1975), often initiated by the infant.

Snow (1983) has explained what these exchanges contain that might lead to learning. Certain important kinds of parental support in the infant-adult exchange appear to promote language growth. Parents

1. expand the topics introduced by their children.
2. extend the information.
3. clarify child questions.
4. give direct answers to questions.
5. provide *scaffolding*, whereby they simultaneously challenge the child and help him or her succeed by reducing confusions.
6. require (of course not always) that their children be "accountable" and complete a task that has been started. (For example, parents require that children supply more sophisticated responses than the youngsters had given previously.)
7. (important to this book) provide routinized settings for learning, such as during picture book "reading" or feeding.

These conditions for parent support are developed through shared effort; the shared experiences are the contexts for talk. The routinization of talk provides a way by which children may focus on the utterances in the give-and-take. In parent-child peek-a-boo games, the turns are routinized so that the infant learns about taking turns while also experiencing the emotional satisfaction of communication (Bruner 1975).

Another and much studied example of the adult-child language exchange routine is the early book "reading" common in many, but not all, homes with young children. Book exchanges provide numerous opportunities for parents to "up the ante" or to expect greater sophistication. Ninio and Bruner (1978) recounted how book reading is structured: The mother secures the child's attention, then asks a question, then accepts a response, and then praises the response. (Such exchanges are described in greater detail in Chapters 2 and 3.)

What adult language—that directed to infants—contains is an issue that underscores the importance of the social context for language learning. Apparently, adult language to infants is not composed, as Chomsky (1965) believed, of imperfect unfinished starts, unclear relationships, and the like. Adult language is regular and special. Called *baby talk*, or *motherese*, it has regular features (Brown 1977). We can predict that baby talk has simplified words like "blankey" for blanket. Baby talk also occurs in language directed at animals, between lovers, and to tease or make fun of someone. In each setting, baby talk has an expressive function. Adults use it to gain a child's attention and to establish an acceptable level of language use. In many ways, baby talk is a simplified form of adult language, with exaggerated stress patterns, slow speech, and reduced structures. As infants develop more language competence, the baby talk features of their caretakers' talk disappear. At this point, baby talk seems to have met its purpose: to encourage verbal communication.

Adult language levels seem to relate with children's level of acquisition. That is, mothers simplify and clarify to establish communication and to help develop meaning. They model language use and confirm appropriate conversational frameworks. Importantly, mothers appear to explore with their infants and to urge the youngsters to take their next steps. Cross (1977) found that as mothers increasingly referred to non-immediate events, their children increasingly experienced more language development.

Problems with the Communication Focus

Our question, the same one asked of the other explanations for growth, is: Does this view explain language acquisition? Our answer is, as it has been before, "yes and no." One difficulty with the interactive emphasis is that the features of a dialogue in one setting are not universal. If dialogues were the *critical* mechanism by which language is learning, then they would have to be experienced by all language learning children, and they are not. Kaluli infants do not experience dialogues; instead, they become a part of three- and four-way exchanges only after first words have begun (Schiefflin and Ochs 1983). Moreover, Heath (1983; forthcoming) describes very different kinds of adult-child exchanges in different cultural groups in the United States. In one community, for example, baby talk does not exist. In that group, children have to interrupt to participate in talk. In each cultural group, however, children learn the ways of language use that enable them to socialize and to understand their world. To be a stronger explanation of language learning, the communication focus must examine communication within the context of how language is used culturally.

Another problem with this approach is that it, like the others, cannot explain what causes the transition from the single word stage to the next level where words are combined, a critical feature of language acquisition (Golinkoff and Gordon 1983). Even though the theories do not explain all aspects of language acquisition, when integrated they provide a framework for understanding how language grows (as we will see in the next section). Moreover, out of this framework, a model for instruction emerges, and this model forms a basis for much of the instructional direction in this book.

INTEGRATION AND SUMMARY

In our attempt to understand the process of language learning, we may draw upon various theories and supportive information to build a workable model for practice. We must remember that such an amalgam is as vulnerable to examination as are the theories upon which it is built. This brief section is an attempt to integrate the valid features of the theories reviewed.

There is an extraordinary leap in language acquisition during the second and third years. As an example of this phenomenon, one child, in one month, moved from utterances like, "doin', doin'," and "different one" to longer utterances made while monologuing during play: "This one, little guy. Cabbage doll, Heidi get. Sitting, cabbage doll. What happened?" (The punctuation is by parents to represent suprasegmentals.) The child's dolls and her talk about the actions are symbols of her thinking. Talk and thought appear to grow quickly together. Piaget and Vygotsky clarified the importance of infants' actions upon and with objects in the growth toward greater competence. Piaget's work, especially, has made us realize that there are natural limits to the expectations we might hold for children at different ages. Childhood maturation and child construction of a conceptual screen for understanding the world provide the boundaries for learning and the stimulation for further growth. Yet, we all know that there are differences in the extent and kind of cognitive and language growth that children experience. Finding an explanation for these differences requires that we look at the teaching influence, a question that keeps reappearing.

During the first year of life, as infants respond to the world around them, their thinking seems to consist of fleeting impressions, unstable links between objects and events. Those objects, events, and people that are more constant in their lives are named. Moreover, they respond enthusiastically to the communicative exchange contained in the give-and-take routines. During this period of life, infants learn the names of people and objects through imitation and reinforcement as they tentatively imitate the name of someone and respond to the excitement and clarity of parental expectation by repeating the response. Through the learned roles in the dialogues experienced by many—but not all—American infants, this process of trial and error, or response and reinforcement, continues.

The fact that the dyadic exchange is not universal does not mean it is not a viable frame for acquiring language. The infant may use many potentially helpful environmental factors as he or she learns language. For example, observation of the dialogue of others, playtalk, and parts to playsongs are elements of some children's language learning (Heath 1983). Interactions with parents and others during give-and-take episodes may increase the clarity of language roles and of the separation of ideas, but it is not a necessary ingredient for language learning.

In regard to the beginning stages of learning, Piaget's explanation that the infant's physical interaction with objects provides the source for understanding the world is basic to our explanation, but it does not explain how words come to be used. The behaviorist ideas about imitation and reinforcement are seen, although altered, in the early development of words. Vygotsky clarified the adult role somewhat. As adults use the language of the external world (naming, for example), they use language "tools." Children learn to say these tools ("hammer") in proximity to the object (hammer); eventually, the tool is internalized. As adults name objects and as they extend children's learning by operating with them beyond where they would otherwise operate alone, adults fulfill an important role. And that role, as seen in the work by those interested in communication, seems to occur in the form of dyadic exchange or, if we accept the idea that there are a variety of means for developing the communicative framework for language, in some other form of communication among infant and others.

When children move into the preoperational stage, at about 18 months, important changes mark language. The interactive communication position and the nativist position both would hold that the combination of children's natural propensity for language acquisition and maturation causes more specific ways of expressing meaning. The difference between these positions is that the environment helps the learning child, according to the communication focus. Toddlers now not only express more, but they also can generalize from specific instances to new examples, and they have more consistent patterns to their language. To the nativists, children's utterances represent a consistency of structure that is explained as the realization of generative rule-based systems.

We cannot dismiss the role of communication even though less study of it exists at these more advanced points of language. As developed in Chapters 3 and 4, dialogue and conversation may account for differences in the acquisition of notions about literacy. While our understanding of the language acquisition process after the age of 18 months or two years is largely influenced by the nativist position, the teaching influence of the language and thinking of parents and others who influence children should be noted continuously.

Thus, in our search through theoretical explanations for language learning, we find variation. However, upon examining these explanations for the purpose of integration, we come to a conclusion that will be helpful in considering the remainder of the book's content: We may do well to think of separate explanations for the psychological and instructional functions. The psychological component is concerned with *why* children achieve certain language learning milestones. This component is different from explanations about the role and the kind of instruction that enhances the maturation process. This distinction is helpful as we turn to the next chapters, for each (to some extent) discusses how parents, teachers, and schools might respond. Chapter 2 describes normal language growth, and Chapter 3 discusses the beginnings of writing and reading that many young children experience before formal training. In Chapter 4, we turn to the question of individual differences and the issue of instructional influence on growth. And Chapter 5 begins a series of discussions on instructional matters.

In conclusion, then, neither the environmental explanation nor the nativist position nor the communication interpretation can provide a full and acceptable account of language learning. A complex interplay between nature and nurture must exist; yet, its forms are not precisely known. Enough is known, however, to form our questions more specifically and to provide both theoretical and practical direction.

SELECTED ACTIVITIES

1. If researchers were to discover that chimps can produce longer, more complex "sentences" than has been shown and that these primates can transmit "chimp" knowledge, which position about language learning is supported: the LAD, the nativist, or the behaviorist? Explain your thinking.

2. Imagine that you have been asked to find out what children say when they first begin to talk. How would you collect this information?

3. Make a chart with a row of these names both across the top and down the left column: Piaget, Vygotsky, Behaviorists, Nativists, and Communicationalists. In each cell, jot down how the intersecting positions agree and how they differ.

4. Do you think fathers and grandparents use features of baby talk? Which ones? Why do you think they do or do not?

5. Tape a mother and child talking together while they are engaged in a typical interaction (a meal, for example). Try to find a child between the age of 1 and 3. See if any baby talk features are used; if so, play the tape back to the mother, and ask her why she used them. For example, if she used very short, simple sentences, ask her why. Then, compare the differences between how she talks with you and with her child.

6. Ask five people who have *not* studied child language or psychology how they think children learn language. Keep probing with questions that make these people specify, for example, how children begin to say words, make simple sentences, and learn the meanings of words. Classify the answers by the theory they reflect, if any.

2 How Language Grows

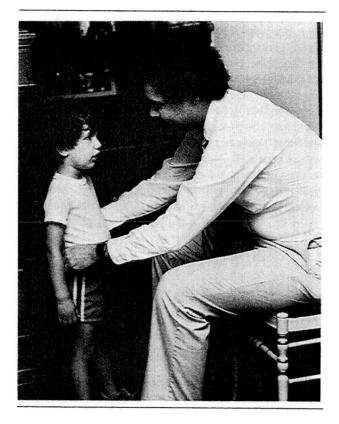

This chapter describes the specifics of children's language. It includes a discussion of how communication occurs and of how utterances may be examined to illustrate the rules children construct. The growth of the phonological, syntactic, meaning, and social systems from birth through the early elementary years is the manifestation of the language rules children construct. The chapter emphasizes the *strategies* of language learning, and it examines the ways in which children learn language so that we can identify potential sources for continued development of language, including literacy. These strategies for learning will influence how we design instruction in early education. Some readers may discern that the description of language learning in this chapter does not consider the critical issues of individual differences. However, because such differences are best understood within the framework in which children learn language, the commonality of strategies or universality of learning provides a basis for understanding differences. Furthermore, Chapter 4 considers individual differences in reference to the beginnings of language and literacy.

This chapter is organized so that the first section extends the discussion begun in Chapter 1 on communicative language. A second section discusses the first eighteen months or so, including the meanings of children's communications and the process of acquisition of first words. The period of critical growth that occurs once children put two words together for their first sentences is the subject of the next section. Studies concentrating upon this beginning "sentence" period have occupied researchers since the early 1960s. We are fortunate to have this work so that we can learn how children construct the rules that generate their utterances. We learn that, during the following period, called here *active language processing*, as children consolidate and expand structures, sounds, meaning, and conversations, the major features of language are acquired. But, as is described in the final section, after the age of five, children continue to acquire concepts of language that stimulate later language and literacy growth.

Major questions that direct the chapter are: What are mothers (and other adults, including fathers) "teaching" and supporting in their children's language acquisition? How do first words emerge? What functional roles do children's first words fulfill? What rules do children construct for themselves in generating their utterances? Do these rules suggest a general learning strategy? How does language reflect the ability of or enable older preschoolers to consolidate their knowledge and to express it in efficient ways? How do primary grade pupils continue to construct concepts of language?

THE CONTEXT FOR LANGUAGE ACQUISITION

As described in the first chapter, it is not altogether certain whether the interaction between adult and child—or, indeed, other types of social interactions—provides a strong answer to the question of how language starts. Nevertheless, the helpful framework developed in the interaction between adult and child organizes the youngster's "immediate surroundings in a fashion to make selected world knowledge more accessible to him in the presence of fine-tuned grammatical modeling." (Bruner 1983, 35). Interaction between adult and child and child and child is critical to language and literacy learning. Due to the importance of communication, this chapter extends the discussion of Chapter 1.

Although our example at the beginning of Chapter 1 describes an adult-infant exchange at two months, Menyuk (1977) reported that such exchanges are found at 12 weeks. In our example, the adult made soothing noises as the infant cooed in alternate "responses." In fact, the adult may have been simply supplying his vocalizations within the sequence of the infant's coos. During the next several weeks, however, such exchanges take on a stronger communicative meaning, and the child participates more actively. She knows her roles better. At first, of course, these exchanges carry no content, although researchers point out that mothers often attach meaning to their children's responses (Harding 1983). These exchanges, chains of alternative vocalizations, establish for infants the experience of turn-taking, which is essential for conversation and human communication.

Bruner (1975) observed mothers with their infants from seven months to the point where first words emerged. He focused upon give-and-take exchanges and found that mothers using exaggerated expression (intonation and behaviorial contrasts) and gestures showed their infants very clearly the beginnings and endings of the "conversation" segments. He suggested that through hide-and-seek, peek-a-boo, and the common "Where's the x" games that are repeatedly played, infants gradually learn to take their parts at the right times. Through their vocalizations and gestures, infants become real partners in these special communications. The mother initiates the exchanges to extend the emotional ties between herself and her infant and to enable routines of feeding, dressing, and diapering to be times of pleasure. Mothers also initiate the exchanges to teach. First, mothers attract the infant's attention and then elaborate. By the end of the first year, many exchanges involve initiation of a topic (by the mother) and comments upon it (by the mother and infant) (Bruner 1978). As they respond within familiar routines, babies learn when to take part. Once they learn when to take part, babies' responses in the slots within the familiar become increasingly stable and finally are words. Routinization facilitates the learning of language and—as we will see in Chapter 3—of literacy.

The Ninio and Bruner (1978) study of parent-child exchanges about pictures in books demonstrated clearly how routinized exchanges provide support for the appropriate production of more advanced language. Prior to the initiation of the picture exchanges, the child had learned to point to referenced objects, and he had learned to utter a sort of "da" as he pointed. The first part of the picture dialogue consisted of the mother's attracting attention to the object (picture), "Look!" with pointing. Next came the question, "What is this?" and its varieties. The child then was expected to respond, and, if the correct label was not forthcoming, the mother would provide the label. Later, when he uttered even his "da," she would confirm and then provide the adult label. As time went on, the mother expected more of her child. If she knew he had the label, her intonation, or stress pattern, changed. Once labels were regularly provided by the child, further questions were asked. The mother was "raising the ante" by asking, "What's x doing?"

Believing that their infants are expressing meaning even before the appearance of stable utterances (as in picture reading), parents often take measures to adapt to their children and therefore intensify the communication (Golinkoff 1983). One of the ways that many parents gain the attention of their infants and share in their youngster's thinking is through baby talk, described in the previous chapter.

Baby talk is an interesting example of how adults attract children's attention and begin communicating with them. Brown (1977) summarized baby talk features and found it contained: higher pitch, longer time in speaking verbs, more instances of primary (strong) stress, more whispering (for contrast effect), and longer pauses. In addition to these suprasegmentals, or phonological features, baby talk usually contains shorter sentences and simpler structures than other talk. In regard to terminology, in baby talk, more names are used than pronouns (pronouns are acquired relatively late). The semantic quality of the talk is reduced, and the talk contains many prompts. Prompts recast children's utterances in such a way as to heighten specific terms. "You want WHAT?" illustrates to the child the sentence order ending for an object.

To consider the role of baby talk in child language development, we must recognize that while neither baby talk nor picture-book reading is universal, both are fairly common in mainstream, western culture. They both, according to language scholars (Bruner 1983; Snow 1977; Snow 1983) appear to enhance the developmental process.

Other forms of talk most likely may help establish a communicative framework for learning language structures. In cultures like the Kaluli (Scheifflin and Ochs 1983), parents do not interact with their infants until certain words appear. Instead, parents give directives to their infants. This form of communication may provide a clear idea about talk. Bloom (1983) pointed out that these babies also overhear dialogue. Listening to others' talk, taking more than one role in monologues, and observing exchanges between toddlers and older children may substitute for adult-child dialogue in some communities (Heath 1983). Moreover, these babies may be involved in interaction with older children. The role of older children's communication with infants deserves study since so many children are not singles or first-born. We do know that older children are sensitive to language learning. For example, we know that children adjust their level of talk downward when talking with younger children (Shatz and Gelman 1973).

Through the study of exchanges like picture-book readings, scholars have found that parents are conscious of the level at which their children are functioning (Cross 1977). Parents can predict the kinds of structures their children will understand and produce (Berko-Gleason and Weintraub 1978). Such knowledge gives parents the ingredients for the other part of teaching, the part referred to as "raising the ante." The mother Ninio and Bruner observed knew when it was appropriate to ask more of her child. The challenge to the next step is successful when the parent also provides a setting and the clues necessary for the child's appropriate response. The parent accepts non-labels for some time before insisting on the label. Similarly, he or she accepts the label before asking for information about the action in the picture. Parental support of this kind illustrates the Vygotskian zone of proximal development. Parents help their children respond and challenge their youngsters through requests for more mature structures.[1]

Language is not solely acquired in social contexts. As we know from Chapter 1, language acquisition is also formed through children's natural ability to develop new structures as they move from single-word utterances to complex statements. This significant aspect of the acquisition process has to do with children's constructive ability, the capability of inducing rules upon which to generate their utterances and through which to interpret the language around them.

Children also practice their new language forms through monologue and language play. Weir's (1962) son monologued in the crib as he generated play with sounds, rhymes, and the like. He also systematically repeated utterances and substituted various structures. While not all children monologue as extensively as others, Garvey (1984) suggests, based on evidence from Black (1979), that practice of a new structure precedes its use in interactive talk. Self-reports of the day's activities, taking roles and conducting a dialogue by oneself, and even planning occur as children try out some linguistic element that has been noticed (Garvey 1984). These overt utterances disappear as children develop, much as Vygotsky (1962) described; language play emerges and continues as children interact with one another, as described in later sections.

The language environment many children experience is one that contains language games during feeding and other caregiving episodes; parental understanding of current functioning; parental acceptance of utterances; probes to elicit more talk; special baby talk to attract attention and to engage them in talk; recast statements to clarify language concepts; and routines through which to practice. These are the characteristics of the setting in which children learn the vocabulary, syntax (order and structure of word combinations), sounds, and meanings of language. In order to understand the role of children's private and social talk in language, it is necessary to understand how the specific structures of language unfold through the early years. We turn next to these structures and, in so doing, focus upon the specific characteristics of child language acquisition.

THE EMERGENCE OF LANGUAGE

The First Words

While this and the following sections are based on chronological stages of development, it is important to point out that children's language acquisition is

---

[1]Interestingly, teacher behaviors that are similar to those found in parents who support their children's learning also are associated with school success: reinforcing, providing cues and feedback, and engaging in the tasks (Walberg 1984). Characteristics found in parent-child exchanges may serve as a model for teaching; they are potentially similar to the social contexts of school learning.

not marked by steady growth indices. The movement from one "stage" to another is often difficult to recognize. Even the point when words first emerge is not clear (Grieve and Hoogenraad 1979). Language acquisition consists of overlapping phases of growth, and it sometimes includes regressions to more primitive forms of communication.

During the first year, infants make many different sounds that are unlike those made after words are acquired. For one thing, we refer to the sounds speakers make to distinguish one word from another as *phonemes*. For example, the initial sounds of "pig" and "big" are phonemes that distinguish the two words and are represented in writing by symbols placed between two slash marks: /p/ and /b/. If the sounds, phonemes, are used only to distinguish words, then babies who have no words have no phonemes. For another thing, we find that the many sounds vocalized during the first year are not used when babies finally do utter words. Thus, while many sounds are produced before referent and utterance coincide, once word acquisition actually begins only a few phonemes are used.

To return to infants who do vocalize, McNeil (1970) has reported that nearly all human sounds are produced during the first year of life, even though all these sounds will not be used in any one language. During the first three months of life, infants learn to cry in different ways so that parents often can identify one cry as a request for food, another as a complaint about discomfort, and so on. Toward the end of the three months, cooing sounds are used to indicate pleasure.

At about six months or so, infants add to their vocalization repertory. They *babble*. Babbling occurs when the infant combines a consonant-like sound with a vowel-like sound in a syllable that is repeated. Babbling continues after the first words are learned.

An interesting phenomenon of this prelingual stage has been observed. Apparently, deaf children go through a similar sequence of crying, cooing, and babbling. However, their vocalizations are fewer when others are present (Lenneberg 1967). The production of these first sounds apparently does not depend entirely on the environment or on feedback, but the extent of vocalization is influenced by environment.

Hearing children acquire one important language-like behavior toward the end of the first year: variations in the intonation beginnings of the language being learned (Dale 1976). Thus, a "language speaker's" stream of babbling is apt to sound like a statement without words or meaning. After learning a few isolated words, some babies combine these words into a kind of pseudo-language. They present utterances that sound like speech, but with an occasional word. Once the author observed a puzzled three-and-a-half-year-old listening intently to a baby who was using this pseudo-language. Finally, the older child said that the baby was funny because she sounded like she was saying something but it did not come out like talk.

Of the vocalizations infants produce in their first year, intonation contours (pseudo-language) (Dale 1976), interactive rules (turn-taking) (Bruner 1975), and a few sequences of sounds consistently used in the same situations mark the real precursors of language. The emergence of the first words sets the stage for language. During the six months following initial vocabulary acquisition, there is relatively little change, but after this period, the growth of vocabulary increases dramatically. At age 1.0, the average number of words used meaningfully by a child is three; at 2.0, it is 272 (Leopold 1971). From this point on, vocabulary grows even more quickly.

Brown (1973), one of the foremost scholars and theorists of language acquisition, identified developmental indices as stages dependent upon the mean length of child utterance (MLU). The one-word stage is his Stage I. This period of single-word utterances, from about .9 through about 1.6 to 2.0, has been identified by many scholars as critical to understanding the beginnings of language. An important question has to do with whether these one-word utterances convey a vague representation of adult sentence meaning (holophrases) or whether the meaning intended by single words refers to more specific relationships. Does "nana," for example, mean "I want a banana right now," or is it just naming? Described as a kind of proto-language by Grieve and Hoogenraad (1979), the utterances, not necessarily recognizable words, do not express meaning as we might convey it. Halliday (1975) studied the use of his son Nigel's utterances between .9 and 1.6 to understand their meaning. Most of Nigel's utterances had interactive meaning; that is, they focused upon his needs and actions. At first (at .9), Nigel's expressions met the following needs:

Instrumental: conveying both general demands and specific orders (e.g., sounds that meant, "Give me my bird.")
Regulatory: making normal and intensified commands
Interactional: both initiating communication with and responding to someone else (e.g., sounds that might be interpreted as, "Nice to see you.")
Personal: making both active and passive comments about self

At about 10.5, Nigel began to consistently use the same sounds—rather than varied sounds—to indicate a particular meaning. These "words" were used to specify personal needs and showed specific intent. By 1.6, not only had Nigel acquired recognizable words, but the functions of his talk also had expanded. The functions now were

Instrumental. Now the specific demands included a word, thereby clarifying the function. ("Fish" meant "I want to be lifted to where the fish picture is." [Halliday 1975, 155].)
Regulatory. The commands now included requests and suggestions. Real words were used to express these meanings.
Interactional. The utterances, not always words, expressed far more specific responses to others and means for initiating actions.
Personal. The child now was able to express a range of feelings and the concept of presence and absence.

Heuristic. This new function reflected assertion of fact through naming, meaning "It's a. . . . "

Imaginative. The initial appearance of the imaginative function at about 1.0 included the early presence of songs, pretending, and rhyming.

In addition to these functions, Griffiths (1979) found that children between 1.0 and 1.6 made references as they attempted to get adults to attend to their interests. Another study of the meaning of first words by Clark (1979) suggests that such words are often overextended. For example, from diary study, one child's "mooi," originally used to refer to *moon,* also was used to refer to a cake, the marks on a frozen window, round shapes in books, and the like (Clark 1973). Because a child has few words but many experiences, and, in some cases, the desire to supply labels and to refer (like in picture book exchanges), the few words are used for many like things. The words also illustrate how infants focus upon certain attributes (in this case, roundness). Moreover, infants often use one term to express like concepts. For example, "big" might be used to refer to something for which *tall* or *wide* would be used by adults.

At this stage, children's word comprehension is much greater than is apparent by the number of words uttered. Children not only overextend meaning, but they also underextend, using a word to refer to a smaller category than adults would for that word. Thus, one child might use "dog" only for dogs like his pet, rather than the whole set of dogs. The process of acquiring the specific terms for relational concepts takes many years (Donaldson and Balfour 1968).

An enduring and not-yet-solved problem has to do with *why* children acquire first words. Golinkoff (1983) proposed that infants may acquire new words through the negotiation that occurs between parent and child when communication fails. The infant with a high degree of motivation attempts to communicate a strong need that the adult does not understand. The subsequent negotiation, as the adult attempts to understand the child's expression by naming the possible objects the child may want, heightens and stimulates movement to new structuring. This format is one in which, it is proposed, children restructure their prelinguistic communications into linguistic ones. The struggle to overcome communication failure is an example of a significant change in thinking, much as described by Piaget. When parents carry out negotiations with children who have developed the faculties for learning words, new words are acquired. Some support for this idea is found in Nelson's (1973) study of first-word acquisition. She found that children, whose mothers were "in tune" with their children's language and aware and receptive to their children's manner of learning, made greater progress. For example, these mothers provided names when children wanted names and linking, function words when children needed them.

An extreme nurture position would suggest that the communication frameworks, practice routines, and direction within the dialogues are the sources for language learning. An extreme nature position suggests, instead, that children acquire words when the youngsters have become prepared through development and from the presence of language in their environment. We have seen evidence for both positions: Children apparently do acquire language without direct interaction with parents (the Kaluli) and by themselves in monologue; they also use a variety of social context supports to practice and learn new words.

Words cannot be uttered without consistent use of language sounds, of course. We might expect to find a change in the sound structure of language when words begin. And we find that once words are acquired, the sounds in them become phonemes. In the first words, only a few primitive phonemes can be distinguished, but when infants are playing with sounds or *babbling*, they continue to use all kinds of sounds. A number of years ago, Jakobson (1971) proposed an explanation of this phenomenon. Jakobson showed that many children's first words were similar, regardless of the language being learned. According to his theory, since the sounds of language are arranged so that some phonemes are far more distinct from each other than others, the most different sounds are learned first. Later, children learn to differentiate among less distinct phonemes. For example, the two phonemes /p/ and /a/, which Jakobson said would be the first learned, contain a basic distinction that exists in many languages. When producing these phonemes, one uses very different parts of the vocal machinery: /p/ is a consonant made at the front of the mouth with closed lips and with a slight explosive sound when it is the first sound in a word; /a/ is a back vowel made with open lips and an open vocal tract. Jakobson stated that, in time, children learn to make more and more differentiations between phonemes that have less and less variation. Thus, the child who has first acquired /pa/ might next acquire a nasal phoneme (/m/, /n/, or /ŋ/), so that /ma/ may be the second word. Next, there would be a division in the vowel system so that /a/ and /i/ (a wide back vowel and a narrow high one) are differentiated and more syllables are possible. With continual splitting of these phonemes, the system gradually is acquired. Ingram (1976) cites evidence indicating that phoneme contrasts on words are not necessarily stable at first.

The first twelve to eighteen months of life are filled with change. In regard to motor development, the changes are very obvious: Children roll over; they reach for objects and eventually learn to grasp what they want, and they crawl, sit, and even start walking. Similarly, in language, infants' growth reflects increased ability to control and understand their environment. The initial crying and cooing sounds demonstrate only discomfort and comfort and underscore infant helplessness, but by the end of this stage, the use of words and engagement in interaction reflect assertion of self. The forms of language become increasingly precise as children induce structures that express their developing concepts.

Words Combined

Between the ages of 1.6 and 2.6, children begin to combine words. According to Lenneberg (1967), it is consistent among normally developing children, regardless of their language environment, to begin combining words between the ages of 1.6 and 2.6. Table 1 shows representative examples of these "early sentences" taken from one study that examined this particular stage in detail. The stage of grammatical development lasts until about 2.6. The mean length of utterance (MLU) at the end of the word combination stage is 1.7; children's vocabularies are between about 275 and 300 words (Garman 1979; Leopold 1971).

The utterances in Table 1 have been called "telegraphic" (Brown and Bellugi 1964). And, while at first glance, they appear to be reduced like telegrams are, to describe these "sentences" as telegraphic is to apply adult thinking about categories of class (such as nouns and verbs) to very primitive language. We are mistaken when we view young children's learning from an adult position.

The possibility that these two-word utterances may simply be imitations of adult sentences reduced to a few essential words relates to a discussion in Chapter 1. However, it is difficult to imagine adult sentences for which the following child utterances are imitations: "outside more," "there bye bye car," and "all gone juice." "Outside more" may be used by the child as he explains that he wants to stay outside longer. An adult would not use the word *more* in expressing the same desire. It could be that just as adults produce an infinite number of new sentences based on a *grammatical rule system*, children's utterances are based on a rule system, too. The novel, nonimitative child sentences listed in Table 1 result from children's applications of their system. This interpretation demonstrates that child language is quite correct and based on a growing and developing language rule sytem rather than incorrect according to adult rules. When a child's rule systems are made explicit, as they are in Bloom's extensive study of the early stages of acquisition (1970), the rules appear to vary somewhat from individual to individual; however, there are some common traits found in the sentence structure of various primitive two- and three-word utterances in the many studies of beginning language (Bloom 1970; Bloom, Lightbloom, and Hood 1975; Brown and Fraser 1964; Brown, Cazden, and Bellugi-Klima 1968; Dale 1976; McNeil 1970). It is clear from all the studies of language learning that children are learning basic grammatical elements even though their expression is very incomplete from an adult point of view. (See more extensive reviews of this point in Chomsky 1969, and Clark 1973.)

Some children show an early use of the subject and object in their sentences. The youngsters sometimes produce the subject part of the sentence and the object of the *predicate*. (Predicate refers to the nonsubject part of a sentence.) "It doggie" is an example of a subject plus object sentence. Another early structure

TABLE 1. Examples of two- and three-word utterances		
	all broke	bye bye papa
	I see	mail car
	no bed	papa away
	see train	all gone juice
	more hot	fall down there
	more walk	airplane all gone
	other shoe	outside more
	dry pants	there bye bye car
	boot off	it doggie

Source: M. S. Braine, "The Ontogeny of English Phrase Structures: The First Phase," *Language* 39 (1963): 1–3. Reprinted by permission of the journal.

includes verb and object ("see train," for example). Sometimes, too, children say the subject and verb part of the sentence (for example, "I see"). In these examples, subject, verb, and object elements are being acquired but are not all combined in one structure. At the same time, children are also apt to be combining words to indicate modification ("more hot"), conjunction, and genitive and locational structures (Bloom 1970).

The descriptions of child language as telegraphic and as representative of simple grammatical structures focus on syntax only. As stated in the introduction to this chapter, researchers now examine the meanings of these simple utterances. This is no easy task, however, since the meanings of two- and three-word utterances are strongly tied to the situation in which they are uttered. One-word holophrases can be interpreted only by knowing what was happening when they were uttered; these words are completely context bound. While the longer two-word utterances are more explanatory, they, too, are bound by the context. It is possible to misinterpret a child's "off a this" if one does not know the child is simultaneously removing a toy person from a toy train. Bloom (1970) was able to interpret the intended meanings of primitive utterances by examining the context, and subsequent researchers have done the same (Bloom 1975; Bowerman 1976; Brown 1973). Brown (1973), for example, combined the findings from a number of language acquisition studies of English-learning children with studies of children learning such diverse languages as Finnish, Mexican Spanish, Samoan, and Swedish to find the types of meanings expressed by beginning speakers. Because children appear to use a similar set of meaning expressions in their first utterances, Brown stated that there are certain characteristic meanings expressed across all cultures. The most common are

1. *Nomination.* Utterances such as "this book" and "a truck" that name and include words following "this" or "that" in simple utterances belong in this category and are universal.
2. *Recurrence.* Words that combine with "more" and " 'nother" are recurring ones. While this category is not as universal as the first, it is a preferred expressed notion.
3. *Nonexistence.* Brown reports that while fragmentary reports do not list statements such as "no more noises" and "dog away" in every child, many English-speaking children show this expression in their language.
4. *Agent and action.* Both Bloom, Lightbloom, and Hood (1975) and Brown (1973) found high preference among children for this category ("car go," "me go"). Because such notions are common in different languages, this category appears to be part of every language in its incipient form.
5. *Action and object.* There is also a high incidence of expressions such as "close it," "turn it," "make house," and "ride Dumbo" in children of many languages. This is a universal category.
6. *Possessor and possession.* As many caretakers of young children know, remarks about ownership are common: "Mommy face," "dolly hat," "dis mine," "girl dress." This is another universal category.

Other categories of language expression have been noted by various researchers, but none have the commonality of those just described. Although scholars do not agree on the exact categories of expression, they do agree that the cognitive level reached during the sensori-motor period influences these universal expressions (Bowerman 1976; Brown 1973). Sinclair-deZwart (1973) described the cognitive functioning at 1.6 as showing stable understanding of action on objects and of knowledge of object permanence, including notions of anticipation and rehearsal. The linguistic expression of these understandings are agent and action, action and object, recurrence and nonexistence. In nomination and possession, children are showing additional awareness of the physical world by labeling common objects and becoming personally attached to objects. Beginning language development appears to be determined by cognitive growth, but Bowerman (1976) suggests that at later points, the learnings acquired through language motivate cognitive growth.

It must be noted that during this period of language expansion, children's vocabularies also grow quickly. In contrast to the time when first words begin, when words are often overextended, children might have command of about fifty words (Nelson 1973); as words are combined into two-word utterances, the vocabulary grows much more quickly. For example, two parents I know kept track of their children's vocabulary acquisition. In both cases, they stopped when the children began to combine words because they could no longer keep up. With about 300 words (Garman 1979), children can refer to six times as many objects and events, and to do so with words placed together to show important relationships (agent and action) is, indeed, an important point of maturation.

The major points about this first period of word combination are

1. There are similar expressions made by children learning many languages.
2. These expressions describe universal characteristics of language learning.
3. The primitive utterances also suggest incipient categories of grammatical structures found later in language growth.
4. The utterances resemble telegraphs.

During the following period of language change, children acquire forms of verbs and nouns, prepositions, pronouns, and other functions of the structure of language so that very quickly their language appears like that of adults.

Active Language Processing

Talk

As we think about the specific structures that emerge with the acquisition of language, it is important that we recognize how children are using their language in their lives. Meaning is demonstrated through the functions of language, as we learned in the discussion of first words. Garvey (1984) has described young children's talk, and perhaps nothing is more illustrative of the meaning of language than young children's use of the negative. To reach backwards a bit to the beginnings of linguistic ability, we all know that "no" is one of the earliest uttered words of most children. Garvey pointed out that the initial use of the negative to refuse and to resist is an indicator of a healthy assertion of individ-uality. Later, when words are first combined, as in "no book" or "Daddy gone," the negative indicates disappearance and termination (like the nonexistence meaning described earlier). As children's language becomes increasingly sophis-ticated, in the stage of active language processing, the negative is part of the child's ability to express and to negate a proposition. One child said, for example, "No, push power off." During this period, children begin to "expand their negative responses by providing the correct *positive* formulation" (italics in original, Garvey 1984, 135). They are able to elaborate comments in conversations and to include reasons for assertions (for example, "Chair too big. Sit sofa."). In doing so, many new language structures are being acquired.

Vocabulary and Syntax

At about age 2.6, children typically have a vocabulary of about 470 words and MLU's of 2.7 (Garman 1979). This period, Stage III, from about 2.6 to about 3.6 in Brown's (1973) scheme, is one of great interest for during it, children make many important additions to their language production. Children acquire the use of important function words and suffixes so that they are able to express number on nouns, and tense, person, and the like on verbs. Prepositions allow children to indicate location precisely; possessives enable children to show ownership, a critical concept to them. The order of these additions to the productive use of toddlers' language helps us understand how the youngsters learn to express important concepts.

How these additional function words are acquired illustrates the extreme efficiency of language learning. There is a larger set of finite rules also relatively quickly acquired during the preschool period; these rules are the grammatical, or syntactic, rules governing word order, inflections (or endings on words), and combinations of structures. Important grammatical structures appear in chil-dren's language just after the early combination of words described in the previous section. Brown (1973) traced the use of fourteen critical structures in three preschoolers' language. He found that while the *rate* of acquisition of the structures varied among the children, the approximate *order* did not—testimony to the universal quality of language. These structures, in order of acquisition determined by their consistent use in appropriate situations, are

1. the addition of -*ing* on verbs to mark the present progressive (as in "Baby sitting in a chair" acquired at ages 1.9, 2.10, and 2.6)
2. use of "in" to mark location
3. use of "on" to mark location
4. plural marking on nouns
5. past irregular forms of common verbs, such as "went," "came," and "did"
6. possessive markers
7. the simple unchanged form of the copula "be"
8. use of the articles "a" and "the"
9. regular past tense forms of verbs, as in "wanted"
10. the regular third person singular verb inflection, as in "the boy runs"

11. the third person irregular, as in "does"
12. the uninflected use of auxiliary verbs along with the main verb, as in "he do not want"
13. inflected use of the copula (to be) in such words as "is," and "was"
14. inflected auxiliary verb with main verbs, as in "he does not want"

These structures appeared consistently in the "correct" situations in three children by 4.0.

When children use these forms, they are expressing relatively new, complex ideas. For example, the difference between a child who does not yet use the plural inflection on nouns and one who does is the difference between one with no number distinctions and one with beginning notions of number. Again, a child who says "a chair" and "the chairs" can distinguish a general and a particular member of a group. Additionally, the fact that the noun plural inflection is acquired before the third person singular form of the verb, although both the addition of the plural inflection on nouns and the inflection on the singular present verb require the same sounds, demonstrates that the syntax determines order of acquisition, not the ability to make sounds. Thus, in numerous ways, the acquisition of these grammatical structures marks the appearance of abstract grammar.

In Brown's list of acquired forms, the *irregular* past tense verb structure (5) appears before the *regular* form (9). Acquiring irregulars before regulars seems counterintuitive. Explanation for this phenomenon comes from Cazden's study (1968), which found that irregular forms were often used correctly at first but later were used incorrectly. In other words, children at the beginning of this stage might say "he ran," "I did," and "we came" as adults do. A few months later, the same children might say, "he runned," "I doed," and "we comed." This phenomenon occurs because in the beginning, the children are using "ran," "did," and "came" as memorized items and not with understanding of the past tense idea. Later, they learn the past tense concept as shown in the example, "he feeled it." When they learn the general rule for an inflection (in this case, -ed at the end of a verb), they apply it to all verbs, whether or not adults use that general rule or a rule for a variant ending. Thus, children generalize about the formation of inflections and apply the generalization to all members of that class. Later, over time, they learn the rules that apply to smaller and smaller groups of words in that class. Overgeneralized learning also occurs in the acquisition of noun plurals ("wash my feets") and with possessive pronouns ("that's mines").

The learning of inflections is a very efficient process and shows the use of sophisticated strategies. Categorization of items in a class occurs first; in the instance above, for example, a verb class was formed. Then comes the formation of a rule that works in most instances; the addition of -ed to verbs when past tense is intended illustrates this point. The rule is then applied to all members of the relevant category. Only much later and with much experience will children become aware of the idiosyncratic rules of their language. For example, the reader has probably heard youngsters of six and seven saying "brang" for "brought," even though "brought" is the form consistently used by adults around them. A moment's thought will show that such children are sensibly associating "bring" and "ring"; if the past of "ring" is "rang," the past of "bring" ought to be "brang." "Bring" ought to belong to the subgroup of verbs with "ring," "sing," etc. Children are very efficient when learning rules.

More illustration of how children's language matures comes from analysis of their questions and negations. The change from initial two-word questions to almost mature questions is dramatic evidence of the rapidity of language growth.

During the earlier two-word stage, question meaning was realized by rising pitch. A child would say "ball go" with questionlike rising pitch or intonation. This question would mean, "Has the ball gone?" In the second column of Table 2, there are many questions beginning with a wh- word (who, where, why) that clearly ask for a missing object, location, or even a cause. The ability to ask these questions indicates a new awareness of sentence function. With the beginning questions, there are also sentences with -ing. In the last column, however, even more learning has taken place. The most important change is indicated by the word order inversion of newly acquired auxiliary (AUX) verb forms (forms of *have, be, do,* and others used to show verb tense, mood, voice, etc.) and the subject. For example, in the last column, one child asked, "Does lions walk?" In this question, he places the AUX "does" first and the subject "lions" next. The inversion of AUX and subject may be one of the first adultlike word order, or transformational, rules that children learn. Transformations enable children to change words around and put sentence parts together. For example, when children learn to put the auxiliary verb form "can" in front of the subject, as in "Can you swim?" they have acquired one of the many transformational rules in our language. Because of the inversion transformation, the first four questions in the last column are remarkably similar to adult questions, and as Klima and Bellugi-Klima (1969) point out, the child's comprehension of adult questions is increasing. What is still lacking, though, is subject-verb agreement and the

TABLE 2. Illustrative questions

Pivot Stage	Beginning Questions	More Advanced Questions
Who that?	See my doggie?	Does the kitty stand up?
Ball go?	Dat black too?	Does lions walk?
Fraser water?	Mom pinch finger?	Did I saw that in my book?
Sit chair?	Where my sleep?	Can I have a piece of paper?
I have it?	Where my mitten?	Where small trailer he should pull?
	What my dolly have?	Where the other Joe will drive?
	Why not drink it?	Where my spoon go?
	Why you smiling?	What I did yesterday?
	Why you waking me up?	What you had?
		What you doed?
		Why he don't know how to pretend?
		Can't you work this thing?

Source: E. S. Klima and U. Bellugi-Klima, "Syntactic Regularities in the Speech of Children," in *Modern Studies of English,* ed. D. Reibel and S. Schane (Chicago: Aldine Publishing Co., 1969). Reprinted by permission of the publisher and Edinburgh University Press.

elimination of double past tense forms. The wh-word questions in the last column seem immature by comparison with the first four yes/no questions, since inversion of subject and AUX has not yet occurred in the wh-word questions. This transformation is acquired in the next few months by most children.

Thus, in eighteen months, children acquire an amazing amount of syntactic knowledge. For example, in asking questions during the two-word stage, children can question only generally a thought or an action. Soon after this point, however, they can ask for a specific missing object, person, location, or cause. By the age of about 3.6 years, children are nearly as specific in their questioning as adults. Of course, they still have not learned all the rules the adult knows; for example, they have not mastered the wh-word question inversion and use of the indefinite "any," as in the sentence, "Don't you want any?"

Sounds

At this time, changes also take place in children's productions of sounds. During the preschool years, all the sounds of English are acquired by most children. According to Carroll's (1960) interpretation of a study by Templin (1967), by the age of six most children have nearly full mastery of the sound system of English. Even at three, most children have acquired many phonemes. Ninety percent of a group of sixty three-year-olds used the following phonemes clearly: /n/, /t/, /g/ (the g in goat), /m/, /b/, /d/, /w/, /h/, /p/, and /k/. Seventy to eighty percent also could use: /f/, /ŋ/ (ŋ is the sound at the end of rang), /l/, and /s/. Fifty to sixty percent had /v/, /r/, /š/ (sh in shut), /ǰ/ (j in judge), and /č/ (ch in church). Among the sounds causing the most difficulty for children at age 3 were: /z/, /ž/ (z in azure), /θ/ (th in thick), ð/ (th in then), and /hw/ (wh in which). These more difficult phonemes are not present in some languages and show less sound distinction from each other than do those learned. For example, the difference between /z/ and /ž/ is slight; some languages do not have either /θ/ or /ð/. These difficult language-specific phonemes are learned late by children, but some adults who are learning English for the first time never are able to learn to use them correctly.

Meaning

From the beginning of their use of words, children have many more images than words to refer to those images, but, later, by the end of the preschool period, children's word production begins to meet comprehension (Fletcher and Garman 1979). (Indeed, when examining closely the language of older children, it appears that production may be greater than comprehension, but that is an issue for the next section.) At this stage, children still are trying to communicate a lot of meaning with relatively few words. The meaning acquisition question has given child language scholars difficulty. One theory by Clark (1973), the Semantic Feature Acquisition Theory, suggests that the process of acquiring words requires learning the attributes, or features, of words. According to the theory, in the initial use of concepts children have only some of the attributes adults have. Because there are few attributes, children use a term broadly (they overextend). When children use terms inappropriately (such as using the term "doggie" to name all animals), they exhibit learning processes researchers can study. As learning progresses, more attributes are acquired.

According to this theory, when children are learning the meaning of relational terms such as *more/less, short/tall,* and *on/off,* the youngsters often become confused. With terms such as "more" and "less," children first learn that both refer to a quantity. Then, they learn that "more" is the positive member of the pair, but they still are confused about "less." Finally, the two terms become sorted (Donaldson and Balfour 1968). Similarly, "same" is acquired before "different," although the two are confused for a while (Clark 1973). "Before" and "after" continue to be difficult relational terms for many preschoolers; in fact, the author observed some middle grade elementary children having difficulty ordering: "Before putting the meat in the soup, you have to put in the onions and then the potatoes."

Nelson and Nelson (1978) observed that young children learn word meanings through action and function. He asked how these children come to acquire a generalized set of word groups—let us call them *clusters*—that speakers of a language hold in common. For example, after seeing an Airedale, a collie, and a springer spaniel, we would all agree that they belong together under the heading *dog.* We all probably would agree about the organization of the following words from most to least general: animal, dog, Airedale. Nelson proposed that this universal organization is evidence of language system knowledge. Children, after having once learned terms as separate items corresponding to certain concepts, may well become aware of the systematic relationships within clusters and thereby construct broader, more sophisticated language systems. In other words, children gradually may move from knowledge of meaning acquired through sensory contacts in their environment to groupings and extensions that form awareness of the hierarchical clusters of language.

One could fairly easily keep tract of a child's language during the time when single words are acquired. Once simple sentences begin, however, it is more difficult to keep up with growth because these primitive sentences are each unique statements of meaning and intent. And they appear with rapidity. Moreover, once a child learns function words, tracking language growth becomes even more difficult. With the concomitant expression possible, the toddler can express a wider range of meaning. And language expands geometrically. Even more impressive than the actual expanding ability is the kind of learning taking place. The patterns of structural changes demonstrate the constructive character of child language acquisition. Children induce rules that they then use across whole classes of syntactic structures, and children's phonological acquisitions also are applied across classes. Toward the end of the preschool period, after this phenomenal growth, language develops differently, as we will see in the next section.

Later Language Growth

By age 3.6 or so, children's conversational skills have developed enormously. While dialogue has been part of language since before language began, real conversation develops through the preschool period described by Garvey (1984).

The early exchanges do not represent reciprocal conversations since adults are providing the framework for the infants' turns. When talking with peers and older children, toddlers gradually learn to repair broken exchanges, to respond more quickly, and to link their thinking into their partners'. At first, in the third year, toddlers talk about immediate objects. Toward the end of the third year, children can maintain the references of the conversation. They use pronouns; they make connections, and they make immediate objects part of talk that extends beyond action upon the immediate. They imagine.

Groups of children in nursery schools engage in pretending; their games are intricately woven with talk that is used to direct and negotiate the various roles of the pretend games. Much of the talk involves domestic play. Sharing and negotiating about "ownership" take much time; the actual passing of objects from one to another symbolizes children's ideas about conversation. The fact that voice quality changes as children take on different roles in their games indicates an important quality of talk. In a sense, the ability to change one's voice and even the words within a role displays an ability to abstract language properties. Children age four and five who are in play groups with peers are quite good at taking roles. They whisper; they use baby talk when appropriate, and they focus upon gender roles of mother and father. Imagination builds within the games and is brought into solitary play as well. One boy I know entertained himself at age four in solitary play by taking on several voices; his roles were part of the planning of his games, and he adhered to them for extensive periods. Similarly, my son regulated his play with small toys by announcing the events and taking the parts of several players.

Conversations among peers are instrumental in providing opportunities for several important aspects of language use: Children learn to tie into the talk of others, to negotiate in conflict, to maintain topics through several units of exchange, to take a variety of roles, and to develop stories in concert with others. Social exchange with peers offers children the opportunity to acquire skills critical to development, and it may differ substantially from exchanges with adults, older children, and babies in the family. Unfortunately, not all children have such group experiences (Garvey 1984).

Vocabulary and Syntax at Nursery School Age

Relative to the previous stages, there is less acquisition of basic syntactic structures after 3.6. However, children begin to acquire the means through which to combine elements of syntax at this point. At Brown's (1973) Stage IV, the MLU is about 3.4 on average (Garman 1979); children's vocabulary extends up and beyond 920 words. At Stage V, the MLU is between 3.5 and 4.0. During this time, children begin to utter complex sentences and to coordinate elements within sentences.

The following sentences illustrate what is meant by the embedding of little sentences into bigger ones:

1. I like the course. It is challenging. It is also personally profitable.
2. I like that course because it is challenging and personally profitable.

The sentences in *1* are simpler than those in *2*. That is, each small piece of information in *1* is expressed in a single simple sentence. The same information in *2* conveys more meaning and is more cohesive. When *because* is added to attach the second "little" sentence to the first sentence of *1*, it signifies a causal relationship missing from *1*. The third "little" sentence of *1*, when added through deletion and attachment to the *because* clause, extends the logic. The rules that govern the attachment, movement, reduction, and transposition of sentence elements are transformational rules. Children acquire and use these rules in Stage IV and V.

One of the difficulties facing language scholars who are interested in this period concerns the complexity of children's utterances compared with the youngsters' comprehension. Do they still understand more complicated material than they can say? Bowerman (1979) has suggested that we may underestimate children's ability to produce complex language. She found that three-year-old children could produce sentences with joined elements in single utterances, as in these utterances with complement structures:

3. I wanna read book.
4. Look it a boy play ball. (Bowerman 1979, 286)

In some cases, a second verb completes the sentence. In *3*, both verbs share the subject; in *4*, there are two subjects.

Also before Stage IV, some children produce *wh* sentences such as

5. I show you how to do it.
6. I don't know who it is. (Bowerman 1979, 287)

In *5* and *6*, *how* and *who* each introduce a subordinate clause. These first embedded clauses are used as direct objects of the main verb or as adverbial clauses of place or manner. Relative clauses appear later.

Coordinated sentences—two independent clauses joined by a connective, usually *and*—are produced after the early appearance of complex structures. It seems, at first, that to coordinate two apparently equal elements ought to be simpler than to subordinate one to another. Coordinations, however, are not like strings of little sentences as in *1*; therefore, the structures in *3* and *5* are preferred. As children learn to use the connectives *and, then, because, so, if, or,* and *but*, the youngsters contend with more subtle relationships, and some of these relationships involve more than simply joining two equal elements. Of those involving the coordination of equal elements, Bowerman found that opposition, sequence, and causation appear before "conditional notions, then conditional and temporal statements with *when* and *then* and finally *before* and *after*" (1979, 287).

During the process of acquiring complexities—as in the process of acquiring any new and different structures—children experience difficulties.

7. I'm just gonna fall this on her. (Bowerman 1979, 302)

In this sentence, for example, the speaker "errs" in the selection of the verb. Just as younger children overgeneralize in the process of acquisition, this child overextends the embedding structure to verbs that adults would not use in the context.

Menyuk (1969) studied the language of nursery school and first-grade children. Although she did not trace an acquisition sequence for transformational rules, we can get an overview of growth between 3.8 and 6.5 by adapting some other data and comparing the two age groups. Table 3 illustrates the number of instances in which certain transformations appeared in the speech of subjects during recorded sessions. Transformations within single sentences are generally more common than rules that enable simple sentences to be combined into *conjoined* or *complex sentences*. Conjoined sentences are composed of two or more simple sentences joined by "and," "but," "or," etc. Complex sentences have a main clause and one or more subordinate clauses and also are called *embedded sentences*. Embedding takes place when a simple sentence becomes a subordinate clause attached to a main clause; for example, "the dog was barking" is embedded in "The boy ran after the dog that was barking." When two sentences are combined by children of this age group, conjoined sentences occur more often than complex sentences.

In Table 3, relative clauses and "because" clauses are fairly common, but "if" and "so" clauses are not. These last two types of clauses are used more often by the first-grade group than by the nursery-school-aged groups, so they are probably learned sometime during this stage by many children. Although this information does not tell us exactly when and in what order sentence combining transformations are learned, it does show that many common transformations of this sort are learned during this period.

During the later preschool period, children also acquire irregular inflections. This later learning occurs after the regular inflectional system is complete and applies to unique subsets of words. In her classic study on inflectional learning in children of nursery school and first-grade ages, Berko (1958) found, while testing inflections (word endings) on nonsense words, that preschoolers of 4.5 could often correctly use noun plurals and third person singular verb forms, but they did so without the degree of success of children of 6.3. Generally, all children had more difficulty with the plural ending in words such as "glasses" than they did with endings on "pictures" and "arms." The younger children also had more difficulty than the older ones with the past tense form "rang." The best performance for both groups came when the form was regular. In general, the differences between the younger and the older group were in terms of the number of errors rather than the kind of errors made. Thus, we find the same characteristic as in the previous stage of acquisition: As language is learned, rules are applied to general categories and then are redefined and applied to specific subgroups. By 5.0, most children have acquired many of the basic structures of their language. But they may not understand specialized structural relationships that exist in mature speakers.

In 1969, C. Chomsky published a study of five- to ten-year-old's acquisition of complex structures. Before her study, many believed that language acquisi-

TABLE 3. Subjects using selected transformations and sentence embeddings

Transformations	Nursery School (N = 48) (Age Range: 3.1–4.4) (Mean Age: 3.8)	First Grade (N = 48) (Age Range: 5.11–7.1) (Mean Age: 6.5)	Examples
Contraction	48	48	didn't
Possessives	48	48	Mary's hat
Pronoun (transformation)	48	48	. . . and *he* can . . .
Adjective	48	48	brown hat
Infinitive complement	48	48	I wanted to do it.
Main clause conjunction	41	48	He sang and Mary danced.
Conjunction with deletion (sub or VP)	40	47	Mary sang and danced.
Relative clause	37	46	The man who sang is old.
Because sentence embedding	30	46	. . . because he said so.
Particle separation	41	44	Put down the box, put it down.
Reflective	29	44	I did it myself
Imperative*	35	42	Shut the door.
Passive*	23	41	The boy was hit by the girl.
Participle complement	19	31	I saw her washing . . .
If-sentence embedding*	12	30	. . . if you want to.
So-sentence embedding*	12	29	. . . so he will be happy.
Compound of nominals*	6	24	baby chair
Iteration	5	13	You have to clean clothes to make them clean.

Source: Adapted from P. Menyuk, "Syntactic Structures in the Language of Children," *Child Development* 34 (1963): 407–22. Copyright © 1963 by The Society for Research in Child Development. Reprinted by permission of the Society for Research in Child Development and the author.
*Numbers are significantly different.

tion—the initial learning of structures—was completed before school entrance. After her publication, scholars had to reassess their thinking. In one part of the study, Chomsky asked her subjects to answer the question, "Is the doll easy to see?" when a blindfolded doll was presented. The question applied to the distinction in these two sentences.

John is eager to please.
John is easy to please.

In the first, the person doing the pleasing is John; in the second, someone else is doing the pleasing. To understand the difference is to understand the basic structure of complex sentence relationships. Chomsky's youngest subjects did not understand the second sentence referent and incorrectly answered *no* because they assumed that the doll was doing the seeing. Most of the oldest in the group tested did understand the referent and answered *yes*. There was uneven acquisition between the youngest and oldest subjects; chronological age did not entirely determine acquisition. Kessel (1970) tested the same structure with a different, and potentially less confusing, method and found generally earlier acquisition that was not completely related to chronological age.

Chomsky also found that when the subjects were asked to respond to another set of sentences by activating small dolls, the youngsters' ability to distinguish between two structures was uneven until the older ages. Sample sentences were

Bozo promises Donald to do a somersault. Make him do it.
Bozo tells Donald to do a somersault. Make him do it.

Chomsky discerned states of acquisition that were not closely related to chronological age. A different contrast between "ask"/"tell" ("Bozo asked/told Donald to . . .") in the Chomsky study was replicated by Kessel (1970) whose analysis showed "tell" is acquired first. "Tell" is then overgeneralized to "ask" until "ask" is acquired.

In a later study, Chomsky (1972) found uniformity across types of structures acquired. That is, children were apt to acquire comprehension of one complex structure at approximately the same time as another complex structure. Furthermore, although the age of acquisition varied among subjects, acquisition related with the exposure to reading the subject had experienced. As in early acquisition, in late language acquisition there is overgeneralizing from the most productive rule to the least. The conclusion drawn from these studies of older subjects is that the processes of language acquisition are similar to those of younger children and relate somehow to reading.

More obvious in school children's language performance than their learning of special esoteric structures is their increased maturing of language use during the elementary years. They combine words in infinite ways based on a set of rules. The capacity for creating new sentences is characteristic of children, too.

School children create longer and longer sentences that contain more information. Loban's (1963) longitudinal study of elementary school children's language showed that there were increasingly longer utterances as children grew older, but that individual variation was extensive. O'Donnell, Griffith, and Norris (1969) studied the language used by children in oral and, when appropriate, written situations. The subjects (in grades K, 1, 2, 3, 5, and 7) were asked to tell (and write) about a short film(s) seen without sound. The utterances were marked off by t-units (minimal terminal units that contained at least one main clause and all subordinate clauses attached to it). While there was growth in the length of these t-units throughout the years, the years of greatest gain were between kindergarten and first grade and between fifth and seventh grades. The t-units grew longer as children learned to make more subordinate clauses. That is, subjects became more proficient in embedding clauses into main clauses and in coordinating clauses together. Furthermore, the older children were apt to delete parts of sentences where applicable. In Hunt's (1970) study, older subjects (in high school) were more apt to reduce a simple sentence to less-than-a-predicate than were younger subjects. Thus, as school children become older, they are more apt to combine elements; they can say more in fewer words, and they have more content in longer utterances.

Sounds

At the end of the preschool period and even in the beginning of the elementary years, children still are learning to produce some sounds of the language. Certain sounds are problems for some elementary grade pupils, such as /r/ and /l/ (Carroll 1960). However, as Ingram (1976) points out, some children can perceive the sounds as contrasts even though unable to produce the sounds. Generally, it is important that teachers do not confuse children who are slow in developing the last learned sounds with children who are unable to make the sounds acquired early by most children. Thus, while a teacher does not need to worry about a child substituting /θ/ for /d/ (*dis*) in kindergarten, she might become concerned with a child's inability to use /b/.

Meaning

While production of phonology appears to be progressing well for most children during the latter part of the preschool period and the beginning of elementary school, the development of phonology perception is acquired somewhat unevenly. This uneven acquisition is a matter of concern in beginning reading, as we will see in a later chapter.

The first years of life are filled with new concepts, new motor abilities, and new control evidenced through language acquisition. At the start of this chapter, we examined the social supports for language acquisition. Although directed to the very beginnings of language, it is also true—as becomes clear in Chapter 4 when we turn to language difference—that the quality of interaction and the quality of children's experiences determine, to a large extent, youngsters' preparation for learning mature language and literacy. From the point of school entrance, children's language development is largely in the realm of meaning. For, as is evident from this discussion, there is an important distinction to be made in comparing acquisition of semantics with the learnings of the other components of language. We have seen that in acquisition of syntax and phonology, the child appears to use the sophisticated learning strategies of categorization, generalization, and application to new instances efficiently. Our question now is whether the same strategies are used in acquisition of language meaning. Although categorization and application may help in learning vocabulary in some instances (for example, experiences with various household brushes will help a child learn that a painter's tool is also a brush), these strategies will not always work. We can imagine the child's confusion in learning the names for the containers used in the home: Some are bottles, some jars, some glasses, some pans, and some pots. Some containers are made out of glass, but not all glasses are made out of glass. Some pots are large, but there are also small pots such as the mustard pot. And what is the difference between a cooking pot and a pan? Because the strategies for acquisition that work in one semantic cluster may not work with many others, trial, comparison with adult use, correction when mistakes are made, and many direct experiences with objects are necessary before full acquisition of attributes, separation of items, and groupings of words in a cluster reach maturity. Consequently, during the preschool and primary years, there is apt to be some confusion in children's minds concerning the attributes associated with terms and the differentiation of one term in a cluster from others.

Conceptual development is different from that of syntax and phonology both in terms of the sheer amount to be learned and in the continuation of the process beyond early childhood. Although adults help children learn vocabulary items by naming, it is obvious that children must have many experiences in order to develop meaning. These experiences should ensure that both positive and negative attributes are acquired so that categorization of words occurs. As was stressed by Piaget and Vygotsky, development of language meaning cannot occur in isolation, although much of the motivation for growth of meaning comes from general language development as children use their knowledge of language to order their experiences.

SUMMARY

Scholars of language acquisition have established that language acquisition is a complex affair. The theoretical shifts that continue to occur stimulate further explorations. Until we understand the motivation and understanding behind children's early utterances, scholars will challenge themselves and one another to further study from which we will all benefit. The activity and success of these scholars' work have stimulated other investigation as well. For example, as we see in Chapter 3, they have stimulated new ways to look at the beginnings of literacy learning.

SELECTED ACTIVITIES

1. Some sample beginning sentences are listed below (from Bloom, Lightboom, and Hood 1975). See if you can identify them according to the six categories of expressed meaning: nomination, recurrence, nonexistence, agent and action, action and object, possessor and possession.

Mommy push	see man	this a dump car, too
my blanket	more cookie	can't do dat
sit lap	look at rabbit	sit orange chair
here ball	where's it	dis a my coat
milk all gone	duck water	bit finger
spank me	Gia book	this a bye-bye boy

2. Explain why a child might say, "Mommy came" and later say, "Look, Mommy comed."

3. Before reading the next chapters, speculate about how teachers might help children develop increased understanding of related terms such as "in," "out," "through," and "over." Think in terms of Clark's Semantic Feature Acquisition Theory. What feature might all these words share for children learning these concepts? What features not yet acquired would prevent children from differentiating the word meanings?

4. Become an observer of a small group of preschool children at their school or in a play setting. Once you know the focus of their talk, listen very carefully for how they each negotiate their turns and influence the group. Watch for how different participants' ideas are accepted or rejected. Indicate how these negotiations are like a conversation.

5. Tape two meetings with the same small child, once when he or she is talking with a peer (see 4 above) and once when he or she is talking with an adult. Transcribe a good set of utterances from each conversation, and count the number of complex sentences in each, using the material reported here from Bowerman and from Menyuk.

6. Compare the level of talk in open conversation in a first grade classroom in terms of syntactic complexity with the complexity of two kinds of books: trade books read to children and readers children use in initial literacy training in school. What are the differences, and what is the significance of the differences?

7. As an "advanced organizer" for the next chapter, write a list of children's language development aspects that you think indicate it is possible for small children to learn a lot about reading and writing before school. Are there indicators in this report about children's language that make you feel early literacy experiences are bound to be limited until the age of five or six?

3
The Sources of Literacy

For a long time, we have known about children who learn to read before they are taught formally in schools. Durkin's (1966) studies of "early readers" revealed something of a surprise: Contrary to widespread belief, some early readers were children of average intelligence. In fact, more common than genius (there were some very high IQ children among her early readers) was the early readers' manifest desire to ask about words and text. With the publication of Clarke's (1976) report on Scottish children and Torrey's (1973) case study of one child, a generalized picture emerged of children who become interested in literacy early. They are not necessarily gifted in the usual sense; they ask a lot of questions about words, letters, and text. They write messages. They have favorites among the stories their parents read. They receive answers to their questions from at least one literate person (a parent or perhaps an older sibling) who is interested in the child's progress. And, thanks to her care in following her child participants through the elementary school years, we know that Durkin's early reading children maintained a lead in achievement through six years compared to equivalently intelligent children who did not read early.

Only in recent years have educators begun to give up a long-held, popular notion about the beginnings of reading and writing. For many decades, school people believed that children needed to attain a mental age of 6.6 in order to profit from reading instruction. Thus, parents were advised not to start their children reading before first grade; some were even told to discourage interest their children exhibited. This author remembers a first grade teacher in her school who complained about children who had learned to make letters at home and who made them incorrectly. Kindergartens used to do very little in the way of introduction to reading, other than some simple reading readiness. The advice given parents that they should not encourage early reading came from educators who had been influenced by the interpretation of a study by Morphett and Washburne (1931) that suggested a relationship between mental age and success with beginning reading. Their study had a persistent impact despite some contrary evidence from work by Gates (1937) and by Gates and Bond (1935–1936). The idea of holding off formal reading instruction also may have come from the overall developmental stance prevalent in American education, a stance that recently has changed.

There are a number of reasons why we have changed our views about the beginnings of instruction in literacy. Not only have we learned of the literacy learning in children with strong home support, but we also could no longer overlook the fact that children in England and Scotland were taught reading from the age of five with no ill effects. Moreover, since the 1960s, a series of demands for greater academic challenge for students at all levels has inserted a wedge in the convention that the first grade is where reading begins. Initially, in response to our alarm over the Soviet Sputnik, science and mathematics curricula were modified during the 1960s. In the process, some effect was felt in language and reading. When lowered scores on national tests began to attract media attention, critics correctly examined the expectations at all grade levels. Evidence from Chall (1967) and from a series of governmental sponsored studies (Bond and Dykstra 1967) demonstrated higher beginning reading achievement

52

for children taught in a strong sound-symbol program. These findings influenced the development of the national television programs *Sesame Street* and *Electric Company* and basal reading programs. When these television programs appeared, a focus on sounds of letters and letter combinations became available to all preschool children. Finally, when teachers became increasingly aware that some kindergarten children already had begun to read and write a little, these educators began to adjust their programs to respond correctly. Today, many kindergartens extend and support the beginnings of literacy.

Parallel with this context for change has been an important area of study, the fruits of which have significant potential for directing the substance of the instruction in kindergartens and first grades. Child language scholars were examining the interaction between infant and adult during book reading (i.e. Ninio and Bruner 1978; Snow 1983) initially because of interest in learning about children's *language development*. Subsequently, they saw these episodes as a medium for learning about *literacy*. Concurrently, scholars of early reading found that language acquisition study provided an explanation for children's acquisition of concepts about reading and writing and also methodological direction for their study. It was reasoned that if language development were supported through the social framework of the exchange, then the written form of language also might be acquired early in life through social exchange, and naturally. Scholars who work with this hypothesis have established a productive field of study and, more importantly, have made observations that suggest new directions for the curricula of kindergartens and first grades.

The study of the beginnings of reading and writing in preschoolers is still young. It has not been possible in a few short years for scholars to describe literacy beginnings completely. There are unanswered questions. In this chapter, we will find an introduction to the study of initial literacy so that readers may understand how young children learn language and literacy simultaneously. Naturally acquired concepts about literacy learned at home without formal schooling—the focus of this chapter—will lead to ideas about instruction. Formal instruction in reading and writing is described in the last three chapters.

Among the scholars who study this area, aptly called the "roots of literacy" by Yetta Goodman (1980), are those who stress the naturalness of the writing and reading growth process. They contrast the literacy acquisition that occurs out of school with the supposedly less natural experience characteristic of formal school instruction. The schools are blamed for presenting literacy instruction in confusing, unnatural ways so that too many children are not successful (e.g., Bruner [1984] and Ferreiro and Teberosky [1982] applied to the United States and South America, respectively). Some writers have examined early literacy among people in different cultural groups within North America and elsewhere (Anderson and Stoke 1984; Heath and Thomas 1984; Scheifflin and Cochran-Smith 1984; Teale, forthcoming). Some scholars have identified similarities between language and literacy learning (e.g., Snow 1983). Donaldson (1984), however, reminds us that there are also important differences. Some scholars focus upon the social context of literacy learning, while others emphasize the psychological processes within the learner. Most scholars agree that interactions between preschoolers and family about words and writing play an important role in the acquisition process. Moreover, all would agree that literacy can begin as language is being acquired. Even those children who do not read or write independently until much later and even those whose families do not read much to them learn something about literacy during the preschool years, as we will see in the next chapter (Heath 1983).

This chapter has three parts. The first describes literacy in its initial stages, comparing its acquisition with language and discussing book reading support during the emergence of literacy. Specific observations about the beginning of reading comprise the second section. The third describes children's early writings, including the phenomenon of invented spelling, which some preschoolers use to communicate through writing. As in the previous chapters, we continue in this chapter to describe children as if there are no important variations in interest, successful learning, and experience. Obviously, there are numerous individual differences in literacy acquisition; indeed, some beginning first graders are strong, independent readers, while others have only a dim appreciation of letters. Moreover, there are variations in success and interest between groups of children. Such differences are, of course, critical to educators; these differences are not neglected in this book. In an attempt to establish the basic concepts of development in language and the beginnings of literacy, general trends have been the initial focus. Chapter 4 addresses the important questions of difference.

THE BEGINNINGS OF LITERACY

Some Precursors to Reading

Bruner (1984) asked why very young children would want to learn about reading and writing since they are engaged in so much other learning and since they do not need reading and writing to communicate. His own answer was that children want to experience the world of stories, the world of dramatic interest, by themselves. One young child took a direct approach, apparently. Sternhell (1984) wrote of her friend:

> A couple of years ago, when my friend Michael was young (he's now 4 years old and sophisticated about the limits of literature), he tried to climb inside a book. Unwilling to believe that so wonderful a world was unreachable, he simply opened the tale to his favorite page, carefully arranged his choice on the floor and stepped in. He tried again and again, certain he would soon get it right, and each time he was left standing out in the cold he cried in bewilderment. (p. 1)

In another way, my own daughter, an avid story consumer during her preschool years, expressed what Bruner meant. My daughter told me, with enthusiasm and great satisfaction after she had read a story or two by herself, "Now I do not have to wait until you're not busy. When I want a story, I can read it myself!"

But we must ask if such clear motivation characterizes many very young children. It appears that children learn many different skills as they approach the beginnings of independence in literacy. And it is difficult to believe that very young preschoolers' desires for independent reading motivate their acquisition of preliminary notions about reading and writing. Did my daughter, for example, have a strong desire to read independent of me during the times she learned that

pictures and text have different functions;
print contains the story;
the words the reader says come from the print;
stories tend to have some predictable segments and features;
it is possible to write messages;
there are words, and written words are made up of letters;
letters are used over and over again in different arrangements to express words;
letters are arranged from left to right;
the letters are in linear fashion to represent the sequence of sounds in spoken
    words;
spaces delineate word boundaries;
letters come in capitals, in small print, and even in script, but they all have the
    same significance;
some marks are used to show beginnings and ends of text?

Young children are simply not future-oriented enough for all of these notions (and there are more) about reading to direct all the learning required prior to successful independent reading. While it is true that young children take enormous pleasure in the stories they hear and see and are thereby inspired to learn about reading, there are other motivations that lie behind the learning of very preliminary skills of literacy.

Durkin (1966) and Clark (1984) both found that many of their early readers initially were interested in writing rather than reading. Many children wanted to learn to write messages. (One day when he was four, my son demanded help in writing the sign *Keep Out of My Room*.) In families in which reading and writing are important—where children are advised not to disturb the adult who is "busy" reading and writing—the written message and the book or other text are obviously significant. To children in such families, each newly acquired literacy skill means they are more like their parents. Moreover, their parents welcome each new skill and each question about reading and writing.

Literacy and Language Learning

This account probably sounds rather familiar. I am suggesting that children of literate parents are able to find sufficient information about literacy to begin the process of learning at home, before schooling. This sounds like learning language, but how similar are the two learning processes? Of course, since reading and writing are language systems, there are similarities. For one, both written and oral language systems are media through which meaning is represented. In learning both, children must have obtained necessary levels of maturation. We have found that language learning is a process by which the language learner constructs for him or herself a rule system from which to generate communication. Because this process happens with no *direct* instruction, and because we understand that reading and writing are acquired in formal schooling, we may wonder about the strength of the parallels in acquisition. Are there features of language learning that might shed light on literacy acquisition? Language learning consists of the child's active structuring of conceptual knowledge into a workable system; does that notion have some bearing on literacy? Indeed, there are several parallels in the two processes that provide insights into the early stages of literacy learning, insights that later influence the design of an instructional model.

One parallel lies in social interaction, even though reading and writing are basically solitary activities as we experience them. The reader will recall that Snow (1983) described features of oral exchange that also occur during book exchanges. In both exchanges, adults use "semantic contingency" to expand child utterances about the topic at hand; the adults extend that topic, answer child questions, and ask pertinent questions of the child. Moreover, in both types of exchange, parents use scaffolding, the adult process of requiring greater complexity and simultaneously providing cues so that their children can respond successfully. Adults insist that children complete the topic.

According to Snow (1983), there is another characteristic of both the oral and the book exchange: Practice through repetitious, routinized events is needed. Just as the give-and-take of peek-a-boo games is predictable and characteristic of early role-taking exchanges in oral language (Bruner 1975), so too is the give-and-take in book reading turns. Ninio and Bruner (1978) showed how the first exchanges involve four distinct, regular steps: the mother attracts the child's attention and focuses upon a feature of a book picture; the mother requests a name for the picture or (later) a response to a question; the child provides a label, response, or facsimile; and the mother reinforces and accepts the response. An episode involving these steps would be followed by another within the same frames. As the child matures, the routines gather complexities; the questions require longer responses, and the reinforcements are links to new questions. Rich environments do include episodes of reading routines that make learning about literacy possible. For example, children listen to the same nursery rhymes many times; gradually, they gain mastery of the word sequences and build a sense of rhyme. Many children also go through a period in which they insist on "reading" the same storybook night after night. Again, the iterative experience allows them the opportunity to gain control over the events and even some of the features of the text.

Another similarity in early language and literacy growth occurs in the process of decontextualization. At the start, children's oral comments cannot be interpreted unless an observer is present and uses the context to understand. One child's "More horse" could not be correctly understood unless someone was at the museum with the little girl who wanted to see the Degas sculpture of a horse again. With more words and more complex rules by which to generate talk, language may be understood without knowing the full context. Similarly, the process of learning about words in print may involve decontextualization. Writing is the essence of decontextualized language. For as long as the page (or the computer disk or tape) lasts, the meaning will last. Snow and others (Ferreiro 1984; Goodman, forthcoming; Snow 1983) have suggested that children learn to separate the printed expression from the context in a series of steps. First, word "reading" often involves repeating memorized labels for familiar objects: *Crest*, for example, on the toothpaste tube. Real reading involves learning the letter pattern so that *Crest* is recognized in any context. Goodman (forthcoming) described a test of reading knowledge she developed. The test involves three tasks, each progressively more removed from the original context of use. First task asks the child to recognize a label in its common setting (the actual representation of a stop sign, for example). The next task involves recognizing the word *stop* with some, but not all, contextual cues. The final task, of course, requires the child to recognize the word in print. The process appears, then, to be one of decentralization, but it also requires some specific notions about words. Comments from others and practice helps in the transition (Heath 1983). And movement from the second to the third step may require children to process phonemes (Ehri and Wilce 1985).

In sum, there are many ways in which the acquisition of language parallels language learning. During book reading, children learn about language and about literacy. There are also important and rather obvious ways in which the two processes differ. For one thing, language acquisition is a universal phenomenon. Literacy is not. Language is acquired by all—except those severely afflicted with a mental handicap—without any obvious direct instruction; relatively speaking, there are few children who become literate who have no direct instruction. Donaldson (1984) pointed out, too, that the acquisition of literacy takes longer than language acquisition.

Other unique characteristics of written language deserve examination as they relate to the questions of acquisition. In contrast to oral language, reading must be obscure to children when they observe their family members read silently. To understand silent reading, children try to develop an explanation for how the marks on paper become meaningful stories (Ferreiro 1984). In addition to learning about words, letters, and the alphabetic properties of text, children also must learn about things such as the spaces between the sequences of letters and the punctuation marks. These demands have implications for instruction, as we will see in later chapters.

The question of practice for competency reveals differences between language and literacy acquisition, too. Kuczai (1983) reported a study of children's language practice, apparently a far more important ingredient of growth than thought earlier. To practice language, children only need to engage in talk with family and friends or by themselves in their cribs. But practicing literacy requires more adult intervention and, at the very least, the provision of literacy materials. More importantly, children need to have available easy books to experience over and over and willing families to respond to their questions.

A final and very important difference between learning language and learning literacy is cultural. Unlike oral language, which is the universal and essential means for communicating, written language is not needed as much. Unless children are raised in a culture in which written language is an essential means for communication, it is not needed. Without language, however, it is nearly impossible for a child to function in any group. Without literacy, it is possible for a child to function in most groups.

These differences between language learning and literacy acquisition are rather obvious, but they have strong educational implications. For our purposes, we need to remember that the support of development in one mode will have an impact on the other. Just as the provision of exchanges will support early understandings of literacy, it also will help children learn more complex language structures. This reciprocity continues to operate during early schooling (Chomsky 1972; Clay 1972).

Sources for Literacy Learning

Since early ideas about literacy are emerging from book exchanges and since the social interaction that occurs during these events appears to be supportive of development, it is important to note that there are other ways in which children gain ideas about literacy. Anderson and Stokes (1984), Heath (1983), and Teale (forthcoming) observed the literacy events of a large number of non-middle-class families. The scholars found many different sources for learning about literacy other than book exchanges that preschoolers could draw upon. Religious activities, bill paying, selection of television programs through schedule reading, watching *Sesame Street* and *Electric Company*, and following directions for home improvements are just some of the family literacy activities found common in the observed households.

Book reading, however, contains actions similar to those in oral language exchanges. It involves the media of school and is the source of much pleasure, and through book exchanges, the parent intends to participate in literacy events with the child. Snow and Goldfield (1982) found that language during book exchanges tended to be more sophisticated than during oral language exchanges. Clearly, book exchanges are rich resources for discovery. For these reasons, we examine them here to discover their potential for understanding the beginnings of literacy and for use as models for formal instruction. But we must remember that preschoolers acquire knowledge of writing (especially) and reading outside such exchanges, too.

Scholars have found that some parents begin to share picture books with their children even before a child's first birthday has occurred (e.g., Ninio and Bruner 1978). As Snow and Ninio (forthcoming) point out, these early experiences are not truly literary; initially, the exchanges include the parts of the picture naming activity. Reading the book text begins later in the second or third year. The aspect critical to beginning literacy is the amount by which sensitive parents highlight essential features of writing to their children during the exchanges over books. These intimate moments in children's experience are emotionally and educationally purposeful. Parents are knowledgeable about the level their children have achieved (Teale 1984). The Vygotskian zone of proximal development exists in the book exchanges: The settings are routinized; the focus is upon topics of childhood. The parent is potentially an excellent guide to literacy.

These situational qualities are displayed in the "prose home movie" developed by Taylor (forthcoming). The details of a family reading (one adult and three children) of the entire story, *Chester Cricket's Pigeon Ride*, comprise the paper. The mother asks questions and focuses the children's attention to points at a level that they can understand. She supports the youngsters; yet, she challenges each child. The children include a daughter age seven, a daughter age five, and a baby boy who appears to be a little older than two. Selections from the "movie" follow:

Mother	**Children**
Focus on Matthew, the baby	
Matthew, do you see the cricket?	*Matthew:* Cricket
Right, there's the cricket.	*Sarah, age five:* Cricket, piggett.
Mother points to cricket. To Matthew: That's Chester.	*Sarah, helping but ignored:* Look at his feet. That's where.
Mother, to Matthew: Can you see the cricket? Where's the pigeon?	*Matthew:* Cricket. *Matthew points to pigeon.*
	Jessica, age seven: Good boy.
Focus on Sarah, age five	
Mother, to Sarah: Do you see the stump in this picture, Sarah?	*Sarah points and asks:* This?
Mm, mm. Where would he sun himself, do you think?	*Sarah:* In the sun.
Right, mm.	*Matthew:* A cat.
What is a stump, Sarah?	*Matthew:* A cat.
	Sarah: A stump? Like this? (She points to a stump in picture.)
Well, what is a stump?	*Sarah:* The tree was starting to grow, and then somebody says, 'I want to find things to chop,' and he chops the tree.
And what is left?	*Matthew, holding his mother's face:* Ma.
	Sarah: A stump.
	Matthew: Mama, mama.
And that's where Chester Cricket used to sun.	*Matthew:* Mama, mama.
Yes, Matthew.	*Matthew, special words for:* I turn the page.

Talk with Jessica, age seven

Mother listens to Jessica.	*Jessica:* We had two crickets in the classroom.
	Sarah: I love putting necklaces on me.
To Jessica: So you've experienced meeting a cricket then.	*Jessica:* Yeah, but we've never heard it sing.
Mm.	*Jessica:* And I've experienced that they die very quickly.
Mm.	*Sarah, playing with necklace, to mother:* I'll read this to you. I'll read this to you.
To Sarah: Go ahead.	*Sarah:* Big Kiss
To Sarah: What does *big* begin with? What letter?	*Sarah:* B
And what does *kiss* begin with?	*Sarah:* K
	Jessica, to mother: Now, keep going.
All right, but Chester didn't only stay . . .*	

In the first part of this record (Focus on Matthew), the mother attends to the baby, mostly. She engages him in a naming episode as she says, "Where's the pigeon?" The parts are clear and have an interesting element: The elder sister reinforces. Later in Taylor's report, Matthew gets bored and wanders from the story. However, during his periodic returns, he is drawn into the reading. And, at the end of the "Focus on Sarah," for example, he indicates a desire to participate by turning the page. He has the opportunity to learn that there is an appropriate time for page turning, as his mother refuses his request then but later asks him to turn the page at the right place. The mother also refuses to be diverted from her discussion with Sarah by Matthew who even holds her face in his hands, a strong example of parental insistence on keeping with a topic until complete. The mother guides these two children at their current level of functioning. She provides scaffolding to enable good responses.

Turning to the brief exchange included here with Jessica in the "Talk with Jessica," we see an example of something quite important to book reading exchanges. The mother's single comment (after Jessica's remark about crickets from her own experience) enables Jessica to take a more distant view of the story information. Instead of saying, "So you've seen a cricket . . . ," which would have resulted in a descriptive conversation, the mother said, "So you've *experienced* meeting a cricket. . . ." In this way, the mother encourages Jessica to reflect upon her experiences. The mother's less didactic role with Jessica appears to help the child understand the difference between the real and the fictional world.

Talk about stories and talk about story information may serve as a means for children to acquire a language about language, a metalanguage (Olson 1984).

---

*Adapted from Taylor (forthcoming) and printed with permission of the author and publisher.

Even Matthew, although he does not actually have the vocabulary, does have a signal that means, "I'll turn the page." Sarah can leave the story for a while and return with no loss of meaning. As Jessica removes herself from the story, she begins to develop an abstract view of the text.

The beginnings of the process for learning a language about language and text have been described by Snow and Ninio (forthcoming). The following are notions acquired during book exchanges, which Snow and Ninio feel are critical to children's understanding of *language* and *literacy:*

1. Books are meant to be read, not manipulated. They are "objects of contemplation" rather than objects upon which to act.
2. The books—not the reader—determine what happens in the "reading." Experiences from the real world are used to help understand the book
3. The pictures represent things; they are symbolic, not real.
4. The pictures in books are for naming.
5. The pictures in books also can represent events. And the discussion surrounding the events begins to resemble the narrative as speakers, mothers mostly, refer to events leading to and subsequent to pictured events. Even the characters may be described.
6. Book events are outside of real time.
7. Books are autonomous; they present a fictional world that exists outside the world of the child but that the child may enter.

The first talk between adult and infant in book exchanges involves naming, and the pictures are the source for talk about pictured events. The talk may change and become like a narrative, thereby leading the child to learn about story structure so he or she later can understand written stories. As separated as book stories are from real world time, children learn that stories are different from their world (Snow 1983). When the talk about pictures wanes and the story text is read, children learn that written stories may excite and entrance. As Bruner (1984) suggested, the world of stories probably motivates the desire for independent reading. We wonder about children who do not have such experience. Teale (1984) indicates that book reading of this sort is not necessary to reading acquisition; other literacy events may substitute. However, a rich reading background is likely to help in reading acquisition and also may encourage long-term interest and understanding of the metalanguage of literacy.

In Chapter 1, the nature-nurture contrast was discussed. In this section, it appears that the environment during the preschool years is important to the development of concepts about literacy. Parents do not formally teach, but clearly, the mother in the Taylor report is teaching her children. The style is interactive; each child participates at his or her level. The environmental, nurturing side of learning has been described and will serve us as we examine instruction. But questions remain about the psychological processes, and we examine these processes in children who learn some reading and writing in the next two sections of this chapter.

THE BEGINNINGS OF READING

Out of the social context of reading, children acquire many ideas, and each one helps the youngsters understand the characteristics of written language. Sulzby (1981) has found that children's knowledge of the distinction between oral language and reading indicates their maturity toward literacy skill. We focus here first on reading, not because it is acquired separately from either oral language or from writing, but for clarity. The discussion of the beginning of reading refers to initial steps taken by children who are progressing on their own (with, of course, the social-family supports just discussed) prior to formal schooling. Later chapters consider school reading instruction. The discussion comes from close examination of a few children, some of whom are highly motivated to learn about reading and writing. Children who learn to read early "on their own" and to write with invented spelling are not typical; how they learn provides insights into the processes of learning important to our instructional model.

Preschool Reading Concepts

We know that children today learn a lot about words and print at a very early age. Goodman (forthcoming) reported that sixty percent of three-year-olds and eighty percent of four- and five-year-olds could read some words in context (for example, *stop* in the form of a sign). All three-year-olds could handle books properly. Many five-year-olds had learned that print carries a message and had a concept of story. Many children knew the parts of a book, and although they did not know the technical words for reading, they had resources to draw upon. Sulzby (1981) studied kindergarteners' knowledge of reading and found that they knew book parts and had a strong sense of the purposes of reading. Additionally, when asked to read their dictated stories, they attempted reading, most with the special prosody, or intonation, of reading. The experiences directly provided by parents and acquired vicariously through television enable nearly all preschoolers to know a good deal about reading before school. In a later study, Sulzby (forthcoming) found a number of different, emergent reading behaviors that appear to be developmental. When preschool and kindergarten children were asked to read their favorite storybook in any way they could, they responded, from the lowest to the highest, as follows: low-level refusals to read; unformed stories (such as labelling); oral language-like stories; written language-like stories (with different intonation); and print-based responses from refusals to word naming, to independent reading. These behaviors suggest that children's awareness of the meaning of print develops after considerable learning about stories and story meaning.

A study of children learning initial concepts about reading by Ferreiro and Teberosky (1982) conducted in Buenos Aires with first grade and younger cross-age groups provides some clues as to how children develop a system for understanding reading. The acquisition of initial reading concepts develops slowly. Learning about the complexity of reading and its functions begins at first, according to Ferreiro and Teberosky, with the idea that reading is not happening unless it is outloud. When children learn that the message remains the same on successive readings and, therefore, that the text bears the message, not the reader, they begin to understand that the reader can do the same thing silently. Ferreiro and Teberosky found that many preschoolers and first graders acquire quite a clear idea of the types of written discourse, including fiction and nonfiction. Important to this knowledge are the talk that occurs during exchanges with children and the explanations provided to the children while parents are engaged in the youngsters' array of literacy activities.

Ferreiro and Teberosky found that when children first encounter books, they do not understand the difference between text and pictures. Once children find that text and pictures do differ, the youngsters believe the text consists of the *names* of objects in the picture, what we know to be nouns. When children's sense of letters and words produces a conflict because more printed ''words'' exist on a page than the simple name of the picture, the children search for a more efficient explanation. As is the case throughout the process of learning about reading, the conflict stimulates the generation of new rules for figuring out the text. At the next level of understanding, children come to know that text represents all of what is said during reading. Once they know that text represents oral language, young children still must learn about both oral and written words within an utterance. We must also recognize that children who have not learned these concepts about the union of talk and written text may find the focus upon individual words and letters in schools confusing. Moreover, children who have not learned the terms used in school instruction of reading—terms such as *letter, word, page,* and *beginning*—which literacy acquiring children learn during the course of conversations with family members, will have additional confusions to deal with.

Another question pursued in the Ferreiro and Teberosky study concerned recognition of letters, which is acquired in cumulative stages. While it is not certain that all children *must* proceed through all stages, there are apparently at least two common issues for children to resolve. First, children must learn to distinguish letters and numbers; once youngsters learn this distinction, they think letters have syllabic value. For example, for a child to name the letter *B,* as ''bee,'' he or she naturally associates it with a syllable, one we would designate in writing as *bee.* There apparently are differences in how children learn letter names. Ferreiro (forthcoming) described how one boy, Santiago, learned that letters ''belong'' to people and that ''his'' letter was *S* (see Chapter 1). As children learn the names of vowels and consonants, the youngsters have difficulty in trying to figure out the sequence of letters in print while attempting to assign the *name* to each letter. Again, a situational encounter in which a previous system does not work causes children to find another explanation. This particular conflict ultimately will result in the abandonment of the syllabic idea and the acquisition of the alphabetic property of our writing system. When that transition begins, children learn first that letters are assigned sounds and then that letters are used repeatedly in different sequences. And reading begins.

A Case Study

So that learning the beginning skills of reading moves toward reading independence without formal training, children must have, at the least, a supportive environment. And the case study by Bissex (1980) is a rich source for understanding this growth within a supportive environment like ones described in the previous section. Bissex's study traces her son Paul's active learning during his latter preschool years as he successfully pursued a quest for literacy. The Bissexes had a book-laden home. Paul's parents read to him a lot, but they did not teach him reading in any *formal* way. He did, however, regularly watch *Sesame Street* and *Electric Company*.

Paul Bissex learned to read and to write during the years prior to formal instruction. His mother reported that he was intensely interested alternately in either reading or writing. She documented that the skills learned in writing were stimulated by reading skills; less obviously, reading supported Paul's investigation of writing. At 2.6, he had favorite books and knew their titles. As was true of several of Sulzby's (1981) kindergarten children, Paul would make up approximate and meaningful story reconstructions of his favorite books, accompanied by page turning when reading on "his own." He also could recognize the sign *exit*. Having learned that there were words in print that were equivalent to spoken words when stories were read, Paul needed only an idea of letters and their sounds to initiate his quest.

At 5.1, Paul turned earnestly to reading after he had acquired essential concepts about stories and print. His initial spelling system was based on a concept of letter names leading to syllables (see the next section). His excited interest in letters was related to printed text, and at 5.3, he announced, "Once you know how to spell something, you know how to read it!" Paul began reading the titles of books, then labels, signs, and the writing on cereal boxes. Even in these early attempts, Paul used the graphic cues that matched his spelling system. He combined these clues with the setting of his words (i.e., the books' appearance, the particular box of cereal, the shape of the sign). His use of these clues indicated a primitive use of context for unlocking difficult words. When puzzled by words that did not make sense to him, he self corrected until his attempts were meaningful. And like his use of context, this strategy remained through his growth toward reading skill. Thus, even at the start of reading, this child was very strategic, using three essential elements for figuring out the words he wanted: graphic cues, context cues, and self correction. However, due to the reading material he chose, simple words did not reappear; thus, he was not building a sight vocabulary.

With increased competence in the use of graphic cues, Paul began to turn to continuous text. His mother suggested a familiar story with repetitious, graphically regular, simple words (words like *cat, hat, dump,* and *grumpy*) when he was 5.6. The next month, he read a similar book nearly independently and aloud. Although discouraged at first, he became increasingly confident and tried out his new skills on a variety of books. Clearly, this child was practicing on materials at an appropriately simple level. Bissex reported that there was a period during this time in which Paul began to concentrate particularly on the graphic cues available to him from his writing experiences. Like other successful beginning readers, he continuously self corrected, especially with words critical to the content (Weber 1970b). Also, like school-taught beginning readers, Paul leaned more upon graphic cues than context as he went through a period of learning the alphabetic principle of writing. Once he was more competent in using the sounds of letters, he experienced less frustration and again used context cues with graphic ones, paralleling what Biemiller (1970) found in first graders observed during formal instruction.

By the time that Paul was 6.0, he began to really enjoy reading and read many simple books. Silent reading (at first with moving lips) occurred just before his sixth birthday. He continued to read to his parents aloud and silently to himself for pleasure. His determination and strategic approach to reading, coupled with acquisition of knowledge about the relationship between oral and written expression, produced an efficient system for reading, one that continued after entering school.

Paul is not the only early reader described in academic literature. Torrey (1973) reported that John, a kindergartner she met in a segregated black school in the South, learned to read without formal instruction. Although his family had books, he did not have as enriched a literacy as Paul Bissex. Like Paul, however, and like the children Durkin (1966) studied, John was rather assertive in his insistence upon reading. Torrey questioned his family (John was the third of five children in a working class family whose parents had not graduated from high school) and found that its members offered John no instruction. John learned about words from television commercials and from the labels on cans and boxes. Since she observed his family answer his questions about arithmetic problems, Torrey inferred that they also had answered a lot of questions about words.

It appears to be characteristic of early readers to ask *very specific questions* and to receive specific answers to those questions. Bissex did not focus upon her interactions with Paul, but it is evident that her answers were direct and clear and that she and her husband provided a challenging environment. In John's case, too, the family provided direct answers to his questions; the challenge apparently came from words displayed before him. Challenge and clarity of responses to specific questions are the critical elements of Vygotsky's zone of proximal development. The challenge drives the child beyond his or her level of current thinking; the clarity aids in assuring success. These children constructed their system for literacy, which, in Torrey's words, suggests that "reading is learned, not taught" (1973, 156). It is evident that the children in these accounts did actively seek to learn to read; indeed, the children of the Ferreiro and Teberosky (1982) study also did the same. Much of these children's success depended upon their concurrent learning of writing, through which they learned the principles of the alphabetic system.

THE BEGINNINGS OF WRITING

Young children do not believe they can read unless they obviously do read; they do believe in their ability to write, even though it is primitive (Goodman, forthcoming; Graves 1983; Sulzby 1981). The acquired skills of writing have an impact on the reading notions they are learning; the reverse is also true. Nevertheless, we should note that the skills and concepts of reading and writing have only "moderate overlap." Much of the observation that writing precedes reading comes from parents. Like children, adult informants are likely to consider different criteria for writing and for reading acquisition. While many accept invented spelling as writing, they are apt to consider only independent reading as reading (Shanahan, unpublished). It is not terribly important to determine which comes first, reading or writing.

Nearly all children do learn something about writing during the preschool years. All the middle and upper-middle class kindergarten children Sulzby (1981) observed could write their names; many also knew the conventional spelling of other words. Moreover, when they were asked how they learned, they identified both parental help and their own efforts at copying, learning the letters, and practicing as significant. Sulzby (forthcoming) describes the kinds of "writing" children do when asked to write; these items are ordered in a hierarchy that only roughly represents stages, since not all children engage in all the activities listed. Sulzby's list includes

drawing
scribbling
forms that resemble letters
well-learned words
invented spelling
conventional spelling

As was true in the previous section, analysis of some children's writing efforts indicates principles helpful in understanding the acquisition process. These principles illustrate literacy learning in informal situations like those in language and literacy acquisition.

Ferreiro and Teberosky (1982) established successive stages of children's construction of a writing system and found that in preschool and first grade children, several stages were necessary for writing to develop. Children's experiments (more evident among the middle than the lower class children) with writing involved (1) the use of straight and curved lines that only the writer could interpret, and even then not for long; (2) after some letters are learned, the writing of letters in different combinations to represent language; (3) then, attempts to assign a sound value to these "letters," thereby illustrating the children's belief that from the print comes oral language. Sulzby (1981) reported one child who used a single letter to represent each word in a story. Other youngsters use single letters to represent syllables. Often at this stage, children face a conflict between attempts to assign syllables to each letter and finding a mismatch between their belief that letters represent *syllables* and the principles of the writing system they are acquiring. Many children (mostly middle-class youngsters) are taught to write their names and, sometimes, the names of others. The knowledge that each person's name has a different sequence of letters is a potential source of information about the alphabet in writing: It provides different instances and stimulates a conflict about length and syllables. Thus, in further discussing children's writing experiments, Ferreiro and Teberosky said: (4) children go through a transition into a stage in which they combine letters representing sounds rather than single letters standing for syllables, and finally, (5) children become comfortable with this notion, and some move quickly ahead in their writing as they use invented and—increasingly—the conventional spelling we know.

We turn to Paul Bissex (Bissex 1980) again to find how he acquired writing. Using the set of processing levels identified by Ferreiro and Teberosky, Paul was in the transition between (3) and (4) when he was first observed. His writing began at 5.1 when, after failing to attract his mother from her reading, he handed her the following message: RUDF? (capitals will indicate children's writing), and asked her, "Are you deaf?" He certainly succeeded in his purpose, since she subsequently paid a great deal of attention to his interest in literacy. Paul already had acquired an ability to write his own name and a knowledge of letter names, which he began to use as whole syllables (R = "are"). He also had attained a primitive sense of sounds (DF = deaf) to represent the *sounds* of the word. Paul's message combines use of the rebus (the symbol—here the letter—for the entire word or syllable) and invented spelling (reported by Read 1971, in his early work on invented spelling) (DF = deaf). Paul's label PAULZBZR ("Paul's buzzer) is illustrative of combining a well-learned unit, his name, and letters to represent sounds. Paul continued to write with great intensity over the next two months before returning to concentrate on reading. During this period, he did not ask for the spelling of words, but rather for the spelling of "sounds," illustrative of his awareness of the alphabetic principle. He wrote messages, signs, price lists, stories, and directions for activities.

Like many other beginning writers, Paul used no spaces to mark word boundaries. Later, when he had, in fact, moved to a new stage of competence, he became aware of word boundaries; he marked those boundaries he perceived by periods between "words." Similarly, Read (1971) reported that one child marked his occasional use of letters used as rebuses with a dot below the letter: STRT (dot under R) to clue the reader to say "ar." One of Sulzby's (1981) kindergarten children wrote his story in a column of single words. Another marked word boundaries with a heavy dot (not a period) between each word. The first grade cousin of a former student, when she was given only one sheet of paper for writing but had a good deal to write, reversed the last letter of each word to signal its end and saved the space for her writing. In cases where the reversed letter was identical to the conventional print, she underlined the letter. She wrote, for example,

IwantSomeicecreamtoday.

Not all children progress easily from use of rebuses and some sound-symbol writing to the alphabetic principle. Ferreiro's (forthcoming) report of Santiago, whose understanding of letters was that each person had a letter (his was *S*), showed that it was difficult for Santiago to move into understanding the purpose of the alphabet as long as he did not grasp the concept that letters related to spoken words. Moreover, for this child, as for many others, the length of a person's name reflected their importance: One's father's name ought to be long! Santiago experienced problems as he tried to justify his idea about letters with this idea of length. Finally, after mismatches between these ideas, at age 3.9— twelve months after his first identification of single letters as belonging—he assigned letters to syllables and recognized that letters were moved about to signal different words. Soon, he would move to the alphabetic principle. For many children, the acquisition of letter names and the ability to write their own names forces this transition. Thus, one would think the direct teaching of name writing—a common enough experience—has important consequences. But as Ferreiro and Teberosky (1982) pointed out, not all children are helped to write their names; indeed, many more middle than lower class children learn to write their names early.

When Paul Bissex noticed that if he took the *b* from *book* and exchanged it for an *l* in *look*, his writing underwent important changes (Bissex 1980). He seldom asked questions about how to write sounds (as he had previously). He tried any word he wanted and wrote intensively. He was operating in Ferreiro and Teberosky's "fourth stage," where children engage in much invented spelling and work to achieve independence. It is an important stage for us to consider in some detail.

Invented Spelling

Fortunately, Read's (1971) work indicates sufficient detail about this stage. He observed the spontaneous invented spellings of twenty children of professionals, youngsters who began to write as early as 3.6. These children used moveable plastic letters as well as paper and pencil. They had the good fortune of having parents who answered their specific questions (like Paul's) about sounds. While Read's intentions were to examine the phonological system in development, his observations are important for instruction. Like children learning language, these children induced systematic ways to represent the sounds they considered important, and the youngsters did so consistently. Their spellings illustrate six writing concepts about important aspects of the sound system; these concepts go beyond the evident help given by knowing the letter names of consonants such as *b, c, d, f, g, j, k, l, m, n, p, s, t,* and *v* (the first, syllabic step toward writing).

In regard to vowels, knowing letter names helped with those words having vowel sounds that are close to the names and having tense or long vowels such as *bite, came,* and *mope.* Words like the following fit this concept (Read 1971, 6):

DA = day	LADE = lady	TIGR = tiger
KAM = came	EGLE = eagle	LIK = like

Problems arose with lax, or short, vowels having sounds like those in *mit, mop,* and *mat.* The spelling of these sounds is so conditioned for us by habit and by our knowledge of word structures and lexical relationships that it is difficult to comprehend the consistency and creativity of children's spellings. We skilled writers do not question that the first vowel in the word *phonic* is "o," like in related words such as *phone* and *phonology,* despite the sound difference. We have internalized this lexical knowledge. Without such knowledge, inventive spellers use the vowel name that is closest to the letter name when the word is spoken. They select these vowel names by using the point where the tongue is placed in the mouth as they say the word. Thus, they find that the vowel nearest to the sound in "fish" has the name E. Similarly, they spell the following words as (Read 1971):

FES = fish	FALL = fell	GIT = got
EGLIOW = igloo	LAFFT = left	CLIK = click

Read also found that when children construct a system to represent the sounds they hear, they do so consistently. Once generated for use in one instance, a rule is applied in similar situations. The rules governing the selection of lax vowels are so strong that some children use a particular rule even with tense vowels: PLEY = play; the vowel is marked with E and Y. Such systematic application of letters resembles the consistency of certain systems in language learning.

A number of scholars have noted the "odd" spelling of the initial clusters DR and TR (Chomsky 1979; Mason 1984). By pronouncing "dragon" carefully, however, it is possible to have a hint at what children do. There is a slight (to us) friction at the start of the word, much like the sound at the beginning of "chicken," and children associate that sound with the sound of "j," "ch," or even "h." The so-called affricatives in initial clusters, as in "dragon" and "try," are spelled like *JRAGN* and *CHRIE,* respectively. Children generate rules for these sounds based on the friction created in pronunciation, rather than on the similarities with other phonetic features of the initial sounds that we "hear" through our understanding of spelling.

Another consistent feature of invented spelling—although it does not last long—involves medial "t's": Children are apt to represent medial "t" sounds with D. If the reader of this text were to quickly and naturally pronounce "water, pretty, better, and letter," he or she would not be surprised to find that the sound is not distinguishable from "d" and that children spell these words: WOODR, PREDE, BEDR, and LADR, respectively. The generalizing character of children's spelling is evident once this spelling becomes conventionalized: Once "t" is represented as T, it occurs with all such medial sounds. (Chomsky 1979; Read 1971; Temple, Nathan, and Burris 1982)

For some time, spontaneous spellers ignore the nasal sounds we hear in situations before consonants. Thus, AD is "and," WOTET is "wanted," and PLAT is "plant." Again, an explanation for these spellings is provided by saying these words and studying the location of the tongue. As mentioned previously, some children operate with the principle that you pay attention to where your tongue is in order to spell; when these children prepare to write "plant," they do not move their tongue for /n/. Thus, they do not represent this merging in their writing. This feature of invented spelling is nearly universal and often lasts into first grade. Children spell according to what they "hear" and what they feel their tongue doing. (Chomsky 1979; Read 1971; Temple, Nathan, and Burris 1982)

If words or syllables have medial nasals or liquids ("l" or "r"), children do not feel they must represent the vowel. Like linguists, these small children believe these "consonants" have vowel qualities. Indeed, when we read their spellings, we have no difficulty with interpretation: BRD is "bird," and GRDN is "garden." Even with words of more than one syllable, as children set nasals or liquids, the youngsters list no vowels, a characteristic that persists for some time: OPN is "open," LITL is "little," and DIKTR is "doctor." (Chomsky 1979; Read 1971; Temple, Nathan, and Burris 1982)

A final systematic feature of the invented spelling of untaught children concerns the final letters used to mark the past tense and the plural (and third person singular vowels). Our convention is to indicate the regular past with "ed," whether or not "ed" actually is pronounced, as in "wanted," "walked," or "examined." Alternatively, we mark the final plural with "es" when it involves another syllable (as in "glasses"). Otherwise, whether we pronounce that sound "s" or "z," as in "bees" or "plays," we write S. Children first represent the past tense as they hear it: LAFFT is "left," and STOPT is "stopped." Soon, children use a uniform "d." With the final "s," they are able to represent the different sounds of the plural from the start, a more abstract representation. This ability to abstract illustrates what conventional spelling requires, and it is induced, indicative of an abstracting ability on the part of the young writers. (Chomsky 1979; Read 1971; Temple, Nathan, and Burris 1982)

With the ability to develop systems to account for spelling through the generation of induced rules, these inventive spellers are able, like Paul Bissex, to write whatever they want. However, this account fails to represent the charm of the stories and messages that these children write. Children's works often combine text and pictures. The arrangement on the page is part of the whole. Expressive and direct, early writers are creative (Chomsky 1979).

The Use of Writing

The children who write with such clever analyses of their oral language eventually do move into conventional spelling without undue difficulty in school. The transition to Ferreiro and Teberosky's (1982) final stage leads to writing independence. This transition is influenced by instruction and is marked by a desire on the child's part for conventional spelling. Paul Bissex's move into conventional spelling appeared to be self-generated, stimulated by his own belief that he ought to spell like the authors of his books did. We may assume that his desire holds true for other inventive spellers (Read 1971). We will discuss the direction of this change in later chapters on school reading and writing. The conclusion we may make from the unschooled writings of these children is that there are several preliminary steps children need in order to move into writing. These notions about writing—starting from the use of letters in "pretend" writing to the use of letter names as rebuses, to the continual attempts to represent sounds alphabetically—denote a growing literacy competency, and many experiences contribute to this increasing competency.

Similarly, the expression of these communications illustrates a growing sense of audience. Much early writing is simply expression; the child writes as if the sheer pleasure of a new expression were purpose enough. There is no real audience. However, when the child writes a message—my son wanted a sign to keep the rest of us out of his room—there is a sense of audience. Letters are an early part of children's writing; often, children are asked or ask to have their letter enclosed with a parent's letter. Again, the audience—grandmother, for example—is clearly in mind. Paul Bissex's lists and his newspaper were replicas of his parents' reading and writing. The purpose of the lists was personal, much like other mature, expressive writing. The newspaper was an early manifestation of writing for a more distant audience. Later, with school and more story influence, children attempt story writing, a complicated matter indeed.

SUMMARY

As was true at the start of this chapter when we specifically examined the social context for learning literacy, even in the descriptions of what inquisitive children do as they read and write, we find suggestions about the presence of parents' supportive responses. Parents answer the specific questions of literacy-acquiring children, and parents provide the materials for learning, including the simple books for practice, the moveable letters, and the paper and pencils. Undoubtedly, parents also respond favorably to children's efforts to grow. Importantly, as Read (1971) made plain, parents do not criticize or label as incorrect the invented spellings of their children.

In summary, some very young preschool children acquire skill in reading and writing; all children probably learn something about reading and writing. With wide variation among experiences before formal school begins, instructional systems must deal with individual differences. Because several notable patterns exist among children who have a good start on literacy when they enter school, we must look closely at environmental influences. Since book exchanges and family discussion about letters, words, and sounds are apparent in the environments of children who become interested and competent in the early stages of literacy, these elements are strong candidates for use in more formal school settings.

We have found that children acquire major concepts of reading and writing in identifiable stages. In both modes, children learn the alphabet concepts as representations of sounds that are repeated in different sequences in oral and written language. In both forms of language, the letter representing the syllable appears to be a critical prior concept. In learning concepts about reading and writing, young children appear to induce from available information a set of rules that are used to generate responses to text. In these basic respects, learning literacy resembles learning language.

But literacy is not universal. When those children whose families have not strongly supported literacy arrive at school, they are behind their questing classmates. What about them? What are the ramifications of their lags for their futures? Chapter 4 addresses the question of difference, perhaps one of the most critical questions in education.

SELECTED ACTIVITIES

1. Watch an entire program of *Sesame Street* and *Electric Company*, and write down every instance of literacy help that you can find.

2. Find a child between 3.6 and 4.6, and read the child a book that he or she really likes. If possible, tape the interaction. List all the indications you can find from your talk about the book that reveal the child understands fundamental aspects of books.

3. Go to your local children's library, and observe how parents and their children talk about books. Identify exchange features that appear to be supportive of the beginnings of literacy, and note features that appear to be confusing.

4. A mother of a three-year-old asks you what she should buy for her child that would help the youngster learn about reading and writing. What would be on your list?

5. In connection with question 4, browse through children's picture books without researching which ones are recommended by professionals, and, with literacy in mind, identify those books that you think would stimulate good book exchanges. Write down the names of these books, and then compare your list to a recommended one.

6. Without referring again to this chapter, list the similarities between the development of language and literacy. And note the differences. Compare your lists.

4 Variations in Language and Literacy Development

The values and laws of democracies hold that all children are entitled to education, regardless of their social class, religion, race or ethnic origin, and sex. Yet, children of poverty in these countries do not experience the level of effective schooling that middle-class children do. In the United States, for example, concern for the schooling of poverty-level children—particularly children from minority groups who made up a disproportionate number of poverty-level children—became an issue at the center of the government's educational policy during the 1960s. The United States developed programs that attempted to counteract the poor performance of inner-city minority children in basic skill acquisition—skills fundamental to the more complex learning required in the country's technical society. In 1966, Coleman found these programs to be unsuccessful in eliminating the inequality of achievement in basic skills between inner-city pupils and their middle-class peers (Coleman et al. 1966).

More recent reports from the National Assessment of Educational Progress have indicated that although still substantial, the gaps between black and white children have narrowed a little (Venezky 1978). Initially, the effects of special schooling appeared to have little effect at the elementary level (Bronfenbrenner 1974). However, some of the special programs developed for preschool children of poverty and supported by the government during the 1960s showed encouraging long-term effects in IQ scores, school completion data, and maternal satisfaction (Berreuta-Clement et al. 1984; Lazar and Darlington 1982). Due to the earlier, more negative reports, however, governmental agencies had withdrawn much of their support for programs for children of poverty. A shift toward more support for such programs may emerge for the latter part of the 1980s as a result of the new longitudinal studies.

Concurrent with the development of new programs to provide more adequate schooling for poor children in the 1960s was the beginning of considerable scholarly speculation about possible causes for the low school performance of large groups of poverty children. Scholarly interest has waned since the early 1970s, although there has been some recent stimulation from work in communicative competence (Feagans and Farron 1982). The issues of inequality in schooling and uneven achievement between children of different social classes provoke questions that are difficult to answer. Nevertheless, there are many citizens, teachers, scholars, and parents of affected children who desire solutions and who believe that we will not succeed in reaching our democratic goals until we reduce the class and racial differences in our schools.

Perhaps *the* critical component in school achievement potential lies in language; it is the source for acquiring literacy and the medium for all other subject learning (Snow 1982; Tough 1973). This chapter assumes that children's ability to understand, produce, and effectively use language in the classroom will influence school achievement. This chapter focuses on the variations in language associated with social group membership; it also considers the effect of such differences on academic learning. These questions are not only for teachers in inner-city schools. Teachers in all parts of North America, for example, find language variations among the children in their classes. For teachers everywhere, to gain an understanding of language variation is to learn further about language development.

74

Several kinds of responses to language variation form the content of this chapter. Contained in the first section is a rather discouraging account of the negative perceptions that many people, including teachers, hold toward users of nonstandardized forms of English. Apparently, implicit assumptions about intelligence and potential are made on the basis of speech, assumptions that may have far-reaching influence. The second section reviews the early explanation that the language of poverty-level children is deficient. An alternate explanation is the topic of the third section: The language spoken by people from culturally isolated groups is a dialect that is different from mainstream English, not deficient. Next, the fourth section discusses a new approach established by the communicative competence work described in previous chapters. And the next section examines the effects of language difference on reading and writing. The final part of the chapter includes some comments about children learning English as a second language during their early years.

THE PERCEPTION OF LANGUAGE VARIATION

Definitions

Central to this entire chapter is the notion that we all—no matter how we talk—have several ways in which to represent our ideas through speech. All speakers of a language, for example, use several *registers*, or styles, for talking about different things in different settings. Hudson's sentences on the right that follow (1980, 50, italics in original) illustrate the registers indicated on the left:

formal, technical	*We obtained some sodium chloride.*
formal, non-technical	*We obtained some salt.*
informal, technical	*We got some sodium chloride.*
informal, non-technical	*We got some salt.*

Adults use different registers in writing, as well. For example, I write the sentences in this text with quite a different style than if I were writing to a close friend.

In addition to these individual variations, there are variations across individuals, variations that reflect social groups. And these social groups are enforced by geographic or social boundaries. *Dialects* are distinct variations within a language that are distinguished by phonology, syntax, meaning, and use. Contrary to what many people believe, we all speak a dialect, and, often, the social variation in our speech is the most notable. For example, there were social, not regional, dialect features that Professor Higgins changed in Eliza's speech in *My Fair Lady*. He taught her to use the features of the prestigious dialect he used. This dialect, the one spoken by educated persons, is called the standard dialect; the dialect of socially depressed, minority persons is called nonstandard.

The standard dialect in Britain (Professor Higgins' dialect) is called the "received pronunciation." Standard dialects usually are spoken by people in the well-educated, socially and economically secure classes. Conversely, nonstandard dialects are those spoken by poor people and members of low prestige groups.

The interaction of social, cultural, and regional variations produces a complex overlapping of dialects in most countries. To complicate matters further, sensitivity to dialect use is often accompanied by negative perceptions of the speech of others. Because children come to school with the language of their homes and communities, any denigration of that dialect is also a denigration of them and their families. On the other hand, if children adhere to a dialect that is low in prestige, they are likely to find few opportunities for successful employment outside their speech community (Shuy 1971).

The Evidence for Language Bias

Linguists have claimed that the use of nonstandard dialect does not necessarily mean that speakers have reduced expression of concepts, even complex concepts (Hess, Maxwell, and Long 1974; Hudson 1980; Labov 1966, 1969, 1970, 1972; Steward 1970). Yet the children of nonstandard dialects tend to be from the lower classes; their lower-class status and different dialect complicate efforts to make schooling equal.

If these social and school achievement issues were not difficult enough, other factors may influence the appropriateness of instruction for nonstandard speaking children. Teachers may perceive the nonstandard dialect of their students as inadequate. In such a case, implicit biases toward their pupil's language may interfere with learning if teachers lower their expectations for their students' success. In other words, teachers may negatively influence learning as their students fulfill the unspoken prophecy that the pupils lack learning potential (Athey 1976; Rosenthal and Jacobson 1968).

To know if bias is actually influential in school achievement, it is important to know if people, especially teachers, form initial impressions on the basis of dialect. As part of a series of studies on evaluation of speech style in Britain, Giles and Powesland (1975) found that speech sample information influenced student teachers, when asked to rate hypothetical children, far more than photographs and even more than written schoolwork. And evaluation of dialect, we find, is learned early and continues without much change through the school years (reported in Hudson 1980).

Teachers' negative attitudes are likely to have a negative impact on their students' learning, studies reveal. In one study, teachers held negative judgments toward black children and their black English dialect (Williams 1970). In another study by Williams and others (Williams, Whitehead, and Miller 1971), younger preservice teachers, who presumably held more liberal attitudes than did older teachers, made stereotypic responses when viewing videotapes of black, Mexican American, and Anglo-white children. These responses showed that the preservice teachers perceived ethnic minority children negatively. Additionally, Williams and others (Williams, Whitehead, and Miller 1972), in a third study, found that negative stereotypic responses to minority children were associated with low expectations for success in language-related learning in school. Low expectation by teachers has been found to result in low achievement (reviewed by Athey [1976]).

Apparently some teachers are very negative toward minority children and expect little in terms of school achievement. Probably not all teachers are so negative. Indeed, in another study, data showed that if the teacher was of the same race as the children, the bias was reduced, but this finding was true only if the children were of a higher, not lower, socioeconomic level than the teacher (Feijo and Jaegar 1976).

An interesting court case illustrates the social and educational issues involved in the question of dialect variation in the schools. In 1979 a Michigan judge ruled that black English is a language. He ordered that *teachers* in the Ann Arbor schools with poor minority children participate in language inservice programs. Interestingly, through inservice education to increase knowledge of language difference, it was hoped that teachers would overcome negative attitudes and learn to accept black English as legitimate. Although the judge's ruling emphasized the need for teachers to be retrained, the press portrayed the decision (incorrectly) as a requirement that black English speakers receive bilingual education (Venezky 1981).

Negative attitudes toward nonstandard dialect are not limited to teachers. There is some evidence that, to complicate matters more, speakers of nonstandard dialects may not respect their own dialect. Seventeen-year-olds in Britain rated the quality of arguments on capital punishments highly if presented in prestigious dialects; however, the teens were swayed more by arguments presented in their own dialects (Giles and Powesland 1975). Similar respect for the standard dialect but personal preference for their own nonstandard dialect has been reported for preschool children (Hudson 1980). Students may admire standard speech, but they may learn better if they speak a nonstandard dialect and have a nonstandard-dialect-speaking teacher.

The elimination of problems associated with bias is not easy to accomplish. The process is complicated on the part of students by identification with their families and communities and on the part of teachers by long-held social values. Change occurs as knowledge about language increases and as teachers introspect about their values. It is important that professionals make every effort to reduce any negative bias they may hold toward students on the basis of those students' dialect. In this way teachers will distinguish educational from attitudinal issues. While only the educational issues can be considered in these pages, hopefully, the review of the three explanations for language differences to follow will influence attitudes toward language as well.

THE DEFICIT VIEW

Several societal shocks in the early 1960s in the United States directed attention to the inequality in achievement among students from different economic groups. In addition to the new availability of federal moneys for Head Start and other innovative programs, scholars worked to discover explanations for these achievement differences. Working under the assumption that the problems stemmed from the kind of language these children brought to school, the deficit concept attributes environmental factors as having a negative effect on children's language.

A group of studies published during the middle 1960s examined the question of whether or not there is a difference between the amount of language knowledge that middle-class children have and the language knowledge that lower-class, disadvantaged children have at various points during the elementary years. For many educators and psychologists, the conclusion that a language deficit does exist for disadvantaged children indicates a need to intervene in the educational process early in the preschool years to offer the child language experiences he would not receive at home. This conclusion has been reinforced by studies that have suggested there are specific areas of language dysfunction in disadvantaged children.

Deutsch and Brown (1964) found that when groups were equated by socio-economic level, the IQs of black children were lower than those of white children in both the first and the fifth grades. The difference between black and white children was greater at the higher socioeconomic levels than at the lower levels. Since IQ is dependent largely on verbal ability, M. Deutsch (1965) analyzed language data at the first- and fifth-grade levels. He found that being poor and/or a member of a minority group resulted in a tendency to have poorer language functioning than being white and middle class. Although Deutsch found little difference between groups in the ability to label, differences appeared in the ability to use language for abstract purposes and were greater at the fifth-grade level than at the first. This discrepancy led to the idea that, as these children continued in school, their verbal proficiency fell further behind that of middle-class children. As support, John's study (1963) comparing first- and fifth-grade black children's performance on various standard measures of verbal fluency showed no difference between lower- and middle-class children at the first-grade level but indicated a significant difference by the fifth grade. Of course, this difference may be due to inadequate schooling of poor children, as Baratz and Baratz assert (1970).

Researchers also have attempted to uncover the *causes* of the verbal deficiencies they found. John and Goldstein (1964) analyzed lower-class children's categorization skills and found these children had more difficulty fitting objects into categories than did middle-class children. These authors thought verbal feedback from the home was essential for learning this skill. In a study by Hess and Shipman (1965), lower-class black mothers tended to provide less verbal explanation to their four-year-old children in problem-solving tasks than black middle-class mothers did.

Another explanation for the supposed language deficiency is impairment of auditory discrimination (perception of phonemic differences). C. Deutsch (1964) found poor auditory discrimination in lower-class black first-graders who were unsuccessful in beginning reading. She explained that the noise level of slum homes caused difficulties in hearing, which produced the perception problem, but this explanation was untested. In fact, Friedlander (1970) showed that excessive noise is not necessarily uniquely characteristic of poor families. Furthermore, Deutsch used a test for auditory discrimination based on standard dialect.

Conflicting evidence for the language deficit idea comes from the study of language structure. Some aspects of the language of children who speak non-standard dialects are equal to the language of standard speakers. For example, Entwhisle's studies (1966, 1970) of word associations showed that poor black and white first graders were superior to white suburban first graders. This superiority of poor children disappeared over the school years. Further, Lacivita, Kean, and Yamamoto (1960) found elementary children equally able to assign meanings to nonsense words that had proper inflections and were embedded in sentences, whatever socioeconomic class they belonged to. Similarly, Shriner and Miner (1968) showed that white preschool children did not differ by social class in their ability to generalize morphological rules, and Cazden (1970, 1972) reported that very early growth in acquisition of language structures demonstrated that lower-class black children were undergoing the same sequence and kind of acquisition as middle-class whites. Ammon and Ammon (1972) reported that training young speakers of black English in vocabulary has a more positive effect than training them in sentences. Cazden (1972) recommends vocabulary training for all children, particularly poor children.

Initially, there was widespread acceptance of this explanation—the language of children of poverty lacked sufficient structure and meaning for appropriate learning. Curricular materials reflected this position; they were developed to restore language concepts thought to be lacking in poor children. For example, one author of such materials claimed,

> The child of poverty has language problems. These are problems far more crippling than mere dialect problems . . . in brief, the child of poverty has not been taught as much about the meaning of language as a middle-class child of the same age.[1]

Materials developed out of this framework tended to present language as consisting of separable items taught through drill and practice. As Blank (1982) pointed out, these materials circumvented the natural language learning process; therein lay the real problems with the deficit position.

Although British language differences have no direct bearing on language difference in the United States, insights emanating from work in Britain were examined closely in North America. Bernstein's (1970, 1971) work identified two categories of language use, categories which differentiated the language of students from poor communities from that of more privileged groups. Bernstein found that the two modes in which persons represent their ideas were the restricted and the elaborated codes. The restricted code was described as context-bound; the elaborated code was portrayed as more specific and thereby less

---

[1]S. Engelmann, "How to Construct Effective Language Programs for the Poverty Child," in *Language and Poverty: Perspectives on a Theme,* ed. F. Williams (Chicago: Markham, 1970), p. 102.

dependent on assumptions that listeners and speakers share. These dichotomous categories referred to conceptual expression rather than surface language features. For example, in elaborated speech, the concepts were believed to be more abstract. The language of working-class persons, the restricted code, had a narrower range of conceptual expression. Persons from more educated classes were seen as having wider choices for the expression of their ideas. Although not an essential part of the psychological literature on deficit, Bernstein's work appeared to some North American educators to reflect that position. While more categorical than we may find appropriate, Bernstein's codes illuminate potential differences in conceptual expression that may have bearing on the educational process (Hudson 1980).

On the other hand, the notion that language learned at home explained the educational gaps between poor and middle-class children appeared to some to be misguided and racist. For Baratz and Baratz (1970), for example, the disparity between the schooling experienced by these groups of children caused educational outcome differences. Schools and the biased attitudes of teachers and administrators should bear much of the blame for learning differences, the Baratzes claimed. Many other linguists agreed that the instruction weaknesses caused by a mismatch of dialects—rather than children's inability to learn well—caused learning differences.

THE DIFFERENCE VIEW

A Linguistic View

In contrast with the deficit view of language (an area of psychological and educational research of the 1960s) sociolinguists of the late 1960s and early 1970s held a different perspective. Rather than looking to the individual and the individual's cognition for the sources of educational problems, these linguists examined the language of nonstandard speakers with the view that different forms (dialects) of language are equally sufficient for expression. Indeed, linguistic study has long held the view that different languages are equally structured for the expression of meaning. One would expect that the same view would be found true of dialects within a language. For persons trained in linguistics, the language variation that children brought to school was seen as a matter of language difference unrelated to a question of deficit.

Nonstandard black English received most of the attention of sociolinguists interested in the language of children. Stewart (1970), a sociolinguist, has traced the history of the English spoken by slaves during the early history of the United States. Stewart finds that many forms of black English today reflect the early *creolization* of English by slaves. Creole languages are modifications by depressed minority groups of the dominant language. Apparently, slaves in the United States spoke a language similar to that spoken by slaves in Surinam and in the Carribean islands which reflected their West African origins. The slaves who worked in the plantation house began to modify their speech toward the Britishdescended English fairly quickly, while the creolized form of English spoken by field hands changed more slowly. When the new language forms were passed to the children, the speech form began to resemble a dialect. Continual modification of the dialect after slavery ended brought this dialect closer to other forms of American English. Black English, however, has maintained certain features from these early beginnings that are fairly common among black English speakers in many parts of the country. And the modifications of the blacks' language have not all been one way.

Standard American English shows influences of black English. For example, the common American use of "uh-huh" to indicate affirmation with rising intonation and to indicate negation with falling intonation has been traced by Abrahams (1971) to language spoken in West Africa. There have been lexical borrowings from black to standard English of such terms as *man* in the sense of comrade, *the man* in the sense of white authority, *cool, hot,* etc. Older jazz terms, such as *gig* and *pad,* existed in black English before they became part of the white person's lexicon. A new expression common to blacks confuses whites: Blacks may say "those are *bad* shoes" to mean the shoes are good.

Despite continual borrowing, certain characteristics of language are unique to black English; these characteristics are summarized in Chart 1. It is important to note first, however, that there are many more points of similarity between the dialects than there are differences; otherwise, we would be discussing different languages rather than dialects! Second, many blacks do not speak and have never spoken black English. Third, not all characteristics of black English discussed here are in the speech of all speakers of black English. Fourth, black English is much closer to the standard English spoken in the South than that spoken in the North; therefore, black English in northern cities is at greater variance from standard English than it is in the South. Fifth, many blacks speak both standard and black English. Sixth, there are many other dialects of English that are at variance with standard. Finally, many bidialectal persons switch, usually quite unconsciously, from one dialect to the other depending on the context.

There are number of black English grammatical factors found in the speech of people in cities such as Detroit by Shuy, Wolfram, and Riley (1966) and New York by Labov (1966) which are at variance with the forms of standard English. Labov (1970) contends that the major differences between black and standard English are phonological. Common phonological patterns in black English are: reduction of /r/ and /l/ at the ends and in the middle of words, simplification of final consonant clusters so that only the first of the two consonants is sounded, a general weakening of final consonants, combinations of these consonant characteristics, some variation in medial vowel sounds in certain contexts, and— mostly for very young black English speakers—/f/ instead of /θ/: "roof" for "Ruth." Chart 1 contains phonological differences, or contrasts, expressed as word pairs. The two words in each pair are pronounced and perceived as separate in standard English but as equivalent, or as homonyms, in black English. Thus, some black English speakers will pronounce words such as "guard" and "God" alike because these speakers reduce the /r/ of "guard."

CHART 1. Characteristics of black English*

r-lessness

guard = God	court = caught	terrace = tess
nor = gnaw	fort = fought	
sore = saw	Paris = pass	

l-lessness

toll = toe	all = awe
help = hep	Saul = saw
tool = too	fault = fought

Simplification of consonant clusters

rift = riff	box = bock	wind = wine
past = pass	mix = Mick	hold = hole
meant = men	mend = men	

Weakening of final consonants

seat = seed = see	feed = feet
bit = bid = big	road = row

Combination

picked = pick	raised = raise
miss = mist = missed	stream = scream
fine = find = fined	strap = scrap

Vowel sounds

pin = pen	find = fond	sure = shore
since = cents	peel = pail	boil = ball
beer = bear	poor = pour	

Th-sounds

Ruth = roof
death = deaf

*Adapted from W. Labov, "Some Sources of Reading Problems for Negro Speakers of Nonstandard English," in *Teaching Black Children to Read*, ed. J. C. Baratz and R. W. Shuy (Washington, D.C.: Center for Applied Linguistics, 1969), pp. 29–67 by permission of the Center for Applied Linguistics.

There are also syntactic contrasts between black and standard English, many of which are influenced by the phonological differences. For example, in saying the black English equivalent for "You'll do it," the characteristic reduction of /l/ and weakening of final consonants would render "You do it." Rather than losing meaning by such reduction, no meaning loss occurs because the statement is embedded in context whether we are talking, listening, reading, or writing. And context explicates meaning. Chart 2 lists major syntactic contrasts.

The first two contrasts in Chart 2 illustrate a rule that does not exist in standard English. In the first entry, "He going," the copula is deleted under

CHART 2. Syntactic differences between black and standard English*

Black English	Standard English
He going.	He is going.
He be here.	He is here *all the time.*
John cousin.	John's cousin.
I got five cent.	I have five cents.
John he live in New York.	John lives in New York.
I drunk the milk.	I drank the milk.
Yesterday he walk home.	Yesterday he walked home.
She have a bicycle.	She has a bicycle.
You go home.	You'll go home.
I ask did he do it.	I asked if he did it.
I don't got none.	I don't have any.
I want a apple.	I want an apple.
He book.	His book.
He over to his friend house.	He is over at his friend's house.

*Adapted from J. C. Baratz, "Teaching Reading in an Urban Negro School System," in *Teaching Black Children to Read*, ed. J. C. Baratz and R. W. Shuy (Washington, D.C.: Center for Applied Linguistics, 1969), pp. 99–100 by permission of the Center for Applied Linguistics.

certain conditions when momentary action is meant. It is present as "be" when habitual action is intended. Note that in standard English, the phrase "all the time" is necessary to translate the full meaning of the second entry. This structure often is used as an example to deny the assertion that black English is a simplified version of standard, since, in this case, standard is simplified to a greater extent than black English. Further characteristics of black English are optional deletion of the possessive marker ("John cousin"); deletion of the noun plural in some instances ("I got five cent"); insertion of a pronoun after the proper noun ("John he live in New York"); alternate forms of variant verbs ("I drunk the milk"); different systems of noun-verb agreement ("Yesterday he walk home," "She have a bicycle," and "You go home"); variant structure of embedded questions ("I ask did he do it"); different transformational rules for some negatives ("I don't got none"); indefinite article differences ("I want a apple"); possessive and other pronoun differences ("He book"); and prepositions that vary in some settings ("He over to his friend house").

According to Blank (1982), the difference position, while a more valid representation of the language of nonstandard dialects than the deficit position, nevertheless did not bring needed educational reforms and improved instruction. Adherents of the difference position did make some suggestions about instruction (see section on "Language Differences in Literacy"), but their essential stance was noninterventionist. We need to know if merely learning the features of black English and adjusting our attitudes toward speakers of black English are sufficient to effect educational change. To learn more about the features of dialects and to adjust one's attitude are strongly recommended; whether the necessary changes are sufficient, however, is another question. Work in communicative competence sheds light on this issue of educational change.

THE COMMUNICATION VIEW

With language scholars studying the interactions between parent and child for answers to questions about child language and for clues about how communication develops, it seems logical for scholars and educators interested in language differences across social and cultural groups to use the communicative approach. This approach appears to be profitable, since neither the deficit nor the difference approach offered strong instructional direction.

Children learn the language of their families; youngsters acquire an understanding of how best to communicate from exchanges with their family members. The communication view suggests that styles of interaction may vary by family and by cultural group. Moreover, some styles of communication may be more conducive to school learning than others. Perhaps, then, the forms of exchange that are characteristic of middle-class, mainstream families are more like the communication patterns teachers expect. As a result, children who are unfamiliar with the expected forms of communication may not be as able to master the group norms that their middle-class peers learn with ease from their parents. Assuming that participation in classroom discourse is actually related to success in learning, the communication view suggests that learning may suffer unless a rapprochement occurs between speakers who are used to different forms of exchange, and unless all children learn to communicate well in school. Like the language difference approach, the communication view suggests that school learning problems may occur because of home and school language mismatch. However, the communication approach suggests that instruction is needed for appropriate learning to occur. The communication view thus gives stronger instructional direction. To understand the communication perspective applied to black English requires understanding more about variations in language functions.

Metaphor in Black English

There are several unique forms of oral speech among black English speakers which Taylor and Ortony (1981) suggest reflect speakers' metaphorical preference. One form is the rhetorical speech of black ministers who may use a Bible story metaphorically to represent current issues. The use of proverbs and sayings to teach and to represent life is common. A child who hears "A hard head makes for a soft behind" (p. 4) probably will correctly understand that he must listen to avoid a spanking. Some metaphoric meaning may be quite unique and not easily understood by outsiders. When one woman says to a friend who is cooking, "Girl, you really put your foot in that" (p. 5), she is being complementary. When black children, usually males, learn to *signify*, they acquire a speech form in which negative meaning is portrayed in an indirect, even hidden, manner. Signifying is a good way to say one thing, but to mean another. *Marking* is a narrative form in which exaggeration and emphasis, including nonverbal emphasis, establish the nonliteral meaning as the real one. As is true of these other forms of metaphoric language, the listener must gather the real meaning through these known indirect means. *Sounding* is a popular form of exchange among adolescents; it begins with even very young children. Although sounding (called ranking in some places) is not acceptable to adults (it is a language form of youth and consists of taboo words), it also illustrates metaphoric expression. Initially an insult about someone's family member, usually a mother, is followed by another retort. Sounding requires that two participants balance between insult and truth. Success depends upon inventiveness. Because these forms of meta-phoric language are admired among elementary children, even very young children learn to play these verbal "games." I have heard first graders start a sound when the teacher turned her back.

Understanding metaphoric language through production and comprehension in these modes is likely to increase users' ability to understand some forms of narrative, and Taylor and Ortony recommend attention to metaphor in classroom story selection, analysis of poetry, use of choral readings, and comparative analysis of story structures. Preference for dramatic readings and oral work may provide a means for involving students whose expressive skills are not being fully utilized in learning. Because classroom talk often stresses the literal, teachers need to learn to stimulate other forms of communication for new ways to help variant speakers. Moreover, children may learn to admire the confrontive features of these communication modes, and teachers may misunderstand and interpret verbal gaming as more violent than meant. Ogbu (1982) suggests that differences in communicative expression cause much of the difficulty between children and staff members in urban schools.

Differences in Parent-Child Exchanges

As described previously, adults do not engage in exchanges with nonverbal infants in Papua, New Guinea (Schiefflin and Ochs 1983), but in middle-class families in industrial countries, mother-infant exchanges are common (Bruner 1975; Ninio and Bruner 1978). It is important to find out if there are differences in parent-child exchanges in other kinds of groups; whether, for example, there are quantitative and qualitative variations in the communication between middle-class and lower-class, and between mainstream and minority group families.

The most extensive study of language and literacy learning among children of different cultural groups in the United States is Heath's (1983). Using ethno-graphic techniques, Heath studied the interactions in communications of children from two communities. Both were small, contained working-class communities in the Piedmont area; one was black, the other white. Their social histories were quite different—their communications, too. The children growing up in Trackton, the black community, learned to communicate in quite a different style. With little dialogue, babies learned to develop ways to present language: through storytelling, play songs, and monologuing. With an emphasis on creation and embellishment, children needed to interrupt to talk with adults. Boys were apt to be more successful; their insertions into adult dialogue gave them opportunities to present themselves through language. Girls tended to monologue; they talked with others, took roles, and participated in the playsongs of the community. Adults explained to Heath that children learn (from the adult model) by listening, watching, and trying. In regard to literacy, these children of Trackton were part of ongoing discussions about reading—the reading that took place over notices and bills. Literacy experiences were conducted in groups; meaning was established through group talk. Much use of reading in religious activities was also a group affair.

When Trackton children went to school, their lack of experience with set times for things, set places for things, set ways of interacting, and set literacy events produced a confusion. The youngsters did not understand the segmentation of time and action in school. Their teachers did not understand the children's inability to follow school procedures. Able to create good imaginative stories, the youngsters' lack of writing experience put them at a disadvantage that compounded the confusion of life spaces. Teachers who studied and understood the communication differences were successful; since many teachers did not, failure in school occurred often.

On the other hand, the children of Roadville, the white community of working-class families who lived along the road, in fact, were also quite isolated in location and in values from the middle-class, mainstream community; they learned a different method for communication. With considerable attention to the set time, the set place, and the set way of talking, Roadville children learned there was a right way to communicate. Unlike Trackton where baby talk by adults was frowned upon, much baby talk occurred in Roadville. The parents spent energy in sharing books with their children until school entrance. Parents accepted the idea that their role was to teach the children; nevertheless, they did not establish links between early literacy experiences and the life of the community for these parents did not use reading and writing very much themselves.

With this emphasis on correctness and rule-bound behaviors, these children had difficulty extending their knowledge into new areas when school came. Moreover, the parents also stopped their "teaching," believing it was the job of the school. The separateness of school and home—indeed, of their reading and writing and their families—was not helpful to the children. For example, the youngsters did not progress when asked "what if" questions. The children's stories were reports, and their expressions of feelings were rare. Their tendency to be rule-bound stood in their way.

Another study of three children, one from each of these communities and one from a mainstream, middle-class family, confirmed these differences (Heath, forthcoming). The middle-class parent was involved in teaching her child and encouraged imagination through conversation. There was a much greater amount of discourse in that family than in the others. In a reported conversation, the Roadville parent neither picked up on the child's interest in a cricket found along the road nor established greater expectations for expanded talk. The mother from Trackton expressed belief in school and her child's learning capacity. In concert with the larger study, the adults from Trackton talked among themselves and encouraged the child's participation only so that he would act out "going-to-school" behavior.

Laboratory study of parents teaching their children specific tasks indicates cultural group differences in the use of language to teach. Anglo-American and

Chinese-American mothers, for example, were more apt to complete the components of the teaching "loop" (attracting the child's attention, providing formal instruction, obtaining a response, and giving feedback) than Mexican-American mothers. Moreover, both sets of parents considered teaching an important part of being a mother. In contrast, the Mexican-American mothers worked more slowly and completed fewer loops (Steward and Steward 1973). A later study of dyadic teaching by African (Gusii) and American parents revealed that the Gusii mothers provided less praise, apparently because they took the child's motivation to perform for granted. The Gusii mothers tended to repeat instructions and successfully contained the children's attention. The American mothers teased, tempted, and encouraged their children to participate. Through such motivational and shaping questions, the American mothers coaxed the children through. The mothers also broke the tasks into components (Dixon et al. 1984). The parents in both countries were demonstrating and teaching their children the functional ways of communicating and learning appropriate for their community.

It is not very surprising to find variation in how parents from very different cultural groups interact with their children; more pertinent to the issue of academic school learning within one society is whether communicative distinctions in child rearing contribute to variation in language competence. Reference was made earlier to the work of the British psychologist, Bernstein, who, with colleagues, examined language exchanges between children and adults before school and during the first years of school (Tough 1973, 1982). Built on the assumption that children need to acquire the ability to use language abstractly to become critical thinkers and to learn literacy skills, Tough concluded that there are, indeed, important class differences in the talk between child and parent, differences that are carried into school. Excerpts from her work illustrate her thinking:

(1) Three-year-old Jimmie comes to his mother:

Jimmie: Look—look what I've found.
Mother: Just look at your hands—black bright aren't they?
Jimmie: Look at this thing—this ladybird—look it's right little.
Mother: Go wash you hands now—just look at the colour of them.
Jimmie: It's a ladybird. I want to keep it. . . . (Tough 1973, 33).

This working-class mother fails, at least in this instance, to follow up on her child's evident interest. This incident contrasts with another incident from Tough that takes place in a middle-class family:

(2) Three-year-old Mark and his smaller sister play with their mother close by:

Mark: What's this funny thing for?
Mother: Let me look—oh yes, see, it's a hook. Can you find something that
    will fasten on behind the lorry?
Mark: Yes—I see—well it might be a breakdown one couldn't it?
Mother: Oh, do you think so? What are breakdown lorries like?—do you
    remember? . . . (pp. 35–36).

This mother takes up the conversation, expands it, and redirects the child's thinking, much as described in earlier chapters. The differences, if pervasive, would have an effect on school learning. A longitudinal study of children from 3 to 7.5 showed that the youngsters of working-class, semi-skilled, less-educated parents had shorter MLU; less clause use; lower complexity of sentence constituents; and less evidence of language used to analyze, reflect, reason, justify, predict, consider alternatives, and imagine (Tough 1982). Tough reported work by Sestini (1975) who interviewed parents about their children. Middle-class parents were more apt to view themselves as teachers of their children, to believe in behavioral change in their children, and to believe in negotiation. Tough suggested that parents influence how their children think; if parents' talk is very categorical, then their children will be discouraged in using talk conceptually with an emphasis on causality, as used in school.

Other study of communication within families demonstrates that children's language prospers when parents' speech is relevant to the child's comments and when it expands upon and uses some of the child's language. "Faster developing children tend simply to receive more speech, as well as a greater number of utterances which incorporate and extend matter previously contributed by the child" (Wells 1981, 115). If the differences Heath found were replicated, we would accept that the modes and extent of familial discourse contribute to children's language growth.

Exchanges in mother-child dyads in two groups—one from poverty families and the other from middle-class homes—demonstrated familial discourse variations (Farron 1982). Although there were no differences in exchanges during the first year of life in how the children and mothers interacted, during the second year, middle-class mothers increased their verbal involvement with their children while the lower-class mothers decreased such involvement. When exchanges that took place between mothers and children of thirty-six months were examined, the children of the middle-class mothers experienced twice as many direct interactions as the others. Moreover, the middle-class mothers were more responsive to their children's initiations. In another study, poor black mothers did not seem to adjust their language to their children's actions as did more advantaged black parents. Instead, the poor mothers repeated their own speech (Snow and Ninio, forthcoming). To add to this picture of class differences in discourse, parents in Israel handled picture book reading differently: middle-class mothers used larger vocabularies and were increasingly abstract in their talk with their children than were lower-class mothers (Ninio 1980).

The communication view of language difference rests upon the concept that discourse styles in families influence language development. Certain modes of communication are associated with stronger language development. The evidence from close observation of a small number of cases and from shorter observation of larger numbers suggests that lower-class parents, after the first year, are less apt to communicate directly with their children, are not as inclined to become engaged in the initiations of their children, do not see themselves as teachers, and carry out teaching and book reading differently from middle-class parents. Nearly all of these differences have been associated with language development;

a few studies suggest that academic learning is influenced by these discourse features. This position appears strong; it offers an explanation for school learning differences. Moreover, a clear direction for instruction emerges. Children with little experience in one-to-one verbal interaction with their parents may profit from instruction that provides such interactive focus. Parents may be able to supplement their interactions through training. (These potentials are explored in subsequent text material.)

The communication view of language differences should not be used simply to identify language problems in the communications of lower-class children. While differences appear to exist, Heath's (1983) work demonstrates that children learn to communicate within the rules and behaviors of their communities. The apparent lack of understanding of school expectations comes from differences in communication rather than from inability to communicate. Our job is to figure out how to bridge the gaps for productive learning. And to do this, we must understand the roots of the language children bring to school.

A note of caution about the communication approach is necessary, however: There is not sufficient evidence to either accept it wholeheartedly or to apply it generally. Children who grow up in crowded homes and who often are in the care of grandmothers and other adult relatives may experience quite valuable interactions with these people. Moreover, other, untested types of exchange that are important to overall communication and language growth may occur. Nevertheless, communicative differences by social class appear at this time; they direct us fruitfully to provide instructional direction, instruction which neither demeans the child nor ignores language needs.

LANGUAGE DIFFERENCES IN LITERACY

In this section, the questions (1) whether dialect and language variation influence reading and writing and (2) the extent of the influence, if any, are explored. Working under the difference approach, linguists and others suggested different methods for alleviating the mismatch between the dialect spoken by some children and that used in school. For example, in 1970, Wolfram identified two basic strategies: either to keep the regular school talk and materials and adjust to the mismatch through teaching or to revise the materials to meet the children's language. If the first were to be followed, teachers either would teach children the standard dialect prior to reading or would encourage dialect renderings in oral reading and talk. If the second alternative were selected, teachers would minimize points in text where features differ (e.g., use of copula). Alternatively, texts and curricular materials could be rewritten to represent the children's dialect, at least at the beginning stages of the educational process.

Suggestions

Clearly, some of these notions do not fit with what we understand about language. Since all children have an underlying language competence, however varied in surface appearance, the concept of changing dialect prior to reading appears to be a waste of time and potentially detrimental to personal identity. Moreover, subtle differences in pronunciation between dialects are not likely to be perceived by young children as meaningful, making this approach a barren one. Indeed, drill and practice oral exercises have been found to be unhelpful (Rystrom 1970). Even sounder programs in language-rich kindergartens did not cause a notable shift in dialect features (Cullinan, Jaggar, and Strickland 1974).

To accept dialect renderings in class and in oral reading is to accept the natural language of children. Given the evidence of stereotypic attitudes toward nonstandard dialects, however, teachers must examine their own attitudes with great care so they are able to accept nonstandard pronunciations during oral reading, for example, and so they do not present negative messages to pupils, however unwittingly. (This suggestion refers only to young children learning reading; the question of dialect change for older students is complex but more properly addressed by educators concerned with pupils at the middle grades and above.) The acceptance of dialect renderings means that real reading errors are differentiated from more superficial dialect features. Such analysis is particularly relevant in tests of oral reading. For example, the scores of inner-city black elementary children in oral reading tests were much higher when the nonstandard pronunciations were separated from errors. This finding was even truer of children with reading problems than of children without (Burke, Pflaum, and Knafle 1980). The newest oral reading tests now caution users about this issue. This recommendation, to accept nonstandard pronunciations is critical; otherwise, children who are asked to change their way of speaking will be confused and will focus upon superficial aspects of language when the other aspects of the beginnings of literacy are far more important. To follow the recommendation, teachers need to know the dialects of their students to distinguish dialect pronunciations.

Wolfram's (1970) third suggestion was to avoid potentially confusing words and expressions in texts. This idea is not practical since such points involve the copula, the agreement of subject and verb, plural forms, and the like. To eliminate such basic structures of the language would be to eliminate language.

A corollary suggestion, to rewrite text to represent the surface features of nonstandard dialect, was more attractive to educators in the early 1970s. However, attempts to do so in Chicago and Washington, D.C., did not have strong support, neither empirical support nor support from the parents of children involved in such experiments (Pflaum 1978).

An alternative approach emerged with the language experience method. More fully discussed in Chapter 7, the language experience approach involves the child's oral language in the acquisiton of literacy. Children dictate stories to a scribe (the teacher) and then, through several means, learn to read their words and sentences. Similarly, as soon as possible, children represent their talk through writing. The strength of this approach is its acceptance of the language of the learner. As children acquire reading and writing skills through the interaction of dictation, reading, and writing, they simultaneously learn the interactive nature of literacy.

Evidence for Direct Interference

With the exception of the language experience method, the approaches suggested as solutions to the mismatch between the language of school and that of nonstandard speakers assume that the mismatch causes reading and writing difficulty. The evidence suggests that such an assumption is not fully warranted. In listening comprehension, for example, nonstandard speakers exhibit competence in understanding oral standard speech. Sentence repetition studies indicate that when asked to repeat fairly long sentences, speakers encode the sentences within their own language system and reproduce the sentences accordingly (Baratz 1973; Garvey and McFarlane 1970; Labov et al. 1968). When listening comprehension of more extended discourse was tested, no interference appeared to exist for nonstandard speaking children (Gantt, Wilson, and Dayton 1974–1975; Peisach 1965; Ramsey 1972). However, standard speaking children have exhibited problems understanding black English (Weener 1969). Given young children's experience in hearing standard speech on television, it is not surprising that standard speech is universally understood while black English is not.

In regard to the assumption of dialect interference in acquiring reading: In one study, general proficiency in language (measured through sentence repetition and, therefore, productive language) predicted success in learning to read, while dialect preference did not (Fryburg 1972). There is some evidence that readers encode written English into their preferred oral productive language, and the written English is best when it is not rewritten to represent dialect variations as in some studies. When rewritten text with black English features was presented to black-English-speaking children, they did not use context clues or sound-symbol clues as well as when reading normal prose; their comprehension of the material was equal in both prose types (Nolen 1972; Simons and Johnson 1974). Jaggar (1973) found that black-English-speaking children comprehended regular prose better than black English rewritten prose. The children began to read the altered prose better with practice, however, suggesting a learning effect in the altered prose condition.

Evidence for Indirect Interference

These studies suggest that there is no direct interference caused by a mismatch between children's nonstandard dialect and that of the *materials* used in reading instruction. However, since so much of what children are expected to learn in order to acquire reading depends upon talk, mostly teacher talk, the interference question must be directed to the oral forms of dialect. With third graders who were asked to respond to word pairs with points of dialect contrasts on auditory discrimination, oral listening comprehension, isolated word reading, and silent paragraph reading, Melmed (1970) found the locus of potential dialect-based confusion. The black-English-speaking children were confused in the auditory discrimination tasks, exhibiting inability to discriminate between *seed* and *see,* for example. There were problems, too, in reading such words orally. When the word pairs were set into context, interference was not apparent.

Teachers may confuse black-English-speaking students when introducing and teaching phonics, or sound-symbol relationships, an important part of most beginning reading programs, if the students do not discriminate the target sounds. Channon's report (1968) gives an excellent example of a teacher's perplexity about her pupil's apparent inability to follow a "simple" lesson. In a rhyming lesson about the phonograph, *old*, Channon's pupils first tried hard to respond correctly. They suggested words such as "cole" and "sole" as their teacher wrote *cold* and *sold*. When someone said "bole," she asked if they meant *bowl* or *bold*. Because the pupils did not understand the distinctions their teacher pressed upon them (*bold* and *bowl* when pronounced sounding alike because of reduced final *d*), they rather wildly offered other ideas: for example, words that began with "b." The lesson ended with confusion, anger, and withdrawal as the children happily turned to assigned written work. The teacher, Channon, later learned the source of her problem and realized that she could have accepted the pronunciation "bole" and pointed out the two ways to spell it. She could then have indicated that the two words needed to be memorized. Thus, she would have acknowledged the confusion as sensible and offered a good teaching approach to prevent confusions. This one confusion illustrates the potential for many misunderstandings that may arise through mismatch of dialects. The solution lies in teacher awareness of potentially confusing feature differences, teacher ability to demonstrate clear answers, and teacher understanding of pupils' use of language learned at home (Heath 1983).

Spelling

A particular kind of interference occurs in writing and spelling. Writing requires the encoding of one's language knowledge into representative graphemes. To spell not-yet-memorized items, one writes the letters according to how one perceives sounds of the letter sequences. So, even more than in reading, the phonological system has some bearing on spelling. And there is evidence of dialect influence on spelling.

Although few dialect influences were found in the spelling of speakers of three *regional* dialects (Graham and Rudorf 1971), Appalachian dialect speakers spelled particular items according to their pronunciation. *Still* was misspelled by the Appalachian speakers 25.9% of the time and written in the direction of its pronunciation, "steal" (Boiarsky 1969).

The extent of black English features in spelling words does account for much of the spelling difficulty of black English speakers in grades two, four, and six (Desberg, Marsh, and Wolff 1976). Comparing second grade black and standard English speakers in southern California, where dialects are merging, researchers found that all children err on similar graphemes; however, black English speakers' errors were predictably dialect based (Kligman and Cronnell 1974). For example, the sound /θ/ was represented as *t* or *f* by black English speakers. These students also tended to reduce the single final consonants (e.g., final *d* in *tired*) and to misspell some final consonant clusters (as in *mist*). Several dialect-based misspellings have been found among black-English-speaking college students (Wolfram and Whiteman 1971).

It is important to understand how dialect-influenced spellings might affect general writing development. We know that employers have been found to be negatively influenced by the presence of black English features in the speech of potential employees (Shuy 1971). Evidence of bias in teachers was presented earlier. It is possible, given their negative attitudes toward low-prestige dialects, that teachers may weigh the dialect-influenced spelling errors heavily in grading written work. Teachers who may not understand the dialect reason why the past-tense marker of *tired* is missing are likely to be amazed about the lack of a very elementary skill and to assume that the written work is generally poor.

Whether dialect-influenced misspellings are amenable to intervention is also important. Taking the case of the past-tense marker, *d*, an instructional approach might be to emphasize the meaning of the marker rather than the sound. Thus, children who are black English speakers should be cautioned to represent the past meaning rather than to rely totally on the sounds they hear themselves make. Consonant clusters that are not associated with morphological meaning (such as *field*, for example) must be treated differently, however. Consistent consonant cluster reduction in speech suggests a potential spelling problem; such a speaker needs help and direction.

Assuring through instruction that all pupils understand how to mark the important grammatical distinctions (such as tense, number, and aspect) in their spelling requires systematic instruction in cases where there is dialect interference. By grades three and four, all pupils should be expected to observe these writing conventions. It is simply unfair not to insist on correct spelling, for beyond the school years, misspellings will become unnecessarily limiting. True, spelling is only one aspect of writing, and how one spells is far less important than what one says in writing. However, if good ideas, exciting language, and coherent argument are masked with what appear to be elementary spelling errors, spelling becomes extremely important.

In conclusion, there appears to be some interference between dialect and learning; instruction may improve the situation. In regard to reading, the interference seems to be in phonology. And, due to the emphasis on word analysis during the primary grades and the mismatch between children's and teacher's dialects, the problem may be exacerbated unless the teacher clarifies the underlying phonological system. Similarly, although spelling is only a small part of writing, misunderstanding by teachers about the meaning of dialect-caused errors may cause other problems.

BILINGUALISM

The number of non-English speaking school children in the United States is growing (Johnson 1975), and schools need to plan for this growth. In Chicago, for example, large numbers of children speak Spanish, Greek, Oriental languages, or Polish. There are, in all, over forty non-English languages represented in the speech of Chicago school children (Chicago School Board 1973). In this section, aspects of instruction for non-English speakers are discussed.

In recent years, schools throughout the United States have seen an increase in the number of southern Asian pupils who have limited English proficiency. The question of how best to educate children whose first language is not English is complicated by the number of different languages and by the geographic dispersion of speakers through urban and rural areas. The questions concerning bilingual education are not limited to the United States. Canadian schools provide instruction in French and English. Belgium has two languages; Switzerland three. In India, there are hundreds of languages; governmental policy has established English as the major language of instruction.

Dictionary definitions state that the bilingual is one who has equal competence (thus, native ability) in using two languages. Writers in education normally use a definition with a broader meaning. According to several writers, bilinguals include those users of a second language with limited proficiency: For example, a child who can produce even a very simple but meaningful utterance in a second language may be considered bilingual (Lindholm 1980). Thus, this definition encompasses even the *introduction* of English to a non-native speaker. The acquisition process for this second language suggests that the educational decisions concerning non-English speakers are difficult ones.

Acquisition of a Second Language at Home

Families, educators, and psychologists have long been interested in the question of how bilingualism affects children's overall language and cognitive development. The issue raises the question of potential interference, and answers vary according to the reports one reviews. For example, the diary studies of toddlers simultaneously acquiring two languages suggest very little harm and some advantage derived from simultaneous acquisition (Lindholm 1980). By contrast, studies of the effects of bilingual education provided for poor, non-English speaking children from uneducated families suggest that "bilingualism" is an adversity difficult to overcome (de Valdes 1978). The explanation lies in social roots. The diary reports come from highly educated persons; often, the reports examine the language acquisition of linguists' children. The families of children who experience difficulty acquiring English in the United States often have quite a different background (Cummins 1981). These two studies represent different aspects of bilingualism and suggest that easy generalizations will not be found.

From the diary studies, there appears to be little interference from one language to the other, even though the children usually learned one language from one parent and the second from the other (Lindholm 1980). I knew a two-year-old girl whose father always spoke Italian and whose mother always spoke Spanish. The child consistently spoke Italian to her father and Spanish to her mother.

At first, these bilingual children appear to acquire two sets of lexical items and one syntactic system. Quite soon, however, they are using the second language syntactic system, and no mixing occurs. Such children experience normal acquisition of both languages; the process is enhanced if the youngsters consistently have a stable context for each language (Lindholm 1980). In the process of acquiring two languages, children learn two labels for events and objects; as a result of having two sets of names for things, children may find it easier to learn to separate referent and word. Some evidence supports the idea that increased flexibility in restructuring occurs with simultaneous bilingualism; this finding perhaps is due to the acquisition of two sets of referents (Lindholm 1980).

Another study of three bilingual (Spanish/English) children by Padilla and associates demonstrated that acquisition of English morphemes paralleled monolinguals reported by Brown (1973). Similarly, Spanish acquisition mirrored monolingual acquisition. Although some forms appeared first in one language, once acquired in the other, there was no mixing of syntax or lexical items (Lindholm 1980).

Acquisition of a Second Language in School

Our greatest school challenge in regard to bilingualism concerns pupils whose second language is acquired through direct instruction. Several questions related to second language acquisition at school need to be addressed.

For one, is there an optimum age for second language learning? We have long thought that children learn language with much greater ease than adults. And while ability to pronounce a second language is much more native-like when the second language is acquired during the early years (Carrow-Woolfolk and Lynch 1982), there is no clear evidence that lexical, syntactic, and meaning structures of second languages are more easily acquired by children. On the other hand, when an adult sets out to learn another language, he or she expects much more skill attainment than the child; literacy, for example, is part of the adult's expectations (Ervin-Tripp 1973).

A more important question refers to the processes used in second language learning: Does a second language learner also learn language through generalization; is there a rule structure basic to communication; do children learn the rules of ordering sentence elements in the same sequence as first language learners? There is some evidence that the same features that characterize first language learning are also part of second language learning, even though the sequence may differ (Carrow-Woolfolk and Lynch 1982).

Ervin-Tripp (1973) has noted a number of characteristic patterns in the language of preschool children acquiring a second language in natural settings such as those just described. For example, she reported about a child acquiring English as a second language who used the negative marker in his primitive English much as a two- or three-year-old who is acquiring English as a first language would. But once this child had acquired understanding of the more mature structure of negatives ("I *did* not do it"), he moved more quickly into mature negatives than would a child learning English for the first time. Further, preschoolers learning a second language are apt to stress those second language words that are like first language words (cognates) as they would stress them in the first language. Interdental consonants ($/\theta/$ and $/\eth/$) were acquired more quickly if the sounds were in the first language than if they were not.

Language mixing often has been used as a sign of detrimental language interference. Adults do mix languages to some extent within a single discourse as a sign of familiarity and meaning (Gumperz 1970). There were instances of lexical substitution in school children; however, few vocabulary insertions (one language to other) occurred. Lindholm (1980) assumed such mixing was not a major problem.

There is little evidence that bilingualism, itself, is harmful to children, either to those who learn a second language simultaneously with the first at home or to those who learn it at school. There is, in fact, some indication of increased cognitive flexibility associated with bilingualism (Lindholm 1980).

Schooling and Bilingualism

Beneficial educational environments should offer the opportunity for children to acquire a second language in naturalistic ways; the classrooms where English is being acquired should be "communication rich" (Cazden 1972; Cummins 1981; Ervin-Tripp 1973). But accomplishing this goal is not simple, for children come to school with a range of language skills for their first language, a range of knowledge for the second, and the need to become literate in the target language while not dropping behind monolingual, English-speaking peers.

In the United States, as in other western countries, there have always been students who are not native speakers. Such children have been expected to acquire the main language, and the extent of maintenance of the native language depended upon personal, family, and religious experiences. Little is known about the general effectiveness of this model. In any case, since the early part of the twentieth century, the situation has become quite different; much higher levels of literacy are required for successful employment, so educational demands are also higher. Several types of programs to teach English have been established.

Teaching English as a Second Language

One such programmatic structure is TESL (Teaching English as a Second Language), which provides training in English by special teachers who take children out of regular, English-only classes periodically. The TESL plan is often used in schools with multilingual children; it does not develop skill in the non-English language.

Bilingual Classes

Because TESL-type programs do not include instruction in the native language, another stucture was developed, the bilingual class. Based on the idea that both the native language and English are to be taught until students are able to successfully handle English only, transition "bilingual" education evolved. Ultimately mandated through the Bilingual Education Act (Title VII), the federal government sought to improve the educational opportunities for limited English speakers. While subsequent governmental redefinitions have attempted to narrow the applicability of federal funds, a 1974 decision by the Supreme Court (*Lau v.*

Nichols) had the effect of widening the availability of bilingual programs. Although it required only that non-English speakers receive instruction in English, the decision has been interpreted to support two-language programs. Subsequent to these developments, because of the availability of federal and state funds, the number of programs has grown (Venezky 1981).

In bilingual classes, bilingual teachers begin training children in Spanish (or the language spoken by the children) and gradually develop more and more English language until the two languages are nearly equivalent. When their skills permit, children are often transferred to other English-only classes to make room for new non-English speakers. Sometimes, bilingual classes have two teachers, or one aide and a teacher. One adult will teach in one language, and the other in the other language. In bilingual classes, the children are expected to move from one language to another and back during the course of a school day.

An important issue concerning bilingual education has to do with the determination of children's transition from the bilingual to the English class. There are no widely acceptable testing procedures, although, again, the communication approach promises a new direction in this area. Gottlieb (1985) measured non-English-speaking elementary children's competence in understanding school language and found it highly correlated with other language and test scores.

Another issue is whether the first language a child learns to read should be the non-English language or English. Much of the research on this question has been conducted in other countries with other languages where the social impact of language choice differs considerably from the United States. In addition, the studies have design problems that weaken their generalizability. A thorough review of the research by Engle (1975) did not produce a clear advantage for learning reading in the first language. On the other hand, it did not reveal any harm resulting from first reading in the first language. Ultimately, starting with the first nondominant language is more likely to result in biliterate bilingualism, an achievement of the educational systems of many other nations. This complex problem is further complicated by the fact that children in the United States come to schools with language skills that may not be fully developed in the first language and that are confused with English structures. Thus, for these children, initial reading in Spanish, for example, will not be the critical instructional question, but language development in both languages will be.

One might think it would be relatively easy to assess the effectiveness of bilingual programs because they have several consistent goals, such as the extent of English facility, the extent of native language facility, and the success of students' transition to regular classes. However, evaluation is quite complicated, as is illustrated by the very different results from two large-scale studies. The National Advisory Council on Bilingual Education reported positive effects of bilingual programs (Venezky 1981); whereas, an independent study by the American Institutes for Research did not find much to be positive about (Danoff 1978). For example, while bilingual programs were meant to be transitional— temporary to the point where children were sufficiently English proficient—it appeared from the Danoff report that the majority of children in bilingual programs were English dominant. Moreover, the students' reading achievement in English was comparably low. With two conflicting large-scale reports, a cautious reader would keep an open mind about the effects of bilingual education structure. Hopefully, careful study of this approach will result from funding decisions.

Language Immersion

There is yet another structure for English acquisition: the immersion program. Lambert and his associates (1970) in Montreal placed English monolingual preschool children in a totally French environment for kindergarten and first grade with English taking over some forty percent of the instructional time after grade one. They found at the end of the fourth grade that the children were bilingual and were achieving slightly below equivalent French-speaking children and equally to English-speaking children. A parallel application of this model would be the complete immersion of Spanish-speaking children in English classrooms. Indeed, this was the traditional model for educating non-English children in the United States for many years.

Educators have discussed for quite some time why the Lambert model has been inoperable in the United States. The explanation is due partly to the social prestige of the home language and the acquired language and partly to the identification with the cultures associated with the two languages. The Lambert children in Montreal already spoke the prestigious language of the country: They came from middle-class families; they had encountered rich preschool language experiences; they had adult models of bilingualism; and (Engle 1975) their parents were eager for them to learn French. By contrast, the Spanish-speaking children in the United States speak a language of low prestige not essential for business in this country; their Spanish dialect is apt to be nonstandard. The majority of the children are from low socioeconomic homes; the youngsters have few close models of true bilingualism.

While not at all common, there has been at least one immersion program for Spanish speakers in English in the United States. In California, children of migrant farm workers and some other Hispanic children have experienced academic success from a program called HELP (High-Intensity English Language Program). It is characterized by small, communication-rich classes and intensive study that is always in English with no translation allowed. Students are encouraged to work hard, and an early emphasis is placed on essential oral skills (Venezky 1981).

A Comparison

There are several problems with each of the program structures just discussed; some of these problems already have been suggested. For example, a difficulty with the early assimilation idea was that it did not take the child's language into account. The failure of many minority language children to acquire skill in school tasks appeared to some to be from the interference of the first language into the second language, an explanation somewhat reminiscent of the mismatch idea among nonstandard dialect speakers. The attempts to combine study of culture with language in bilingual classes has not appeared to work as well as hoped; Cummins (1981) pointed out that it slowed literacy training of Finnish immigrants to Sweden. The problems associated with the transition bilingual classes are many and thus reflect the complexity of the issue. Just one example of the complexity is the failure to establish a consistent criterion of what constitutes English language proficiency in limited English speakers. Immersion may be more successful. Though expensive, if two or three years of immersion were sufficient to achieve English language competency, then immersion might be worthwhile.

Immersion and Underlying Language Competency

An explanation for the apparent failure of most second language programs has been put forth by Cummins (1981). Cummins' idea is that many second language programs were incorrectly built upon the idea that children learning a second language were learning an independent system. Instead, he suggests that there is a common underlying proficiency for language. Calling this proficiency the "cognitive/academic language proficiency," Cummins claimed that it operates across languages in this way: A student who is strong in language and literacy in his first language (Lx) will, upon acquisition of a second language (Ly), become strong in that language, too. Central to this notion is that students need training in one language to promote this proficiency, and Cummins cites the Canadian immersion programs as evidence of where a strong French emphasis was associated with growth in both French and English. Cummins predicts:

> To the extent that instruction in Lx is effective in promoting cognitive/ academic proficiency in Lx, transfer of this proficiency to Ly will occur provided there is adequate exposure to Ly (either in school or environment) and adequate motivation to learn Ly. (1981, 141)

My own experience as a teacher supports this idea. Many years ago, I taught a group of seven sixth graders in a private English-speaking school in western Puerto Rico. The student with the most impressive language ability—and excellent writing and reading—was a student whose Spanish-speaking parents were worried that her six years of instruction in English (one hour of Spanish a day) had limited her Spanish literacy skill. They placed her in a Spanish-emphasis parochial school for the seventh grade. To their surprise—but not mine (and supportive of the single proficiency model)—within weeks, this girl led her class in subjects requiring reading and writing in Spanish.

Another student in that school, also a native Spanish speaker, entered only in the sixth grade. He had studied the English of his local school (in those years a fairly minimal amount). This boy was befuddled by English spelling. When I advised him to use the same sense of sounds and letters in writing English that he did in Spanish, he pointed out that you did not have to think about spelling in Spanish. Correct, I agreed, but the way in which Spanish is written, as you might expect from the way words sound, provides clues about English, too. He did begin to use his sense of symbols and sounds; English did start to make sense to him. I had advised him to rely on his general language knowledge.

The native English-speaking children in that school, with only an hour of Spanish a day, did not have the parallel skills of the Spanish speakers. However, those who had significant social use of Spanish—with playmates, for example— did have good Spanish. Many years later, one of these children discovered, to his surprise, that his Spanish was good enough for oral and written communication to help in his law practice.

These studies support the idea of the existence of an underlying competency in language which is best supported by strong immersion in one language, even a non-native language. Immersion programs in English obviously limit cultural sharing; they have not been tested on a large scale outside of Canada. Thus, while immersion appears to be supported theoretically, there may be better solutions. There is not, however, any disagreement that children learning a second language should be learning in a language-rich environment.

SUMMARY

This chapter has focused upon language issues revolving around deviations from the norms of mainstream society. While there are clear differences between the educational needs of children who speak a nonstandard dialect and speakers of a different language, there are similarities in the direction their education should assume. It is recommended that teachers of both groups of children have the following knowledge, skills, and abilities:

Knowledge of language and its variations, including both dialect and non-English language;
The ability to perceive underlying competencies in language and to support them;
The ability to respect pupils' communications;
High expectations for progress that temper any residual negative perceptions of nonstandard English;
Change in attitude toward language variation as needed;
High value given to communication richness;
Ability to conduct instruction so that all pupils are involved in exchanges that are meaningful and to teach the communicative strength of informational exchange;
Class work that develops conceptual ability;
Sensitivity to the strengths students have for metaphoric language use and for cultural identity expressed through oral talk and in literature.

This list contains skills and attitudes within reach. They are not essentially different from what is suggested for all school children. For those teachers who have nonstandard speakers in their classes, points of potential confusion in lessons involving phonological knowledge, including spelling, should be predicted and the instruction should be designed to eliminate them.

Chapter 5 describes a metaphor for instruction. Based on many of the explicit and the implicit instructional recommendations from the first four chapters, this metaphor provides a way to think about a direction for language teaching. The metaphor for language instruction assumes that instruction can influence children's futures positively. In order to help prepare children for later learning, we must be realistic about what counts as success in our society. Thus, it is important to share the learning processes found to be characteristic of successful students with those students who have less education. But this pragmatic view does not mean that there are not important strengths in the language of children who come from nonmainstream families. We must develop the ability to capture the strengths and to build upon them.

SUGGESTED ACTIVITIES

1. While observing or teaching in a class with black English speakers, listen carefully to the speech of one pupil. Make a list of all the black English structures you hear. Then do the same with the same pupil during play, and compare the changes that occur.

2. Try to obtain a written piece by a seven or eight-year-old black speaker, and find the black English features in the spelling. How would you, as this child's teacher, interact with the writer about these spellings? How do you think your approach differs now that you understand the source of the spelling "errors"?

3. Locate several oral reading inventories (from a school or college curriculum library). Examine each carefully to find any recommendations for teachers to use in assessing pronunciations that reflect a nonstandard dialect or the influence from another language. How do you view these recommendations in light of what you know?

4. Over two days, list all the people with whom you have a conversation. Check those who speak a different dialect from yours. When you are finished, review the speakers of different dialects, and determine if you have any negative responses to them based on the dialect features.

5. Find an adult who entered school with a non-English language. (There are many older persons in the United States who fulfill this description.) Ask this person about his or her first reaction to school, how he/she learned English, and what happened to the first language after English became easy to use.

6. Visit a bilingual class, and keep track of the activities and of how each language is presented and by whom. Keeping your attention focused upon one or two children, is there evidence that one language predominates? Is there any indication that pupils use facility in just one language?

PART II

Preparation for Literacy and Beginning Literacy

5 Preschoolers at Home and at School

The characteristics of language learning have been described in the previous chapters. The purpose of this chapter is to describe what is believed to be an appropriate approach to language and literacy instruction for preschool children. It includes information about parental input and formal instructional programs. The intent of the discussion is to make instructional recommendations for home and school as if the teaching efforts of parents and teachers are actually easy to accomplish.

But an ideal world in which needed educational change is accomplished without much effort does not exist, of course; the contexts of families and schools influence strongly what can occur in the way of change. For example, in some schools, teachers are required to use materials that are antithetical to their understanding of learning. During the past decades, we have seen an increase in a managerial view of education in which curricular decisions are made by nonteaching professionals. Some of this trend is due to the need for consistency in school and district-wide programming. Some may be due to teachers' acquiescence to external decisions. Some is the result of mistrust and concern about educational attainment in the classroom from outside the school walls. Whatever the reasons, I believe the present situation, particularly in large urban school systems, is quite different from the professional autonomy that I experienced when I began teaching in 1959. In the present context that many teachers experience, teachers are not free to select programs and materials that reflect their theory of instruction. All teachers, however, are free to interact with their students in accordance with their beliefs about language, and this level of interaction is the focus of this chapter.

In regard to instruction by parents, there is a wide range of need and potential for change. Many parents have a strong and sound approach to their role as teachers; they depend upon this sense and search for ways to enhance their children's experiences. Some parents, however, are very anxious to find out the latest wisdom about child rearing. These parents tend not to rely on their own observations sufficiently; moreover, these parents do not build a consistent approach to family experiences. Many others are not aware of the impact of their "teaching" on their children's acquisition of conceptual systems, including language. Many parents, even if aware of their impact, simply cannot accomplish much because the family situation is too emotionally, economically, or even physically stressful. For example, parents who are concerned about putting sufficient food on the table will not be able to attend to their role as teachers of their children. Mothers who are being abused by their husbands cannot be effective, positive influences on their children's sense of independent learning.

In addition to the difficulties associated with parents' receptiveness to learning is the problem of reaching them. Teachers are trained in formal settings that can include theoretically based instructional recommendations that can direct their teaching. But parents, as teachers, are relatively isolated. Thus, they rely on their own experiences as a child in a family, possibly on the advice of neighbors, possibly on the advice of medical professionals (although few poor families get sufficient medical services), and, in the cases of parents who reach

106

for professional advice in their reading, on authors of popular books and magazines.

Ideally, parents with children in preschool classes also will have the opportunity to learn by observing the modelling of effective instruction by teachers. And through the teaching professionals, some change may occur in this difficult-to-reach group of parents. Nearly two decades ago, for example, I observed a skilled teacher talk with a small group of three-year-olds, which included my daughter, as she showed them a watermelon. I was struck by the quality of the descriptive comments the children made in response to her initiations. I learned to stop and observe objects carefully in interaction with my children as a result. Modelling of good teaching by someone parents respect is a way to reach them effectively. And research supports this position. Long-term, positive effects have been found in children whose mothers participated in a home visit program that consisted of modelling behaviors surrounding the use of educational toys (Lazar and Darlington 1982).

It is hoped that teachers will include the modelling of effective interactions with children among their concerns. Thus, the recommendations for parents' roles as teachers are meant to be important for teachers, too. The first part of this chapter presents a framework for instruction in preschool language and literacy. Based on the discussion of previous chapters, the framework in diagram form represents theory; it is a metaphor for instruction. Subsequent sections present relevant information from the study of various early childhood programs, then specific examples of how the literature and the metaphor combined may be realized in parental teaching and in preschools. A few final comments about testing and assessment are included at the end.

THEORY AND A METAPHOR

Teachers (and parents) whose decisions about and behaviors toward young children are founded upon a coherent framework are likely to establish a strong environment for children who are acquiring language and communication skills. The following pages contain a framework built upon theoretical ideas and information from the previous chapters. The framework is diagrammed to illustrate the role of instruction—adult guidance, the characteristics of the learning environment, activity selection, and direct interactions—in language learning. The diagram may be thought of as a metaphor to represent the instructional influences upon language learning.

A theory is a working hypothesis validated by evidence, both factual and conceptual, of relationships among observed facts that have not yet been established as laws. A theory ought to be specific enough so that the elements (observations) and their relationships are precisely stated; precision leads to accurate prediction of behavior patterns. A physical theory (for example, relativity) is described in very precise terms upon which predictions may be made. The tests of the predictions establish the theory's validity. Such testing requires sophisticated methods.

Like scientists, teachers ought to work from a theory of instruction that is precise enough to stimulate specific predictions about educational outcomes. A mechanism is needed to operationalize relationships within a theory for the making of predictions. Even though an instructional model is never as precise as one in the physical sciences, a model of a theory may be operationalized; the model then can be tested with sophisticated research and testing procedures. Prior to the development of a model strong enough for such application, a modified approach is possible, and the instructional metaphor in these pages represents such an approach. In using the metaphor rather than a model for implementing theory and in using critical teaching tools rather than research methods, I propose that valid, theoretically based teaching will result. Teachers who accept a theoretical position, who have some sense of how theory might be operationalized, who use the explanation of the theory in their teaching, and who test the outcomes against the theory are thinking, critical teachers.

The metaphor for an instructional theory of language learning presented here is built on theory. Not sufficiently precise, the metaphor ought to provide teachers with the means for creating instruction out of a cohesive, theoretical stance and for testing the validity of instruction against learning outcomes. Ultimately, it is hoped that modifications representing teachers' fine tuning of the metaphor will enrich teaching.

The Theory

The basic notion, or theory, throughout the previous chapters is that children learn language by constructing a rule system: The system governs the interpretation of the language children hear; it governs the structure of the utterances made; it directs the forms within which communication occurs; and it is malleable so as to be influenced by new information. Growth in language occurs as children accommodate their language system to new language structures, patterns, and communication events. The theory also holds that the extent of children's capacity for language and academic learning also influences their ability to construct systematic understanding of the world and, especially, the world of conceptual knowledge. In its basic structure, the theory establishes the notion that children, given sufficient mental ability, physical health (such as hearing and nutrition), lack of chaos in the home, and the presence of language and stimulation, will acquire language. Children will do so because they have a natural propensity for language; they desire to communicate a range of feelings and ideas; they are able to select salient language notions from their environment; and they build a language system that governs their comprehension of language, the manner in which they communicate, and the form of their utterances. All these factors form the elements of the natural learning component of the theory.

The theory also holds that the sensitivity of the language learner to new concepts, structural elements, and language and literacy experiences is influenced by adult guidance, which stimulates and expands the malleable language system. Most of the adult guidance occurs during direct interaction with children. The environmental factors that influence the extent of language learning include adult behaviors in interchange with children as well as other *variable* elements: the number of people interacting with the child; the kind of interaction; the presence of books and magazines shared with the child; the development of routines within which communication occurs; and the ability of adults to challenge the language learner to new structures. These environmental features may occur both in the family and in the school. The theory of instruction holds that the amount, type, and mode of language and communication exchange during the preschool years influence the size and strength of children's language knowledge and academic preparedness.

Finally, the size and strength of children's language knowledge and academic preparedness are thought to have an influence on the extent of children's sensitivity to learning and to accommodating to new features in the language environment. In all, the essential idea of the theory is that the richness of the environment in which language and concepts about literacy are acquired influences the strength of children's academic preparedness, which, in turn, stimulates learning potential.

The Metaphor

The metaphor for language instruction in early childhood is pictured several times in the following pages. Each representation is like a different X-ray of the same structure. Superimposing each X-ray results in the whole metaphor. We begin with the bare essentials. In Figure 1, the natural propensities of the child are represented as "Natural Learning," which leads to "Academic Learning Preparedness" by the simple presence of minimal familial and nutritional support.

The Beginning of the Metaphor

The arrow between Natural Learning (NL) and Academic Learning Preparedness (ALP) represents how children learn language given natural propensities (and normalcy) without regard for the instructional impact obtained in family and school.

The Instructional Component of the Metaphor

In order to represent the influence of the environment upon ALP, the metaphor draws upon a known concept and applies it in a new fashion. The known concept is an accordian, an instrument in which wind is forced through reeds

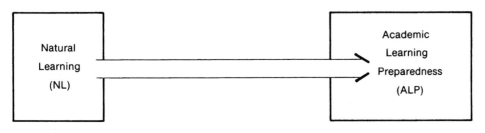

FIGURE 1. *The metaphor without the instructional component*

by the means of a hand-operated bellows. The handles on both sides are held in either hand; one is pumped to force wind through the reeds. The sounds are regulated by the manipulation of the keyboard at one side.

The accordian, applied to our metaphor, represents environmental influences—including instructional impact—upon language and literacy learning. The instructional part, the Variable Environmental Influence (VEI), is the accordian. It is placed between the NL and ALP segments (Figure 2). The sides of the Variable Environmental Influence are expandable; they signify the potential for extension, and they help us understand the metaphoric meaning of VEI (comparing it to the accordian idea of pumping to increase the force of the wind). We imagine some force for learning initiated in NL progresses naturally to ALP, and the "doors" on either side of the large arrow through VEI indicate how the VEI force enters. The doors may open as "the wind" is forced through or may close with no force. Thus as the Variable Environmental Influence is pumped and the resultant wind force is increased, the doors open and strengthen the learning begun in NL.

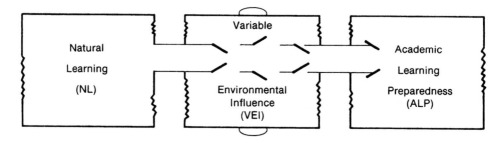

FIGURE 2. *The metaphor with the instructional component*

The accordian metaphor represents all of the teaching influences upon young children in the youngsters' learning of language and about literacy. As the VEI is pumped and as force is added to the NL in the arrow, the strength of the influence upon ALP is increased. The size, then, of ALP increases according to the strength of the VEI: The teaching impact extends children's learning potential. Since children's acquisition of language skills in turn influences their natural learning potential, NL is represented as expandable, too.

To extend the accordian metaphor perhaps to its limits, it is also possible to relate the use of the keys to learning. Just as a musician plays melodies and creates chords by depressing the keys and various combinations of keys, the activation of certain instructional elements will produce variations in learning. Controlling this variation is the ultimate goal of using this metaphor, and that goal outreaches present knowledge; we do not know exactly how some instructional features (in VEI) specifically produce certain learnings (in ALP). However, the metaphor may be specifically interpreted. Certain oral language experiences are likely to lead to oral language facility; certain elements of exchange (such as scaffolding) are likely to lead to greater comprehension of language; certain experiences with books and stories are likely to lead to understandings of reading; and certain experiences with letters and words are likely to lead to ideas about writing.

Oral Language in the Metaphor

First, in regard to oral language and language comprehension, we may specify the elements within the metaphor to bring the concept to a pragmatic level. The following components of each of the constituents of the diagram include much of the material from earlier chapters. (The list, like others in this book, is neither exhaustive nor definitive; it represents current "best guesses.")

The components of NL, the natural and essential learning potential of young humans, are

Natural Learning—Language

Physical Characteristics of the Infant
Sufficient mental ability
Sufficient physical health
Sufficient speech capacity
Sufficient hearing

Natural Propensities for Learning
Ability to structure language systems
Desire to communicate
Ability to select salient language features

Minimum Environmental Requirements
Sufficient nutrition
Presence of language in home
No physical or emotional abuse

Given these characteristics, Academic Learning Preparedness occurs as follows:

Academic Learning Preparedness—Language

Oral Language
Use of lexicon to express meaning
A system of rules that structure utterances
Understanding of some communication rules
Ability to communicate
Consistent use of phonology of native language(s)

Comprehension of Language
Understanding of the meaning of a set of words
A system of rules which govern the encoding of others' utterances
Ability to understand others' communications
Perception of different sounds

Within the metaphor, these natural abilities and minimal levels of academic preparedness are contained within expandable segments. These segments are, of course, somewhat influenced by the extent of certain aspects of NL. For example, natural mental ability varies from individual to individual, resulting in differences in the size of the expansion of ALP. However, for our purposes (and of some importance generally), the impact of the several components of VEI in regard to oral language and language comprehension is the critical element.

The following list contains the instructional elements thought to be encased in VEI, according to theory and research. These elements are, as we will see, applicable to all children. I have used this metaphor to present how the extent of learning experiences is represented by the idea of the force exerted in the bellows of the accordian. These experiences, like the bellows, amplify the natural learning taking place. Represented here, then, is the idea that the greater the amount and type of one of the elements in VEI, the greater the potential for language learning in ALP. The elements of VEI in regard to oral language and comprehension are

Variable Environmental Influence—Language
Setting for Language Exchange
Establishment of routines and exchange games
An adult (parent/relative/teacher) desirous of communicating
An adult interested in negotiation for meaning
An adult who values child's meaning
An adult able to pick up directly from child initiations
An adult sensitive enough to child's current level to adhere to it and provide increasing and appropriate challenge
Adults and siblings interested in holding and extending communications
Activities and objects about which to communicate
Specific Exchange Elements
Extent of actual communication
Amount of adult expansions of child utterances
Amount of adult redirections
Amount of comments upon child's utterances
Specificity in explanations about word meanings
Number of specific answers to child questions
Kind of scaffolding to encourage use of greater complexity
Use of oral exchange games
Amount of interactive talk surrounding play with objects
Amount of interactive talk surrounding story experiences
Use of simplified language to child and concomitant ability to gradually and appropriately increase the complexity of the exchange elements

It is quite likely that not all these components are essential to maximum learning; it is equally possible that certain combinations of instruction are more beneficial than others. In this way, the metaphor is limited. Nevertheless, in general, it indicates how familial and school influences may support language learning.

Literacy in the Metaphor

The metaphor may be used again with regard to the acquisition of concepts about reading and writing. As indicated at the beginning of this section, although this metaphor is described separately from its application to oral language, in reality the elements of the metaphor in both applications are merged in the child's experiences. In this way, the impact of strong oral language acquisition and of strong storybook experiences is shown to influence both oral language and literacy development.

The elements that need to be included in NL for literacy are

Natural Learning—Literacy
Physical Characteristics
Sufficient mental ability
Sufficient physical health
Sufficient speech capacity
Sufficient hearing
Visual acuity
Natural Propensities for Learning
Ability to structure language systems
Desire to communicate
Ability to select salient language features
Interest in stories
Interest in words
Desire to acquire the skills of the community
Minimum Environmental Requirements
Sufficient nutrition
Presence of language in home
No physical or emotional abuse
Presence of reading and writing material in environment
Use of reading and writing material in environment

In regard to literacy, the "preparedness" of ALP is critical. The metaphor has been designed to explain the instructional influence upon children's acquisition of basic knowledge about reading and writing rather than independent reading commonly acquired through direct instruction during the first years of school. Therefore, the elements within ALP represent skills and knowledge thought to be essential to the beginning of independent reading and writing. They are

Academic Learning Preparedness—Literacy
Reading
Understanding that there are different purposes for reading
Knowledge that pictures and text have different functions
Knowledge that the print contains the meaning

Knowledge that the words spoken during story reading come from the print
Knowledge of books, the handling of books, and simple terms
Knowledge of story structure
Knowledge that discourse is composed of words
Knowledge of alphabet
Knowledge that words are represented by letters
Knowledge that letters are rearranged to represent different words
Knowledge about spacing and sequencing of letters
Ability to rhyme and analyze sound segments within words
Writing
Knowledge that meaning can be written
Knowledge that writing is used for a variety of purposes
Knowledge that letters are arranged in order to express words
Sense that the sequence of letters corresponds to the sounds in words
Ability to write one's own name

It is clear that the path from NL to the abilities contained within ALP for literacy requires considerable input from VEI. Since, of course, literacy is not universal, it is quite clear that environmental influence makes a particularly strong impact. With increased knowledge about the emergence of reading and writing (Chapter 3), it is possible to begin to specify those elements of VEI.

Variable Environmental Influence—Literacy
Specific answers to child questions about reading and writing
Reading
Extent of storybook experiences
Adult-child exchange over elements within stories, about pictures, and about meaning
Amount of explanation about reading uses by family members
Participation in favorite rhymes with playful input from child
Appropriately placed talk about print and about how print contains the story
Appropriately placed talk about words
Appropriately placed talk about words in stories and on signs in the home and school and on trips
Instruction on letters, beginning with the child's name
Appropriately placed explanations about the use of letters to represent words
Appropriately placed explanations about spacing and sequencing
Writing
All elements listed under *Reading,* plus the following:
Careful demonstration of how writing is used to express messages
Encouragement and acceptance of "scribbling" and other primitive forms as "writing"
Demonstration of how to write letters, beginning with letters of the child's name
Encouragement of attempts to write messages

The metaphor asserts that these elements of exchange about reading and writing will lead to expansion of ALP, relative to the strength of the instruction. Because reading and writing depend upon the presence of definable skills (e.g, writing letters), it is easy to understand how the direct impact of several of the literacy-acquiring VEI elements relates to the skills of ALP. For example, repeated readings of the same story will establish a routine through which the child may learn that the print contains the discourse of the story. Likewise, talk about letter formation, when presented at the appropriate time and in the best way, most likely will lead to the ability to write one's name.

The Metaphor Completed

It is possible now to combine the separate representations of the metaphor into a whole. (See Figure 3.) In so doing, it is important to realize that the oral language and the literacy segments flow into one another, demonstrating how the learning of a skill in one depends upon and supports the learning of the other.

In conclusion, the use of the accordian metaphor to represent the influence of the environment and its instructional qualities suggests these factors have an important role in determining academic preparedness. The accordian represents how the environment influences rather than initiates the learning. That is, the metaphor rests upon the notion that learning is characterized by children's active processing of experiences. Thus, the arrow area that represents learning is open throughout; learning occurs as children interpret their experiences. The best instruction, then, is truly interactive. With this idea in mind, the following section describes instruction at home and at school.

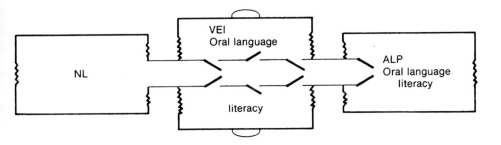

FIGURE 3. *The metaphor with the instructional component identified*

CHILDHOOD EDUCATION AT HOME

Several years ago, a number of innovative preschool programs were initiated and intended, for the most part, to help children from low-income homes become better prepared for school learning. The programs varied in terms of curricula, duration, designs for evaluation, theoretical underpinnings, and instructional direction. Some programs provided direct adult-child interaction; some, for parents, modelled interactions with the children, and some involved group learning in schools. In addition to studying the immediate impact of such programs on intelligence and achievement at the beginning of the elementary school period, long-term effects have been examined. This work provides an informal test of the metaphor and suggests direction for the metaphor's instructional implementation.

Preschool programs, of course, have been available for many years. The programs have had different purposes and have been of uneven quality. Most served middle-class children who attended a few hours a day. Beginning in the 1960s, private and public resources were used to make preschool education available to children of poverty. Long-term evaluation of program effects has yielded positive results: Preschool education, when of high quality, makes a difference in the achievement and lives of participants years later (Berreuta-Clement et al. 1984; Lazar and Darlington 1982). Many people believe there ought to be increased opportunity for more children. Yet, as of 1980, only 39% of children from low-income homes were enrolled in preschools (Chorvinsky 1982). Moreover, with 43% of the children under age 5 in the United States with working mothers, early childhood education is particularly important. However, in the middle 1970s "there were 1.2 million licensed spaces in center- and home-based care for 13 million children of mothers employed full-time outside the home" (Berrueta-Clement et al. 1984, 111). The availability of preschool education is far too limited; the impact of its influence on the lives of the participants is quite strong. Clearly, change is needed in policy and the delivery of effective education. Home-based programs are a good solution.

The Programs

A number of home-based programs were initiated in the 1960s in recognition that the most critical teachers of young children are their mothers. Home-based programs involved the mother either directly or as an observer. It was hoped that a number of changes in child rearing would result and therefore have stronger effects than a few hours in a preschool.

The Florida program initiated by Gordon (Gordon, Guinagh, and Jester 1977) involved weekly home visits. With the intent of focusing upon the parents, paraprofessionals demonstrated mimeographed lessons to the mothers (with the child). Early results indicated favorable benefits; the longer the treatment, the better the results. Lazar and Darlington's (1982) study of the lasting effects of the programs (some of the original program participants had reached age 19), however, did not show lasting effects after grades two and three. Nevertheless, it appeared that the treated participants were not referred as often for special education as their untreated peers.

Like the Gordon program, the Mother-Child Home Program by Levenstein (1977) focused upon poverty children and upon the mother. In the Levenstein program (still underway in many sites), paraprofessionals model to the mothers how to involve children in play and talk about toys and books brought and left in the home. With the goal of enriching mother-child dyadic interaction, the teaching approach is to model talk about the toys and books rather than to didactically demonstrate. The toys and books are chosen for the purpose of steadily increasing the complexity of the interactive experiences. As the materials are modelled, parents learn to expand their child's talk, to encourage silent listening, and to describe what they are doing to their child.

Believing that family teaching is critical for learning within an "emotional haven," the program provides forty-six semi-weekly home visits for seven months in each of two years. In both the original and newer sites, program results are quite strong. In regard to IQ, those who were in the program maintained a significantly higher IQ average through the age of 10 compared with control children. Moreover, fewer program children were assigned to special education classes; through grade five, these children also had higher reading achievement. Finally, mothers of program children were more satisfied with their children's progress than control children mothers (Lazar and Darlington 1982).

Levenstein stated that the positive effects are due to the interaction of three factors: the child's socioemotional competence, the mother's parenting, and the child's cognitive development. Not knowing which leads to which, this triad resembles our metaphor. The close modelling of interactions between adult and child is likely to have influenced the mothers' ability to stimulate beneficial, long-term effects on language and literacy. Because costs are low due to volunteer and part-time paraprofessional workers, this system is relatively easy to implement: $250-$900 per child (Levenstein 1977).

Effective Language Teaching at Home

Effective interaction between parent and child involves a number of factors listed under the Variable Environmental Influence of the metaphor in the previous section. Some of these characteristics are part of many parents' repertoire. While research studies reported in Chapter 4 revealed less interaction and differences in the kind of interaction in low compared with middle-class families, suggesting the former families are in greater need of intervention, it is also true that all parents need to examine their form of interaction with their children. It is not the intent of this section to imply that parents, by virtue of their poverty, are perforce inadequate teachers of their children. It is true, however, that if parents of young children have not, themselves, experienced stimulating learning environments in their own upbringings, then they are likely to need intervention more than parents from families in which talk is believed to be important to children's development. Improved interchange has both cognitive and emotional benefits for all young children acquiring language.

The list of oral language features on page 112 contains several critical elements under *Setting for Language Exchange*. These features are critical to interchange, and they apply to all families. Since in some low socioeconomic groups, parents may not believe that teaching is an important part of their role (Heath 1983, forthcoming), these parents may not provide sufficient opportunities for interchange with their children (Farron 1982) and may not respond to children's initiations to enhance their thinking (Tough 1982; Wells 1981). Thus, any help in the area of parental communication with children is likely to be critical. Following the Levenstein program (1977), the modelling approach of teachers to parents appears to be an excellent way in which to help parents. Probably less effective, but perhaps helpful, are written and spoken directions to parents. Whatever the process, parents who understand that their communications—the sheer amount and the quality—are important to their children's future are likely to interact with increased facility. Teachers of small children are in an excellent position to model effective strategies to parents and to provide guidance on communication in general.

A second important concept in regard to the setting for exchange is that meaning is negotiated through communications. Parents who view language as control over their own and their child's actions will have some difficulty accepting this notion, but teachers can help parents understand that consideration of the child's intentions may be more fruitful than controlling through talk. One of the salient distinctions between talk at home and talk at school is that at home, children may be more secure to assert themselves and to disagree. While negotiation at school is also recommended, at home it is important. Talk with give-and-take allows children to learn to negotiate meaning. These negotiations, rather than representing a disregard for discipline, instead clarify and extend meaning. Parents can be as forceful when they explain as when they order. For example, when it is time for a child to leave a comfortable situation, acceptance of the child's denial and reassertion of the need to leave teaches the child that her desire is at least acknowledged. This response is far better than ignoring the denial with continued assertions.

Another feature of the setting above is the establishment of routines within which regular exchanges occur. These may be implemented in families as teachers encourage mothers to play the games taught at school ("Pop Goes the Weasel"), to talk about foods being eaten, to establish ways of listing clothing items during diapering and dressing, and to establish a few moments each day for exchanges during picture book reading.

It is very important for parents to learn to comment directly on the initiations and comments of the child. Even when meaning is relayed through gesture and movement, mothers should learn to comment upon the meaning of the action or vocalization. For example, when a child reaches for a brightly wrapped candy at the supermarket, an item the parent has no intention of buying, the action displays meaning and should have a direct response such as, "No, Imogene, no candy today. Candy is not very good for small children." Again, a child who points and comments on the arrival of the bus at the corner should receive a direct response, "Yes, Michael, here comes the bus. Where shall we sit?" Whenever possible, these responses should encourage further talk. It is important for parents to focus on the direct meaning of the child's comments.

In this way, parents learn more specifically the level at which the child is operating and thereby are in a position to begin to expect and demand greater input. This insight cannot be taught; it is learned as parents involve themselves more and more directly in interactive talk with their children as meaning is negotiated. Specific questions to parents about whether their children would understand a particular comment or would be able to produce a particular structure will suggest that attention be paid to this issue.

Since there are certain aspects of the setting in which communication occurs and since the greater the amount of interactive talk, the better, specific exchange characteristics also need consideration. Moreover, many times, parents are in direct contact with their children; these interactions provide opportunities for good talk. Good daily opportunities for meaningful talk are

Morning dressing and feeding
Errands and travel (by car, bus, or train)
Visits to or from people
The trip to preschool, clinic, etc . . .
Laundry and other chores
Lunch and nap preparation
The return of siblings and others for supper
Supper talk
Explanations about TV programs
Preparation for child's play on floor
Bathing
Talk and picture book reading before sleep

Whatever the family schedule, there are innumerable times during each day for productive talk. It is necessary, however, to consider that many parents have difficulty in implementing much change because of the stress of their lives. A single mother of two small children I knew well described her feelings at the end of work each day as she organized her family: She picked up her small son from his day-care center; she had to get her daughter from a neighbor's; if necessary, all had to go to the market; dinner needed preparation; and the children needed to be readied for bed. With worries about paying bills and the dangers of the neighborhood, these days were very stressful. As a teacher, she knew full well the importance of her communications with her children. But as a highly stressed parent, she found it quite difficult to be productive and suggestive to her children. And this mother had a good job and other supports that many mothers do not have. Professionals cannot assume that all situations are like their own experiences.

Specific types of interchange are listed in the Variable Environmental Influence of the metaphor. Chart 3 lists and gives an illustration of each interchange.

Literacy Development at Home

The last example in Chart 3 represents how oral language and literacy experiences are developed jointly. All of the elements that apply to the development of communications in oral language also apply to the acquisition of literacy concepts because literacy concepts rest upon a strong language base. The type of inter-

CHART 3.   Specific types of interchange in Variable Environmental Influence

	Exchanges	
Type	Definition	Example
Expansion	Adult restates child utterance in greater complexity.	*Child:* Look. Bus. *Adult:* Yes, the bus is coming.
Prompts	Adult attempts to get child to use language specifically.	*Child:* Milk *Adult:* Milk? Milk for me? *Child:* Me. Want milk.
Comments	Adult comments to child initiation.	*Child:* Pencil *Adult:* Oh, you want a pencil. No. How about a crayon?
Word meaning	Adult supplies clear, unequivocal meaning and uses contrast to explain.	*Child: (looking at book, points to dog)* Kitty. *Adult:* Not a kitty. That's a dog. Dogs say *RRR*; they're big.
Specific answers	Adult gives very clear answers with no extra explanation, unless asked and child wants it.	*Child: (pointing to snowplow)* What's that do? *Adult:* That's a snowplow that pushes snow away.
Scaffolding	Adult raises expectation for child participation.	*Adult: (child with book)* What is this picture? *Child:* Bunny. *Adult:* What's he doing? *Child:* Bunny getting food.

actions for oral language are recommended as the means by which parents can facilitate basic literacy concepts. In the Levenstein (1977) program, the teachers brought books to the home and modelled ways to use the books with children. Mason (1984) also found that simple books sent to homes with directions about use extended children's knowledge about literacy. An excellent book by Butler and Clay (1982) provides parents with some advice about book use and a beginning list of good books for interactions that many parents can use. For parents not accustomed to picture and storybook reading, however, more information is needed. Through teachers' modelling the exchange with books and writing, parents will learn how to use materials effectively. Moreover, teachers should help parents get library cards and should negotiate use of the library with family group trips, for example. Since the home is filled with materials for literacy discussion, advice on talk about how to use magazines and food parcels also is recommended.

Just as was true of oral language at home, where the setting for learning was important, the setting for literacy needs attention. For example, most parents are not sufficiently aware of their impact on their child's reading; many believe their child's reading is the concern of the school, and some believe they might mislead their children if they "teach." The metaphor for instruction broadens the definition of teaching to include the outcomes of meaningful direct exchanges with children. Minimally, the setting must have written and writing materials. Parents should understand that talk about the materials is part of the setting for learning literacy.

Although not often considered by most of us, there are innumerable ways in which literate adults use reading and writing; it is recommended that parents make these explicit. Letters and bills, magazines, newspapers, written words on television, television guides, recipes and other directions, as well as books can be pointed out as sources for adult reading. Parents can point out their writing as they write letters, respond to bills, fill out forms, and write lists. Thus, children will become conscious of the purposes of reading and writing.

In addition to the setting in which first literacy knowledge is acquired, the interaction with small children over home materials and storybooks is the medium through which notions about literacy are learned. Chart 4 contains several literacy exchange settings and lists examples of how discussions with children might occur in these settings. The examples serve as ways to model literacy exchanges to parents. Parents should be advised that notions about literacy are developed over time; new ideas are suggested only when children are ready, as indicated by their questions and responses.

CHART 4. Literacy exchanges

Type	Activity	Example
Reading		
Specific answers to child	Provide the child with just the information asked for; on occasion, relate it to previous knowledge.	*Child:* What's this? *(pointing to word on box)* *Adult:* That's a word, CHEX. What letter do you know?
Book experiences	Provide the child with daily storybook experiences.	*Adult:* Which book do you want to read? You pick it . . .
Exchanges during storybook reading	Read through stories, and be able to stop and ask questions.	*Adult:* This is your book. Let's see what it says.
Questions during reading *Are You My Mother?*	Ask the child to name, expand, predict, talk about the setting, discuss concepts, and talk about overall meaning.	*Adult:* What's this? *(picture)* What's he doing? What's going to happen? Where's he going? Where's his mother? Why didn't he know who his mother was?

CHART 4, *continued*

Type	Activity	Example
	Reading	
Rhymes and sounds	*Play* with sounds in talk and readings: rhyme and beginning sounds.	*Adult and Child: (repeated unison Mother Goose poems, letting Child fill in line-end rhyme)* *Adult: (emphasizing initial B)* Baby bought a blue ball *(and other silly alliterations)*
Talk about print	1. Focus on the significance of print. 2. Discuss the print and picture.	*Adult:* See, these words tell me what to say. *Adult:* The picture shows what the words say.
Talk about words	1. Show words. 2. Identify a few words.	*Adult:* This is a word, and this is a word . . . *Adult:* This is XXXXX.
Words in stories	Point out one or two important words to well-known stories, signs, etc.	*Adult:* See, here is the word that says XXX.
Letters	1. Point out letters of the child's name. 2. Relate the child's first letter to the first letter in other words. 3. Gradually show other letters.	*Adult:* Look, Sue, here is your name. S U E says Sue. *Adult:* There is an S like in SUE. *Adult:* Here's a U like in the middle of SUE.
Alphabet	Introduce the alphabet with songs, "Sesame Street," and books (not for recitation, just awareness).	*Adult and Child: Sing alphabet song. Read alphabet books. Talk about "Sesame Street."*
Letters in words	Comment on letters in words for general notions.	*Adult:* This word has many letters; this has a few.
Spacing and sequencing	Point out spaces, sequencing ideas, and word sequences.	*Adult:* The word begins here and ends here. *Adult:* To write SUE, the letters are always S U E. *Adult:* The words are XXXX. *(points as reads)*

CHART 4, *continued*

Type	Activity	Example
	Writing	
Demonstration of writing purposes	Show how messages are written: letters, notes, lists, and forms.	*Adult:* I'm going to write to Aunt Lizzie. I'll start *Dear Lizzie.* What should we tell her?
		Adult: Let's leave a note for Richard to tell him when we'll be back.
		Adult: Let's see, milk . . . *(etc.)*
		Adult: Look they want me to write something here and here and here.
Acceptance	Encourage and accept the child's writings, emphasizing meaning.	*Child:* See what I wrote? *(shows scribbles)*
		Adult: Good for you! What does it say?
Writing of name	Encourage interest in writing name.	*Adult:* Watch me write SUE. Do you want to try? Funny snaky S . . .
Other writing	Use writing to challenge notions about letters and words.	*Adult:* Here's SUE. Look at MICHAEL's name. What do you see?
Encouragement	1. Act as a scribe.	*Adult:* I've written to Gram. Do you want to say something to her? I'll write it.
	2. Use labels.	*Child:* See my picture? *Adult:* Let's make a title.
	3. Move the child to his or her own writing attempts.	*Child:* Please write *Keep out* for me. *Adult:* I'm too busy. You do it yourself.

The chart may give the unintentional impression that parental input ought to be directive. The conversations that evolve around reading and writing experiences should not be directed by the parents. Parents need to learn to accept responses from their children that do not seem "correct." As they model to parents the interactive setting for literacy experiences, teachers should take the opportunity to talk to the parents about the child's level of understanding demonstrated in the exchange and should comment on the developmental process underway. Teachers should be clear that meaning, new ideas, and the child's unique contributions to the talk are far more important than the parents' notion of correctness. Perhaps the most important part of the exchange is the acceptance and interest of the parents in regard to their children's ideas.

By themselves, the examples in Chart 4 represent only suggestions about activities that should be repeated over and over, that should vary by setting, and that should become more complex as the child's questions indicate the need for additional challenge. The activities also depend upon the dual opportunities for having lots of good books and the chance to read and reread favorites until they are almost memorized. Teachers should take every opportunity to ensure that parents get books to read with their children. As they suggest books for parents to use with their children, teachers should be mindful of the parents' own educational levels. And because parents are not the only family members who can provide storybook experiences for children, parents can ask older siblings and others in the family to take on this responsibility. Indeed, as we will soon see, children can benefit from similar experiences with other adults in settings away from home.

CHILDHOOD EDUCATION AT SCHOOL

Recommended teaching practices of the preschool are like those of the family. The essential challenge is how to apply the elements of the one-to-one exchange between adult and child in the home to school situations that include one adult and a number of children. Moreover, because teachers do not have the emotional ties with children that exist at home and cannot know so specifically what children can produce in regard to language complexity, it is more difficult for teachers to provide the best kind of response than for the knowledgeable parent. Since the setting, itself, influences instruction, the setting must be considered in the instructional model applied to the school.

Our metaphor suggests that the force of the accordian's bellows is strongest when applied early and consistently by parents. Indeed, history would suggest that when education is applied that way by literate parents, preschool education is not necessary. For generations, children began school at age 6 with no prior formal instruction; obviously, great numbers successfully learned language and literacy. In fact, of course, the idea of the accordian metaphor applies wherever people interact with young children. It is only critical that there be sufficient force generated somewhere for children to obtain knowledge sufficient for successful learning in the primary grades, something all children are entitled to. For those children whose families do not provide enough interaction for fruitful learning experiences, preschool education is extremely important. For many children, preschool experiences reinforce those at home; for some, they extend home experiences. In both environments, the bellows should operate similarly.

It is, however, more difficult for school learning to have the same effects due to constraints associated with numbers of children, limitations of time, and the need to fulfill social goals in the school community.

Preschool Programs

During the middle 1960s, the traditional preschool concept was applied, sometimes unchanged and sometimes modified, to the education of children of poverty through the federally funded Head Start Program. Differentially defined and applied, participants were post tested when they left the programs and again at school entrance. Generally speaking, the early results were disappointing (Bronfenbrenner 1974). It generally was accepted that early intervention provided recipients with only short-term benefits; as a result, considerable reduction in federal support for childhood education occurred. Based on these early findings, however, Project Follow-Through was funded by the government, and many programs were continued through the primary grades in school, again with uneven results (Tavris 1976). From several independent sources, however, new longitudinal studies indicate significant, long-term positive effects from quality preschool experiences (Berreuta-Clement et al. 1984; Lazar and Darlington 1982).

In one example of the longitudinal studies, participants in the Perry Preschool program (ages 3 and 4) were tested at several points during their schooling and interviewed at age 19 and older (Berreuta-Clement et al. 1984). There were significant differences between them and randomly selected controls (good design) in IQ at the start of school, differences that diminished. Despite the diminished IQ differences over time, participation in the program was related with fewer assignments in special education and greater academic achievement. By age 15, program participants valued their schooling more highly and had higher school grades. At 19, program participants scored higher on a test of everyday competence, had higher employment, earned more, and saved more money. Moreover, there were fewer pregnancies and arrests among participants. The authors analyzed costs for the preschool program versus the costs for special education, the criminal justice system, welfare, and the like. As one may imagine, program costs were far lower without even considering the human savings.

Twelve preschool programs that had not been part of Head Start were evaluated for their impact on long-term educational outcomes. Lazar and Darlington (1982) compared the treated participants with their controls from twelve programs; most participants were at least in the upper elementary grades at the time of the retesting; many were in high school and beyond. The researchers found that students who had been in the preschool intervention programs had been assigned less often to special education classes in the interim than had controls, even when controlling for IQ. A number of programs made an impact on reading and math, at least through the third grade. Many program participants had significantly higher IQ scores compared with controls for three or four years after participation. Only the Levenstein program (previous section) continued to present IQ differences beyond that time. Program girls especially mentioned achievement-related reasons why they were proud of themselves compared with controls. For those who were between 15 and 19 years of age, the program students rated themselves as higher achievers than their peers. In all, there was a 16% better school survival rate among program participants than among controls.

Among the successful programs evaluated by Lazar and Darlington was one limited to boys in Harlem (ages 2 and 3); it focused on the acquisition of essential concepts (such as *up, high,* and *skinny*) (Palmer and Siegel 1977). (See list in Appendix A.) In this program, children were given one-to-one tutoring two hours per week for eight months. Using objects to clarify, there were two treatments, one highly structured and the other called "discovery." Mothers were encouraged to observe the teaching but were not otherwise involved. Both types of treatment were found to significantly and favorably influence conceptual knowledge and IQ two years after training ceased. Moreover, in the study of even longer effects, Lazar and Darlington (1982) found that treated children had higher IQ's than control children through grade five. This minimal amount of treatment presented one-to-one (like mother-child) direct interaction about specific concepts for the children's maximal benefit.

Several other successful preschool programs included regular home visits. Long-term IQ benefits accrued to program participants in Philadelphia (Lazar and Darlington 1982) who were involved in a program designed on a fairly typical developmental model plus a one-day-out-of-five home visit. Another program involving summer school participation linked by weekly home visits during the academic year for either two or three summers favorably influenced participants' IQ's for three years after the program's conclusion. Overall, participants were less likely to be placed in special education (Gray program, Lazar and Darlington 1982). Another program involving home visits was the Perry Preschool project (just recently discussed), a developmental, Piagetian curriculum with weekly home visits; the project has had a significant long-term impact on the lives of the participants (Berreuta-Clement et al. 1984).

In their conclusion, Lazar and Darlington stated that the longitudinal results of their studies did not support particular school patterns; they concluded that it was not clear that home programs were better than school programs, that teachers were better than paraprofessionals, or that programs for infants were better than those for older children. Despite Lazar and Darlington's conservative claim, I believe that home visits were part of the most effective programs; in all but one of the most successful programs, there were regular home visits, a common feature also noted by Berrueta-Clement et al. (1984) and Bronfenbrenner (1974). The one successful non-home program, the Palmer program, involved close talk with program children in an interactive mode.

The findings of these longitudinal studies do not mean that any form of preschool, even with a home visit component, will produce strong effects. The programs that have been studied were carefully designed and directed by leaders in early childhood education who, although they may have disagreed about some features of the curriculum, were theoretically oriented; they had explicitly detailed the purposes and directions of the instruction, and they held to scientific methodology for the good of future children. Generalization to other programs will require sufficient creative leadership and the ability to make program goals known to all workers and the community. With the recent accumulation of evidence that early childhood programs—with little cost—do begin to break the cycle of poverty, legislators in state governments and policy makers in Washington are being persuaded that special money for the education of children at age 3 and 4 is money well spent, particularly when it is spent on children who would otherwise have less chance to be stimulated to learn well in school.

In many ways, the recommendations in regard to language and literacy development in the preschool can be fit into any type of program, particularly developmental programs that encourage dyadic and group interactions. Perhaps more than is true of an older, traditional nursery school which emphasized socialization, a strict Piagetian program which focuses on doing (Kamii and DeVries 1977), an experientialist program with a similar focus (Biber 1977), or a Montessori program, the language and literacy focus of the present recommendations are more explicitly verbal. If they are applied to a quality program, the interactions recommended will be natural. The adult role as leader in language will be easily accepted.

Effective Experiences at School

There are two kinds of language environments in which children participate in preschools, situations with and without an adult participant. When adults are involved, they are either leading a formal experience with language (e.g., storybook reading or a discussion about a class activity), or they are responding to questions and taking part as a member of an exchange. Adult impact on language can be preplanned only for the formal settings. Since their participation in a spontaneous exchange cannot be planned, and since these encounters, as direct exchanges with individuals, are likely to have considerable impact on language learning, it is important that adults working with young children in schools have incorporated a general position in regard to their role in language learning. And that role ought to reflect the concepts embodied in the theory presented in the metaphor. In addition to the influence of the adult, the children's play with one another is also important. Interactive talk among children serves important purposes (Garvey 1984). The social life in the preschool is very important. Exchanges between and among preschool children provide the beginnings of social learning beyond the family. Children learn a lot while interacting without adults in the protective community of the preschool. They learn the rules for exchanges parallel to the negotiation over "ownership" of toys. The play corners of the preschool enable children to focus upon particular kinds of imagining; the imagining provides richness for practice. As discussed in Chapter 2, language practice appears to be important to language development.

Throughout the discussions in these pages, we have stressed the importance of strong links between school and home. Sharing the school goals, methods of interaction, and activities with the adults in the family through early-morning and day-end conversation will provide the child with coherence. Teachers also can demonstrate exchange features through videotapes at parent meetings. The adults in the family can use some of these new ways for talking at home. Similarly, the parents can use these times to tell the school people about family experiences and insights. I suggest that in addition to the typical teachers' reports to parents about children's progress, teachers need to share what they have done, why they have done it, and what would be good ways to follow up. Moreover, teachers should ensure that each parent visits the school for an entire morning, if possible, to observe the interactions involving their child. This modelling may make as great an impact as any family interaction, since this modelling has the potential of integrating home and school methods of talk with children.

Effective preschool programs, following the metaphor for language and literacy development, are likely to include: (1) specific attention to concept building in an interactive framework; (2) adult attention to the characteristics of effective exchanges with children (such as routinization, scaffolding, clarity, and direct answers); (3) the provision of literacy experiences to expand the potential for learning in formal instruction; and (4) the provision of opportunities for children's play.

Several features of the preschool demand special recognition. Group exchanges cannot substitute for one-to-one exchanges. On the other hand, although one cannot know for sure, children must experience some of the benefits from exchanges through listening, even if they have not participated. Thus, social activities and structures may have important cognitive benefits in addition to the social goals. Nevertheless, the language and literacy impact potential of the preschool is less than that of the family because the adult-child exchange in the preschool is diluted somewhat as a result of numbers. Teachers have less time for talk with individual students. However, if children come from families that do not promote supportive language growth and that are unable to change, the preschool can compensate to some extent.

Insuring that specific language activities are incorporated into the school program requires planning for the formal part of the instruction and internal evaluation of the informal part. To illustrate how language and literacy ideas can be integrated into preschool group lessons for four-year-olds, Chart 5 presents parts of a storybook exchange from Leaf's (1936) *The Story of Ferdinand*. Chart 5 includes only a few illustrative examples of language and literacy exchanges. In planning, the teacher should note the main appeals to young children: the bee sting and the nonfight in the bullring; the teacher should focus the planning on these points. (My teenage son, upon watching my preparation of this section, related his memories of *The Story of Ferdinand* to a friend on the phone. With great excitement and without even looking, he told of the sting and the unwillingness of Ferdinand to fight. I was struck by the permanence of his memories of Ferdinand and by the symbolic importance my son gave the book as he described it as "pacifist.")

There are many language and literacy experiences to be gained from just one story. From daily stories, the talk about books may indeed be described as

CHART 5. Illustrative storybook experience, language and literacy

Focus	Activity	Example
Planning (Just thinking through and listing these major points are necessary for planning.)	Select concepts	Teacher selects concepts for discussion: fight, peace, smell, and sting
	Discern literacy ideas	Sounds of Ferdinand, bulls reading sign, and signs to Madrid
	Find points for discussion	Teacher selects Ferdinand's preference for smelling flowers, the sting, the selection, the fight, and the return.
Concept development	Make concept explicit and clear	*Teacher shows picture of Ferdinand about to sit on bee:* What is going to happen? *Child:* Ferdinand is going to sit on the bee. *Teacher:* What will the bee do? *Child:* Bite! *Teacher:* Has anyone here been bitten by a bee? *(Accepts "bite" for time being.)* *Child:* Yes, it hurts. *Teacher:* It's called a sting. No one wants a bee to do what? *Child, Child, Child:* Sting!
Predict	Reveal idea of peace	*Teacher:* Well, Ferdinand is going to Madrid to fight a big fight. What do you think he will do? *Child:* Fight. *Child:* Sit down. *Child:* Nothing. *Teacher:* Let's see. Remember what he likes to do.
Answers questions	Stress specificity and clarity	*Child:* Do bulls really sit? *Teacher:* No, they lie down or stand. The artist liked it this way.

CHART 5, *continued*

Focus	Activity	Example
Prompts	Ask for greater specificity	*Teacher: (Ferdinand sitting in arena)* What's Ferdinand doing? *Child:* Sitting. *Teacher:* Ferdinand is sitting down, and he's supposed to what? *Child:* They want him to fight!
Scaffolding	Expect greater sophistication	*Teacher:* The matador does, too. He wants Ferdinand to fight. Tell me who wants Ferdinand to fight. *Child:* All the people and all the bullfighters and the matador want Ferdinand to fight.
Differentiate prose and pictures	Focus on the meaning of the print	*Teacher: (picture of bulls "reading" sign of bullfight)* What are the bulls doing *(pretend)*? *Child:* They are supposed to be reading the sign. *Teacher:* Yes, it says . . . What the story says is . . . It shows that these bulls want to fight.
Talk about words	Focus on the sign	*Teacher: (Ferdinand on way to Madrid)* See Ferdinand in the cart. There's a sign that tells where they're going. It says "Madrid."
	Focus on the words in text	*Teacher:* Look on this page *(one with few words, one of which is Ferdinand).* Where do you think it says Ferdinand?

"communication rich." The reader ought to avoid interruption and talk that diverge from the main story so that the experience is extended and fruitful. The example with Ferdinand indicates how both language and literacy ideas are simultaneously developed out of good storybook exchanges.

There are many other occasions for the development of language and literacy ideas in the context of group activity. Chart 6 illustrates these group activity opportunities.

CHART 6. Language and literacy in group activities

Experience	Activity	Example
Reading	Recognizing name	*Teacher:* Let's do something to help everyone know where to hang their coat. I want each person to look on this table to see if they can find their name. (*And she helps as needed.*)
Reading	Matching letters	*Teacher:* Each of you try to find a card with your name letter.
Reading	Rhyming	*Teacher includes as many rhymes as possible each day; she leaves a rhyming word slot for a child to fill:* "Hey, diddle diddle, The cat and the XXXX."
Reading	Playing beginning sounds-alliteration games	*Teacher:* Bob, Betsy, Barbara, and Bill
Reading	Pointing out words	*Teacher:* Here is the book, *Are You My Mother?* Which is the word "mother?" *Child:* This one because it's the biggest. *Teacher:* What else helps you know?
Reading	Discussing sequence and space	*Teacher:* (*same book*) Look at the name of our book. See how the words go. (*She points and says*) *Are You My Mother?* What tells you where "are" ends? (*She points to space.*) *Child:* It's empty there. *Teacher:* Good. And the next word, "you," where does it end? *Child:* It's empty there, too.

CHART 6, *continued*

Experience	Activity	Example
Reading	Using the alphabet	*The teacher hangs alphabet cards around the room and uses commercial materials as they fit class activity. She focuses upon single letters, shapes, and sounds; then, she begins to compare them.*
Writing	Demonstrating uses	*Teacher:* We have to write to Mr. Brown to thank him for the new table he made. What should we say? *(same for other purposes)*
Writing	Writing name	*Teacher:* If you want to, you can write your name today. You can write it all by yourself, or you can write it over where I wrote. *(Teacher accepts all work.)* Where do you want to put your name?
Writing	Comparing names	*Teacher:* OK, who wants to show us their name? Tell us about your name, Duane. *Child:* Here is a D, a U . . . I forget. *Teacher:* It's fine, Duane. Who has a name that looks like Duane in the beginning, right here?
Challenge	Discussing word size	*Teacher:* Look at Benjamin's and Bob's. How are they alike? How are they different? *Child:* That one's bigger. *Teacher:* Right, Benjamin's name is longer. Why do you think?
Encouragement	Furnishing beginnings (Teacher is willing to be scribe, if needed)	*Teacher:* Everyone has to write a letter to take home about the party tomorrow *(details discussed).* I'll help, but I want you to try. Here is the day and the time written for you.

Each of the examples in Chart 6 are to be applied many times in many instances but only when teachers are certain the children can handle the questions and the challenges. Children at the preschool level can accept the idea that different people do things differently; as a result, the fact that some write and read a lot and others do little is not a major instructional problem. The concepts and skills of language and literacy outlined in these pages and others may be presented informally as long as teachers plan to include the concepts and skills in a sensible, coherent order in their lessons and their talk with children. The best use is made of commercial programs and workbook materials when they are applied to a program designed by the teacher with *her* class in mind and when they clearly represent the instructional views and directions. In this way, the materials properly support the class program and are, therefore, built upon a theoretical position that the teacher has assimilated.

The accordian metaphor used to draw theory about child language and literacy acquisition to practical levels is simple. When applied to language and literacy instruction in the home and at school, the kind of instruction does not differ substantially. Indeed, when parents and teachers operate out of the same theoretical position and understand the impact of environmental influences similarly, the bellows/accordian concept is strongest. But the accordian is not always used to its fullest; moreover, too often the goals of the school and the family differ. As was true of the participants in the special programs described previously, parents and teachers involved in the education of young children will want to determine the effectiveness of instruction. The next and final section of the chapter discusses this rather thorny issue.

TESTING LANGUAGE AND BEGINNING LITERACY

Critical teaching depends upon the recognition of when new concepts and abilities in language and literacy emerge; thus, one might conclude that informal, diagnostic, instructionally directed tests would be encouraged. It is true that close observation and the recognition of shifts in development are important to teaching. But, as we will see, good use of tests is not automatic, since there are problems with typical test development, the claims made about tests, and, most importantly, the negative impact that results may have on children's development. As a researcher interested in programmatic effects, I have conducted a number of instructional studies (e.g., Pflaum and Pascarella 1980). In fact, in previous editions of this book, I have stressed diagnostic testing by teachers so they could rationally determine teaching level. We do need empirical studies of experimental programs to determine effectiveness, as in the case of the preschool programs. However, difficulties with classroom use of tests must be recognized.

It seems that newly emerging abilities do not appear suddenly and consistently. In the process of literacy acquisition, for example, some children experience retrogression for a short time (Sulzby 1981). Thus, a single measurement might be misleading. Another concern involves the reliability of tests given small children who can become confused by the demands of the task, even though they may understand the process. Finally, the scores from tests are used both to measure skills and knowledge and to design appropriate instruction. The results, when applied to groupings, result in labels. Children whose initial starts in school may be slow may have the capability to develop quite well later. If, however, children are labelled negatively, they may not be appropriately challenged.

Because they are the products of tests, scores tend to be treated as facts. Indeed, the development of the initial, educational, normative test in the United States was intended as a method to provide a more scientific approach to education (Johnson 1984). The production of scores that represent knowledge and skill is both the embodiment of this history and the manifestation of our weakness. And scores may be seriously misused. For example, they are misused when viewed as a reliable measure of stable knowledge, when based on an outmoded notion of early education, and when developed inappropriately.

Yet, to plan effective instruction, teachers need to understand their students' current level of functioning. Parents, we asserted earlier, do know which kinds of language structures their toddlers can and cannot understand (Berko-Gleason and Weintraub 1978; Cross 1977). That knowledge is the product of many hours of personal interaction, something not available to the teacher. Yet, teachers' observations about their students' functioning have been found to be fairly reliable. For example, researchers have found that determination of children's reading readiness is as effectively done by teachers as traditional reading readiness tests when the teachers used an observation instrument (Feshbach, Adelman, and Fuller 1974). It may be that teachers' observations are enhanced when they use a direct instrument.

An important consideration in observations to determine functioning level comes from the ideas of Vygotsky. Although discussed in Chapter 1 in regard to the adult role in learning, Vygotsky's (1978) zone of proximal development may be correctly viewed as a way to understand testing. The level at which children function independently, without help, is determined by most tests. The other, higher level of functioning also may be determined by measuring the complexity of tasks successfully completed when the child is prompted and aided by an adult. Theoretically, then, one can obtain two different functioning levels: The lower one would represent the child's overlearned, independent level, and the higher one would represent the child's potential. If teachers had a good method for determining these two levels and *comparing them*, they would have the correct information for instructional planning.

Referring to the metaphor once more, it is clear that teachers need to know children's current understanding about prose to ask the right questions during storybook reading and privately. If, for example, most children have acquired the notion that the visible length of a word parallels the extent of the word's sound, then they will take more interest and find more value in talk about which word on a page is "Ferdinand" than if they have no such idea. However, unless one knows that the children have begun to find interest in letters at the beginnings of important words when working with adult guidance, one might not extend the talk from finding "Ferdinand" on the page to talk about "F" words. Using a guide for observation helps focus attention. When the observation includes indications about where children function independently and with help, the observations are enriched. The checklists below are intended to help in observations that underlie teaching decisions and approximate the two levels of the zone of proximal development. The checklists contain reference to language and beginning notions about literacy. The examples provided are at two levels, one the independent level (the lower) and one the level at which the child can reach with guidance. Each chart includes very rough age ranges for two age groups, a nursery school age (three and four) and an older group, including kindergarten (four and five).

Occasional use of Table 4 as a broad observational aid ought to help teachers review their children's progress. When, for example, not much change has occurred in a two-month period within a particular area of language, the teacher can evaluate whether the students have had sufficient opportunities for growth. If children are viewed as having achieved the independent level but have not shown further growth with adult guidance, a different interpretation is called for. This result may indicate that this area of language growth is not currently expanding. Greater attention through teaching may be needed to encourage growth.

TABLE 4.   Checklist for observing language

Language Type	Independent Level	In Adult Exchange
Ages 3–4		
Concepts		
Conceptual knowledge	Uses most terms in Appendix A. Answers questions about concepts	Uses all terms in Appendix A. Concepts emerge in talk with adults
Labels	Easily uses nouns for class, community, and family	Can name objects in picture books seen once or twice
Talk		
Monologues	Plays with toys and directs play with monologue	Does not monologue, having replaced it with discourse
Conversation	Has the ability to sometimes interact with peers on the same topic	With an adult, has a real exchange of information
Imagining	Imagining directs interactions with peers. Thinks up and accepts various roles in play	Tells an adult that he or she played "family" (or whatever) and discusses the role taken
Sounds		
Consonants	Uses nearly all consonants but /v/, /r/, /š/, /ǰ/, and /Č/. Cannot do /ž/, /z/, /ə/, and /ð/	Tries /v/, /r/, /š/, /ǰ/, and /Č/

TABLE 4, *continued*

Language Type	Independent Level	In Adult Exchange
	Ages 3–4	
Sounds		
Rhymes	Enjoys Mother Goose rhymes	Takes parts in rhymes
Structures		
Regular inflections	Uses regular endings	Has learned to use a few irregular past and plural markers
Pronouns	Uses pronouns rather than proper nouns in direct reference	Uses pronouns correctly
MLU	At stage IV, uses 3.4 words per sentence	Uses sentences slightly longer than 3.4 words
Use of AUX	AUX appears uninflected in some questions and negatives, and inflected in some	Displays some use of AUX inflected and AUX transformed
Sentences	Uses basic sentence constituents mostly	Uses well-formed sentences most of the time
	Uses occasional complex sentences	Uses complex sentences with adult comments
	Ages 4–5	
Concepts		
Conceptual knowledge	Can make categories of things that belong together	Can, with help, supply name for category
Labels	Has wide vocabulary: over 500 terms	Seeks names for unknown
Talk		
Monologues	Uses occasionally	Disappeared almost entirely
Conversation	Is truly interactive with peers	Is always interactive with adults
Negotiation	Begins to hear the other side	Can deal with wants as negotiation
Adjustment	Can adjust to different listeners	Uses advanced language in interchange with adults
Roles	Negotiates many roles in complicated games	Can alter roles and use different language for each
Oral stories	Can take part in a group-developed story	Can help provide resolution and coherence to story

TABLE 4, *continued*

Language Type	Independent Level	In Adult Exchange
	Ages 4–5	
Sounds		
Consonants	Uses all but /r/ and /l/ with ease	Uses clear and confident speech
Rhymes	Can supply rhyme on familiar poem when asked	Has a variety of rhyming games and knows part of poems
Alliteration	Enjoys and offers an occasional word in sequence: boy, boat, bomb, blast. . . .	Participates in sequences of words
Beginning analysis	Can say that "grand" and "father" are parts of grandfather	Has a growing sense of word parts
Structures		
Inflections	Knows all regular inflections as they are used in the community	Knows large groups of irregular inflections (e.g., rang and sang)
MLU	Is between 3.5 and 4.0	Is sometimes much greater than 4.0
Sentences	Occasionally combines sentence elements	Clearly understands the beginnings of complex sentences
Connectives	Uses a few connectives: and, then, because, so, if, and WH words	Is challenged to use many connectives

In regard to the acquisition of literacy, commercially available tests exist for beginning literacy. Clay's (1979) tests that examine children's concepts about print are used quite often. While not originally examined for validity with other tests, it appears that the tests (named *Sands* and *Stones*) show strong consistency with other tests and skills (Day and Day 1979).

In order to simultaneously observe current levels of functioning and to determine the directions in which children appear to be gaining facility, teachers can chart a zone of independent children's skills and skills activated in concert with an adult. Teachers can compare their notations with the skill levels detailed in the two columns in Table 5 (which parallels for literacy the material of Table 4 for language).

The guidelines in Table 5 may be used in the same way as the guidelines in Table 4: to heighten a teacher's awareness of her pupils' development. The use of the checklists every two months will provide a helpful ongoing picture of growth in the classroom, at least in language and literacy beginnings. Since young children often respond differently in different settings, observations,

TABLE 5.   Checklist for observing beginning literacy

Type	Independent Level	Level with Adult Help
	Ages 3–4	
Storybook		
Interest	Has one or two very favorite books and poems. Knows them well, so recognizes when they are "misread"	Can become interested in new stories; asks questions
Story understanding	Can relate sequence of events	Can tell about a story in its absence
Story seeking	Is happy to participate in storytime	Is eager to help an adult find books
Notions about Reading		
Print and picture	Can point to where story is contained	Can verbalize difference in what picture and print show
Purpose for reading	When asked, can find newspaper, book, etc.	Talks about the kind of reading done in various media
Parts of stories	Can answer question about sequence	Talks about parts of story explicitly
Notion of word	Picks out word in title	Can identify where words begin and end
Writing		
Practice	"Writes" when asked (scribbles)	Is eager to show "writing" to an appreciative adult
Words	For example, has notion that big people ought to have big names	Talks about ideas regarding print
Letter	Learns letter of own name	Learns letter of name and asks for more
	Ages 4–5	
Storybook		
Familiarity	Knows several storybooks by name	Has specific things to say about several books
	Knows passages of at least one book	Knows several book segments by heart
Routine	Experiences a school and a home reading routine	Can be explicit about routines for reading
Preference	May have preference for one type of book	Is beginning to like certain types of storybooks

TABLE 5, *continued*

Type	Independent Level	Level with Adult Help
	Ages 4–5	
Storybook		
Purposes	Is quite specific about various reasons for reading	Can identify several purposes for reading
Notions about Books and Print		
Books	Knows which way to hold a book, where beginning and end, pages, title, etc. are	Can describe how to handle a book for reading, and uses terms well
Reading terms	Points correctly to page, sentence, word, and letter; says sound	Uses terms correctly: page, sentence, word, letter, and sound
Notions about Reading		
Print	Has no confusion about where a story comes from	
Stability	Knows that a story is always the same because of the print	Can explain why print tells the story
Words	Is familiar with terms and words and can point to printed words	Can identify oral and written forms and tries to describe the difference
Printed words	Has observed and spoken of the way words are printed with the same letters	Knows that words are written with the same letters and sequence each time
Sequence	Participates in talk about oral and written sequences in writing	Can identify how oral and written sound/symbol sequences occur
Letters		
Letters	Knows several letters in different settings	Can name many letters in different settings
Notion about alphabetic principle	Puzzles about word size and consistency of use for sounds	Begins to talk about stability of letters in different words to represent sounds
Writing		
Name	Writes name (possibly uses magnetic letters, but pencil use is preferred)	Asks for help to write other names
Practice	"Writes" when asked. Makes signs and labels	"Writing" may take on spontaneous spelling. Has a variety of writing purposes

when conducted regularly and carefully, may be more reliable than a single testing. In any case, when this test or normative reading readiness tests are used, the observations can enrich and expand the interpretations given any individual.

SUMMARY

The discussion of this chapter has reiterated the need for language and literacy to occur in an interactive environment. Even the charts used to gauge the pupils' development presume this interactive learning setting. Thus, although the book is concerned with language and literacy, neither is viewed as separate from social knowledge and development.

The stimulation in the environment was depicted through the metaphor of the accordian bellows, a representation of what good home and school programs appear to provide children. The message of the chapter is optimistic and simple: Children are well served and well prepared for the academic expectations of school when they interact with adults who stimulate language growth in ways that are consistent with prior language, that are set in routines to make the new easier to attend to, and that include challenge. With the intelligence of understanding adults and not much fancy equipment, young children can become engaged with objects and with stories that will enhance their ultimate success in school.

We turn in the next chapters to the question of reading and writing. In some ways, it seems that school reading and writing instruction does not rely on strong language learning. This situation exists in the first months of reading learning, but not for long.

SELECTED ACTIVITIES

1. Observe a preschool child in the context of his/her class for an entire morning. Using the charts at the end of this chapter for language and for literacy, see if you can describe his/her language and literacy levels.
2. Write a list of all the specific components of language/literacy you would include in a preschool curriculum.
3. With the metaphor for instruction in mind, pick one or two language stimulation activities, and trace their presumed effects on language development specifically.
4. Many of the preschool programs that had strong effects on participants' later experiences were based on notions about child development that emphasized group play and varied language experiences. Classrooms usually had special areas for special kinds of play (such as a house corner and building blocks areas). The day would be marked with both free-choice and scheduled activities for storybook time, talk,

group experiences, and some focus upon conceptual development. Why might such a setting be appropriate for the application of the metaphor as compared with a more structured, elementary school-like organization?

5. Imagine that you have planned an activity for your four-year-olds. You want them to write their names for drawers that will hold their things. What will you do about the fact that Paul and William always are together, and their skills are very different: Paul reads and writes like a second grader; William has no interest? How will you make sure that William doesn't feel bad in comparison?

6. Make a list of all the ways in which you will be able to provide the parents of your imagined three-year-old children with the information they need about talk with their children, provision of books for their children, and ways to elicit children's interest in words, language, and literacy. Make your list as long as possible.

6 A Look at Beginning Readers and Writers

When they enter classrooms that have formal instruction in reading and writing, children experience considerable excitement and fundamental changes in expectations and behaviors. Usually, this reaction occurs in the first grade; increasingly, however, kindergarten classes are having long periods of time devoted to formal instruction.

The changes children experience upon entering first grade involve the scheduling of daily activities, children's physical movements, the kinds of materials they use, the children's interactions with the teacher, and the responses the teachers expect. Compared with preschool, some kindergartners and most first graders find far less time devoted to whole body involvement in play activities; their time is scheduled in fairly long periods, and the names of these periods conform to school disciplines (such as reading, writing, and arithmetic). Instead of work tables and room areas for imaginative play, children are assigned permanent spaces at desks where they must sit for much of the day. Instead of play with objects and only occasional paper and pencil activities, now children work with paper and pencil most of the time, and their work often requires exact, correct responses. Children are expected to listen to and follow teacher directions and to remember explanations. Now, more than before, children are expected to respond to specific questions. Rather than enticing their fantasy, these new classroom conditions impose a new kind of expectation on children.

These new school experiences may seem overly restrictive. However, nearly every young child looks forward to the acquisition of skills associated with maturity. Children look forward to independence with books and writing. Just because the acquisition of reading and writing requires discipline, something children recognize, the experiences of formal classrooms need not be restrictive. In fact, while teacher-directed classes have a negative influence on learning in kindergarten, direct instruction has a positive influence at the beginning of first grade (Soar 1973).

Children have their own notions about what reading is. In one study, first-grade children were interviewed by a five-year-old youngster who asked, as directed, how to prepare to be a good reader in first grade (Sanders 1981). The children revealed considerable awareness of the social and academic expectations of reading in school. They asserted that reading is knowing words. If one has to rely on methods to figure words out, one is not reading words. One child said, "First grade is like a test. When the teacher asks a question like, 'Who knows the first word on this page?' you can just raise your hand and tell her what you already know. Then she will think she taught you." (p. 269) As we see in the succeeding pages, getting to know the words is critical to initial reading and writing; in contrast to the opinion of these first graders, however, teaching children how to figure out new words is part of reading in the first grade.

The first section of this chapter describes what children are learning about reading in the first year of formal instruction. The discussion relies on analyses of children's errors during oral reading; as is true in language study, unexpected, non-adult responses reveal what children understand as well as what they do not. The next section contains a description of the enduring conflict between

144

two quite different instructional approaches to beginning reading. And finally, the third section describes both the traditional and innovative approaches to beginning writing.

OBSERVATIONS OF READING-ACQUIRING CHILDREN

Several studies have traced the oral reading behaviors of children through the first year (in some cases, more) of learning to read. These works demonstrate that the first year of formal reading is characterized by developing control over various strategies for figuring out more words. Children who are developing well begin to integrate different strategies as they try to figure out unknown words (Barr 1974); through practice, the new words become familiar until they are recognized immediately (sight words). For the most part, the first year of reading is characterized by steady increases in reading vocabulary and concomitant increases in fluency or speed (Allington 1984).

Typical Reading Programs

Although we will examine published materials used in the first year of formal reading instruction more thoroughly in a later chapter, those who are not familiar with school reading need to have some insight into the classroom context for first-year reading, including classroom organization, materials, and procedures. Most children in the United States experience some common instructional features, but readers should bear in mind that variations do occur, especially among educators who take one or another extreme view of beginning reading.

In regard to structure, most classrooms develop some method for organizing students to meet individual differences in word knowledge and rate of learning. Because some children come to formal reading with considerable experience in contrast to others who have little, meaningful instruction certainly requires attention to differences. The most common means for attending to this range of reading potential is through the formation of different groups; children typically are assigned to one of three such groups on the basis of previous test scores (e.g., reading readiness tests; see Chapter 7), informal assessment by the teacher in the first weeks of school (often including assessment tasks like letter naming, identification of letter sounds, and simple reading and writing), or some means external to the classroom, such as school-wide preschool testing. The children of each group have separate materials, class instruction, and assignments.

Although critics complain that grouping encourages labelling which may, in turn, have a negative impact on individuals, grouping eight to ten children of like learning capacity appears to be the best solution to meet individual educational needs (Rosenshine and Stevens 1984). Grouping is clearly better than whole class instruction (Barr 1974–1975). Nevertheless, teachers should be aware that children know which group they are in and the significance of that assignment. My daughter told me, for example, after two weeks in the first grade that she was in the "top" group, but her friend was only in the "middle" group. Teachers must assure students and parents that individual progress is important;

indeed, they must believe it themselves. Any negative impact of grouping may be mitigated as teachers determinedly and consistently assess if each pupil is working to capacity and readjust groups accordingly. Because children have such different levels of preparedness when they start formal instruction, a decision not to group is likely to be more negative than grouping may be.

Most basal programs have a single strand of hierarchically arranged materials. Regardless of preparedness level, children experience similar content. The speed with which the successively more complex materials are completed marks differential learning. The beginning reading basal materials consist of a set of simple preprimers, soft-covered books with excellent illustrations that increase in language complexity from one to the next. Preprimers have only a few stories; much of the content is contained in the illustrations. The vocabulary is controlled quite carefully, and planned repetitions of each story's new words are carried to the next. As the vocabulary load increases, the text in the books begins to carry more content. After completing usually three preprimers, children read the primer and then the first reader. (Some programs have additional, transitional primers.) First readers are hard-covered books with more stories, more content, and fewer illustrations. Accompanying all the books are workbooks, which provide practice in the skills being taught. In many classes, these workbooks are supplemented by worksheets for additional practice. Many basal programs indicate the successive books with alphabetic designations in an attempt to emphasize the nongraded aspects of reading learning.

Perhaps the most important component of the basal program is the teacher's manual. Teacher's manuals have, in addition to the entire child's book (even the colored illustrations), explicit directions on how to teach, how to introduce the new words, how to guide the story reading and rereading, and how to introduce, explain, practice, and test new skills. The skills lessons often combine small segments of single skills rather than presenting an entire, single skill, a curiosity discussed in a later chapter.

The financial investment that school systems make in these materials is sizeable. While the books may be reused, new workbooks must be bought each year. Moreover, there are new editions every few years, and wealthier districts purchase new programs fairly often. Given this large investment, school personnel want to assure that the materials are used. Moreover, because administrators and teachers often have strong beliefs that the basals must be followed closely and because skills organization is extremely intricate, basal programs have a considerable influence upon reading instruction. (See Chapter 8 for a further discussion of basals.)

In regard to procedure, much more explicit and exact responses are expected now than in preschool. Indeed, in keeping with the interactive focus, what actually happens in the instruction is thought to be critical to reading acquisition. Common to many classrooms are the small group meetings with the teacher at which new words are introduced, stories are read aloud in turns, skills are presented, and assignments are made, each step typically following the teacher's guide. Following the small group instruction, teachers explain which workbook and worksheets to complete and how to do the work so that children receive practice with new words and skills according to the schedule of the program. Most basal programs include a system for monitoring specific acquisition of skills. By establishing a skills emphasis, reading is being redefined.

Since so much is provided through the basal programs in reading instruction, one might wonder why they are the topic of so much interest. Why, indeed, should teachers be prepared in university classes to teach reading when they are only required to follow the directions of the teacher's manuals? The answer to this question lies in how well teachers present the stories and how they adjust to children's responses. Learning is affected by interaction over materials, modification of the materials to suit day-to-day learning, and decisions about the rate of movement through the program.

Oral Reading of Successful First Graders

Through the careful study of errors children make during the first year, scholars of reading have found significant shifts in children's strategies for handling the most difficult aspect of initial reading: figuring out words that are not immediately recognized and, ultimately, knowing the words. These errors on difficult words, then, demonstrate how children are acquiring reading. Because the programs introduce new words with each new story, thereby building vocabulary, a constant challenge is presented to young children. By asking what children do when they meet words they do not know, researchers have focused attention on reading behaviors during the period of emerging achievement.

We have known for some time that the type of oral reading errors children make changes with experience. Ilg and Ames (1950) found that between the ages of 6 and 9, children improved their use of graphic cues to figure out unknown words. Increasing control over meaning and text structure was indicated by greater use of meaningful substitutions for unknown words. Overall, less reliance on teacher pronunciation plus the integration of cues characterized reading development.

Applying Ilg and Ames' findings with first-year readers, we might expect fewer strategies, less integration of different strategies, and more dependence on outside help than with middle-grade readers. In an important study of first graders, Biemiller (1970) found three phases in children's oral reading. During the first months (while reading preprimers), upon meeting difficult, unknown words, children made substitutions of other words that made sense and that were among those words taught in class. Toward the middle of the year, the children's reading had many more no response behaviors (not trying to substitute a word), less use of contextually appropriate other words, and more use of first letter cues. The incidence of no response behavior was interpreted by Biemiller as a demonstration of children's awareness of the importance of the graphic information and the inability to use such information, an interpretation supported by others (Allington 1984; Barr 1974). At the end of the year, children reduced their no response behaviors and combined more first-letter and contextual cues. The combination of contextual and graphic cues grew during the year. At the beginning of the year, only 30% of the errors showed the ability to use both contextual and graphic (first letter) cues; at the end of the year, 70% of the errors had integrated cues.

Other strategies used by beginners amplify this developmental picture. Successful beginners made surprisingly few errors during classroom reading: an average of 3.4 errors per hundred words in Weber's study of (1970a) first graders. But there is a range of error rate. In Clay's (1969) study, the children in the upper quartile made only 2.67 errors per hundred, while the next quartile averaged 6.58. Good readers moved steadily through the books, acquiring vocabulary with relative ease. With few errors, the good readers were able to use their knowledge of language and their expectation for stories as cues to unknown words. Indeed, when she examined the word substitutions in light of sentence meaning and grammar, Weber (1970a) found most substitutions were like the unknown word and fit meaning and grammar. The range of those substitutions that are grammatically like text words and appropriate to the first part of the sentence ranged from 70 to 91% (Biemiller 1970; Clay 1968; Weber 1970a, 1970b). In regard to the meaning of the passage, 92.8% of the substitutions were semantically acceptable (Weber 1970a).

Successful first graders experience growing ability to use graphic and meaning cues. Their increasing independence in reading also is marked by sensible self-correction, reading behavior thought to indicate children's ability to keep track of (monitor) and restore meaning (Pflaum and Pascarella 1980). Rates of self-correction of initial errors ranged from 28 to 38% (Clay 1969). Good readers were found to use this fix-up strategy very appropriately. Out of ungrammatical errors (unsuited to sentence syntax), self-corrections were made on 85.3% incorrect responses; by contrast, self-correction of errors that did not need to be corrected as much (self-correction of errors of the same grammatical class as the text word) was much smaller: 27.4% (Weber 1970b).

Less Successful Beginners

The picture of beginning readers who do not experience such a strong, strategic start is quite different. Since these children appear to learn words more slowly than others, they move more slowly through the first-grade materials. The stories they read have fewer words, and the children have less opportunity to practice. With less practice, the youngsters are less likely to build independence through the use of strategies for figuring out new words. In many ways, this situation causes a cyclical pattern of problems.

For example, children in the lower groups make more errors during classroom reading, despite the fact that they read easier books. For example, in one report, the lowest quartile of readers made 38.8 errors per hundred words, not a very helpful environment for developing new and effective strategies (Clay 1969). Poor first-grade readers make less use of graphic cues compared with the better readers (Biemiller 1970; Cohen 1974–1975; Weber 1970a). For example, in a program that stressed acquisition of skills to use graphic similarities instead of memorized sight words in learning, poor readers began the year making responses that had no relationship with the story at all. Later, however, these children began to use strategies reminiscent of the better readers at the beginning of the year, suggesting developmental lags that were likely to continue (Cohen 1974–1975). In fact, it was noted that the poor readers were unable to use more than single, or at least minimal, cues at a single effort.

Children experiencing difficulty with beginning reading do not seem as able as others to use more than one cue at a time; this problem may reflect children's cognitive levels. If they cannot decenter (have not achieved concrete operations), they will not understand the component parts of words (letter combinations and sound sequences). The inability to handle multiple elements of words may adversely influence reading acquisition (Zutell 1981). Moreover, if the children have had few experiences with reading and writing, complex analysis of written text is not likely.

While strong differences have not been found between good and poor first-grade readers in the grammatical and semantic acceptability of substitutions in oral reading, self-correction does differentiate their reading. Good readers self correct between one-fourth to one-third of their errors. Poor readers do not self correct as often. For example, in one study, the poor readers self corrected only 11 to 14% of their errors (Clay 1968); in another study, only 2 to 4% of poor readers self corrected (Cohen 1974–1975). We have seen that good readers self-corrected errors that needed it the most, the errors that cause meaning change: 85.3% for the meaning-change errors and only 27.4% for grammatically appropriate errors. Poor readers corrected only 41.5% of the meaning-change errors and 32.7% of the others (Weber 1970b).

The contrast between the good and poor beginning readers suggests rather serious differences in the application of useful strategies for reading. And scholars interested in the instructional context for learning to read have examined whether instructional practice has contributed to these differences.

The Instructional Context

Observing three teachers, Roberts (1973) found they gave their low readers the correct words at hesitations instead of what the teachers gave their better readers: sufficient time to figure out hard words. Moreover, first-grade teachers were found to interrupt their poor readers more than the good readers and to tell the low-ranked children the words more often (Allington 1980). My colleagues and I wondered if teachers were responding to pupil status levels in their feedback or were simply responding as best they could to ineffective reading behavior. Teachers' responses to errors predicted children's reading behaviors more than the youngsters' relative status (Pflaum et al. 1980).

Given the contrasting reading behaviors of good and poor first-grade readers, attention to how teachers respond to errors is needed. For whatever reason, teachers give the low readers more "help" by telling the words the youngsters do not know and by interrupting more and more quickly. When cueing on difficult words, teachers tend to provide graphic over meaning cues for poor readers. The practice of immediately supplying difficult words is associated with poor reading progress (Hoffman and colleagues 1984). The interactions that slower children experience may be so confusing that the purpose of reading is not revealed in the reading groups. For example, if teachers call out words to try to achieve story fluency, children may learn to call out, too. For example, it seemed to me as we observed the reading classes in first grades that student call outs were far more common in the low groups. One boy who could barely read constantly gave words to others, even words he later erred on when it was his turn. Did he understand reading to be successful call outs? Since the best reader in the room, the teacher, made a lot of call outs, this conclusion is a possibility. He certainly believed reading was a matter of word recognition. Call outs by anyone reduce the opportunity for individual readers to figure out words.

The context of learning to read is complicated even further. Acquisition of skill in reading also depends upon how much is read. It appears that how much material is covered (or perhaps stories read from the program) predicts the number of new words and phonics learned (Barr 1984). Yet, there is little uninterrupted contextual reading. The average length of first-grade reading lessons (using basals) was recently reported to be 30 minutes, with only an average of 4 minutes devoted to contextual oral reading and each child's individual reading lasting less than a minute (Gambrell 1984). While practice in reading prose is recommended in most texts as the kind of practice needed for learning, such small amounts of time given to actual reading is most worrisome. Even though children may read in small segments, there are differences in how much is covered according to which group a child belongs to (Barr 1984), and teachers make grouping decisions rather idiosyncratically (Barr 1974). Teacher decisions about pacing, contextual reading for practice, and grouping are extremely important, probably more important than decisions about which materials to purchase.

From these observations of initial reading and teaching practices, several recommendations may be made about instruction. Even though much more material on beginning reading will follow, it does seem appropriate to recommend that teachers of beginning reading attend very carefully to critical practices and consider the recommendations in Table 6.

Thus far, our discussion has been focused upon children's reading without examining how the method by which children are taught might influence their reading. And method does appear to influence how beginning readers read.

DEFINITIONS OF BEGINNING READING

There are two major influences upon current practice in reading instruction. In describing what occurs as children learn to read, most educators believe the position they each hold is the best explanation. In truth, a continuum of explanations exists, and it has an extreme position at each end. Most educators would place themselves somewhere in between the two ends of the continuum. But the juxtaposition of the positions has excited controversy about beginning reading since the nineteenth century (Mathews 1966), and the controversial positions have stimulated a search for more knowledge. We will be concerned

TABLE 6. Instructional recommendations for reading groups

Instructional Goal	Recommended Practice
Assessment of pupil group placement	(1) Carefully move students from group to group until individuals fit well with the skill level of others. (2) Prepare all children for reading, even if it means providing preliteracy book and writing experiences.
Provision of practice for all students	(1) Provide repeated contacts with new words, even if it means developing new exercises to supplement the text. (2) Insure that low readers read and reread easy stories often. (3) Encourage practice at home with easy, success-producing materials.
Explicit directions about using strategies	(1) Teach students to self correct and to combine sense of sentence and graphic cues. (2) Include strategy use in skill instruction (e.g., explanations and demonstrations on how to use skills with low readers).
Development of independence for all	(1) Provide sufficient wait time (up to 5 seconds) for all students to figure out words. (2) Reduce word supplying for students who have to figure out difficult words. (3) Provide meaning cues to all students.
Movement through materials	(1) Determine coverage on the basis of success rather than on efforts to cover the program materials. (2) Provide children who have a poor start with more than average time for reading.
Self-evaluation	Occasionally tape reading lessons for evaluation of kind of feedback, equality of practice, and pacing of the instruction.

with the two extreme positions, not necessarily to side with them, but to understand the dimensions of beginning reading approaches.

Decoding Aspects of Beginning Reading

Defined as *"Reading is the translation of written elements into language"* (Perfetti 1984, 41, italics in original), the position toward one end of the continuum is that children must learn to decode words into meaningful speech, or, to put it another way, to decode print into language (Perfetti 1984, 41). We examine the implications of this position for instruction by first describing the features of the orthography that effect learning to read. We then examine what this suggests that reading entails for the beginner.

An orthography is a written system to represent the oral language. Developed through history and influenced by political change, the various orthographies are conventions that need to be fully absorbed for literacy to develop. Examining first orthographic demands that are quite different from learning to read English, we turn to Japanese. The first orthography that Japanese children learn thoroughly (normally before formal schooling), hiragana, is syllabary. For example, the spoken word "takai" meaning "high" is represented by three units of hiragana, each corresponding to a syllable (Sakamoto 1980). Japanese school-children also learn another orthography, kanji, a logography where each logo-graph represents a meaning unit. The two are combined in most Japanese texts (Sakamoto and Makita 1973).

It is proposed that at the initial stages of reading acquisition, logographies like the kanji system are easiest to learn, that syllabaries like the hiragana are next easiest, and that alphabetic orthographies are the most difficult (Liberman et al. 1980). To learn a logograph is to learn the direct sign of the meaning without the mediation through sound. To learn a syllabic marking that is used over and over according to sound, not meaning, is efficient, too; it is as if we used a symbol for the sound of "bal" in the words, *ball, ballistic, balloon*. But to learn an alphabetic system requires the manipulation and analysis of units and graphemes that represent smaller segments in words. Study of prereading Japanese children indicated that logographs, although visually more complicated, were easier to learn than syllabic symbols (Sternberg and Yamada 1978).

These differences provide some perspective about learning to read in English since, of course, there is no choice available. Like other alphabetic systems, written English is based on the "rule governed generation" of a large set of words with a limited number of graphemes (Perfetti 1984, 42), and this base is believed to be critical to reading and writing acquisition. While beginning acquisition may be somewhat more difficult, once acquired, the alphabetic property of our written langauge has the advantage of not requiring the memorization of thousands of different visual symbols (logography) and the constant mediation of sound (syllabary). In fact, with alphabetic systems, children may acquire skilled reading more easily than with other systems; the generativity allows for greater and quicker word and meaning accessibility.

Some alphabetic orthographies more closely resemble the spoken language than others. Finnish, for example, has only thirteen consonants and eight vowels; almost exact sound-to-symbol correspondence between sounds and letters; no consonant clusters; consistent stress on the first syllable; free word order; and use of syllables (Kyostio 1980). In English, by contrast, while there are only twenty consonants and five written vowels (and *y*), they are recombined to represent twenty-two different vowel sounds and twenty-four consonant sounds (various phonemes) (Ives, Bursuk, and Ives 1979); consonants may be doubled or not; there are many double and triple consonant clusters; there is variable and complicated stress; and word order is constrained. When visual patterns are examined rather than oral phonemes, there are hundreds of letter combinations used to express these variations. While initial acquisition of reading in Finland may be much easier than in English-speaking countries, as one could predict, there is no evidence that such an advantage is long-term (Thorndike 1973).

It is difficult to learn to read English, then, for one reason, because there is no clear correspondence between English sounds and letters. English is difficult because its phonemes (the differentiating sounds) are really abstractions. The reason why four-year-old Jocelyn, for example, writes JUP for *jump* is because the written *m* has no articulatory value for her in this setting. Later, she will develop a much more global sense of *m* and perceive its presence in *jump*. Children have to learn that really quite different sounds are called the same thing and used similarly. The final sound of *fat* and the initial sound of *table* are not really alike; children abstract as they acquire literacy and thereby build a system for understanding the phonemic basis of our orthography.

In order to accomplish this generalization, children learn the concept of words and a few visually memorized word items (Ehri and Wilce 1985), a form of reading like the first stage noted by Biemiller (1970). As they gain increased experience with words and letters, children learn that words are made up of segments. At first, the youngsters are much more successful at perceiving syllabic than phonemic segments (Liberman et al. 1974). This characteristic is important because the range of ability in children's phonemic segmentations accounts for much of the variance in successful beginning reading (Juel 1984). Once phonemic segmentation occurs (perception of the separate sounds we hear, such as the four sounds of *jump*), children learn to manipulate units within words, both letters and their phonemic equivalents, and thereby acquire working knowledge of the alphabetic principle.

Since the demands of English and its orthography are difficult, many believe it is unprofitable to focus on them in initial reading. However, the consequences of not learning the code, complicated as it is, may restrict growth toward reading independence. For beginning readers to progress well, they must acquire the ability to read many words and to read them very quickly. If not—if they are not responding automatically and if they have to remember many items based on external cues—they will not be able to give sufficient attention to comprehension (LaBerge and Samuels 1974; Perfetti 1984). Scholars argue that since the orthography is alphabetic, the ability to manipulate it is necessary at the beginning (Gough 1984). The argument in favor of learning the alphabetic principle, however, does not necessarily mean that children must learn it in a particular manner.

For children to learn the alphabetic principle, they must be able to perceive phonemic segments within words (Juel 1984; Perfetti 1984). Children can be taught to segment words into phonemic elements; such learning enhances knowledge of letter-sound correspondences (Bradley and Bryant 1983), which, in turn, is associated wth better reading (Juel 1984). There is evidence that children profit from repetitive experiences with words having recurring and predictable letter patterns (Perfetti 1984). Repeated exposure to such combinations (such as -mp, -at, and tr-) will enable children to build expectations about the relationship between the visual form and the phonemic combination. Juel and Roper-Schneider (1985) found that during the first months of reading acquisition, children were helped when they read materials that had vocabulary controlled by common letter combination patterns. If young readers meet the same letter patterns in text as they simultaneously learn about letter combinations, letter sequences, and sound realizations, initial reading becomes easier. Children can become independent in figuring out new words as their predictions are fulfilled. Eventually, the ability to analyze in this way is not necessary for children as they build memory for printed words in their lexicons.

Among the several instructional contexts in which children learn to apply the alphabetic principle is the induction of the system from wide experiences with print. For example, the early reader, Paul Bissex, whom we discussed earlier, figured out the word *look* for writing purposes. He knew that if he took the *b* from *book*, a word he knew, and put in an *l*, he made *look* (Bissex 1980).

Not many children learn this skill by themselves. Some children learn to relate common letter patterns with sounds from instruction that has them synthesize single letter-to-sound associations. For instance, when learning to read *dog* through blending sounds, children are asked to say /də/../ə/../g/ for *dog*. Then, they are taught to blend the three sounds, /də..ə..g/ for *dog*. In another approach, children can be taught the set of letter settings that produce the predicted phoneme; for example, /o/ is found in the following settings (where T stands for a consonant that fits): *oTe, oaT, Tow, Toe* (The Headway Program, the Open Court program, 1979).

In contrast to these methods, another way of directly teaching children to map predictable letter combinations through phonemic knowledge to orally known words is to have them analyze common word segments. For example, the common letter combination -ow in the set of known words, *cow, how,* and *town,* can be applied to a new word, *gown.* This process can be learned either directly as children are taught to realize the initial phoneme with the known combination, the "analytic" approach. Or, in a "linguistic" approach, children can be encouraged to induce the relatedness of the letter combination through reading materials that contain vocabulary controlled to represent the letter combinations being presented.

Initial reading often is characterized in literature and in classrooms as a process of gaining control over the alphabetic property of our written language. Some scholars claim direct instruction is required. Others stress that reading skills, including the ability to analyze words, are best acquired naturally, given an optimum literacy-rich environment, in a manner reminiscent of language acquisition. Whatever the instructional interpretation, the position that reading requires cognitive activity focused upon the print often is described as a "bottom-up" position, since it views reading as beginning at the lowest level, the letters and words (Smith 1979). According to many other scholars of reading, it is, instead, a "top-down" process. Reading is the application of a reader's knowledge about the content and skill of reading.

Beginning Reading Is Mostly Thinking

With a much broader definition of reading, the advocates of the position at the other end of the continuum view reading as a problem-solving activity. The concept is that reading, even the recognition of words, is driven by higher-level processes. The task of instruction in beginning reading is to establish in beginners the full range of skilled reading behaviors. For both beginners and skilled readers, the essential task is to obtain meaning.

How the extraction of meaning occurs is explained on several levels. As part of the process of creation, beginning readers have expectations about meaning, and they search for confirmation of these expectations. They learn best when they are in an "apprentice" position, following the model of the skilled person. Although not an expert, the novice reader acquires the mindset and the facility to approach reading as the expert, albeit with simple texts (Smith 1971, 1984). To follow the apprenticeship idea, we easily see that beginning readers must have a reading vocabulary.

It is important to the success of beginning readers that they learn a set of highly useful, immediately recognized words to help in providing a rich context so the readers can learn the behaviors that skilled readers have. Thus, words common to the language (such as *to, and, the,* and *run*) are learned first as memorized items. Early in the instructional experience, beginners who find these words used in sentences with predictable syntax, who learn to apply their oral inflections to written words, and who have a growing sight word vocabulary will, in fact, almost be able to read like a skilled reader.

There are, however, important differences between the skilled and the beginning reader. Skilled readers who are reading easy material may not *read* every word (Smith 1974). They certainly bring a great deal of information to their reading. Some of the information comes from within themselves and some from their experiences with the world; much information comes from building up knowledge from the material being read: the plot movement, characters, setting, mood, and style.

From the work of Goodman comes the idea that reading is a "psycholinguistic guessing game" (1967, 1976). As such, reading depends upon the ability of readers to use their language and conceptual knowledge to recognize words sequentially. As a result of outside knowledge, language ability, and familiarity with the material, readers build up expectations for the material that reduce the need to read every word. These expectations are treated as predictions to be tested. Readers swiftly sample the written material and use as little data as possible to verify predictions.

This type of reading is possible because readers have many cues available, cues of a syntactic and a semantic nature. Readers have more information, in fact, available to them than they absolutely need. According to Smith, Goodman, and Meredith (1970), readers use punctuation to find sentence units; they use spaces to know word boundaries; they use inflections on the ends of words to find plurality of nouns, tense and aspect of verbs, and comparison of modifiers; and they use knowledge of acceptable English word order to cue expected words to follow, such as where subject and predicate are likely to appear, and how articles and prepositions indicate following nouns. Thus, every piece of graphic material does not need to be analyzed for meaningful interpretation; readers supply their language expectation and find the information necessary to confirm.

In addition to the careful development of an efficient sight word vocabulary and text that supports use of language knowledge, scholars point out other factors characteristic of reading for meaning. One factor has to do with world knowledge. To obtain meaning from text requires that readers have previously acquired knowledge of the prose content or the story elements (prior knowledge) (Anderson and Pearson 1984). Beginning readers meet narrative text, for the most part, and the content of the narrative must relate to the experiences of the reader. For example, in order for the young child to understand a story about "The Grumpiest Man" (Holt, *A Place for Me,* 1973), the notion of a grumpy person and the effect of a grumpy person on others must have been experienced. The idea is that a reader has a notion already formed about a topic, a schema or several schemata. As the reading progresses, the text information is fit into the prior knowledge. To ensure that children bring their prior knowledge to bear on the reading for maximum comprehension, teachers elicit children's prior experiences. Teachers encourage readers to test prior expectations with information as it is being processed. But reading is not just in narratives. Because advanced readers are expected to read expository text, too, modern beginning reading texts include simple explanatory and descriptive segments.

Accessibility makes a difference in beginning readers' ability to obtain meaning from text. Like a computer program, text can be more or less "friendly." That is, text can be more accessible to young readers when it is coherent, when events are logically related, when text contains no extraneous leads, when there is clarity in reference, and when the relationships among concepts are clear (Beck and McKeown 1984). Beck and McKeown describe how they clarified a traditional tale and succeeded in making it more comprehensible to young readers. For example, they modified the text sentence, " 'This coat is worn out,' Jane cried. She took the old rag and threw it into the trash basket" (Beck and McKeown 1984, 77), so the meaning of "old rag" would be clearer. Since beginning readers have small reading vocabularies, the texts they read often contain short, simple sentences. Often this form of text requires readers to make many inferences in order to understand story meaning. Clarifying the relationships and making the references explicit increase text "friendliness."

Still another way to look at text is to analyze its large component elements. Just as sentences are composed from rule-generated grammars, it seems that stories are constructed from story grammars (Stein and Glenn 1979). Children having wide experiences with stories expect and find settings, initiating events, episodes that develop the initiating event, conflict, and resolution. Just as skilled readers read well when they have a schema for the structure of the particular text, children read narrative well when they have a schema for stories. Moreover, in meeting expository text, children do well when they acquire a schema for its various structures, for example, cause and effect.

If one is designing beginning reading instruction out of the notion that beginning reading is mostly thinking and therefore the attainment of comprehension is essential, then, among others, one implication is that children must learn a set of common words as memorized items. There are several reasons for this: (1) so beginning readers have sufficient context from which to use linguistic cues to figure out new words, (2) so the children can identify most words on sight and thereby experience the fluency needed for comprehension, and (3) so there are sound reading behaviors established as a basis for the next steps in reading competency. Thus, the developers of initial reading programs provide slow and steady introductions of a few basic words through the first year. These words often are presented as items to memorize; they are repeated in the texts so that sufficient meetings insure sight recognition (Gates and Russell 1938).

Another feature of beginning reading instruction is for teachers to encourage children to use their sense of what to expect based on preceding text. Children are encouraged to self correct in order to obtain meaning. Some texts are developed with repeated sentence structures to enhance the process of language cue use.

As teachers prepare children for stories and guide them through the material, they focus upon the prior knowledge needed to understand concepts and content fundamental to the text. By structuring children's prior knowledge, teachers demonstrate how reading involves the use of prior knowledge to understand the story concepts and how new information is highlighted by its addition to the old. Textbook writers, if they attend to the advice of researchers, will shift from an older stance of reduced text to enable word recognition to more explicitness and clarity so that prior knowledge and story expectations will increase comprehension (Anderson, Osborn, and Tierney 1984). As children learn to identify story elements, their knowledge of text is made explicit and becomes part of their schemata for reading.

Having examined the roots of two different views of beginning reading, we may well ask whether they are mutually exclusive. The publishers of most of the popular basals do not seem to feel that they are, as the basal reading programs include a strand of skills to develop word analysis skills through phonemic realization and strands of skills to encourage comprehension. Most programs teach a set of common words at the start for immediate contextual reading. There are, however, some that focus more upon one of these positions than upon the other. Evidence from the observations of oral reading behaviors in beginning readers suggests that the position does make a difference.

Method Influences in Beginning Reading

Two first-grade observation studies were conducted with children learning reading under quite different instructional approaches: One stressed decoding (Cohen 1974–1975), and the other stressed reading for meaning (Biemiller 1970). From the start, the children learning through decoding made relatively fewer grammatically and semantically constrained substitutions. Among the better readers of each study, the errors of the children in the reading-for-meaning program indicated use of context 86% of the time, while Cohen's readers used context only 7 to 73% of the time. Alternatively, the children in the decoding program used at least first (or last) letter cues from 95 to 100% of the time, while those in the reading-for-meaning group used first letter cues only 29% of the time, a clear difference among successful readers.

During the winter months of the first grade, the reading-for-meaning children maintained approximately the same proportion of context use and began to use graphic cues more; 50% of their errors were no response errors, and 61% of their substitutions used first letter cues. The decoding-taught children used progressively more graphic cues, and, despite the lack of emphasis in instruction, began to respond to the context. At the end of the year, the differences due to method of instruction appeared to be reduced; the decoding-taught children used context in 59 to 73% of their errors, compared with the reading-for-meaning children at 84%. The self-correction rates of the decoding-taught children began to resemble those of another reading-for-meaning group (Weber 1970b). In regard to graphic cues, however, the differences due to method continued to be apparent. Nearly 100% of the errors in the decoding group reflected observance of graphic cues; only about 50% of the substitutions in the other group did.

Readers appear to use what they have been taught to use. Those learning that reading is decoding use the information provided through direct instruction to unlock unknown words; these readers give less attention to the maintenance of meaning, at least during the first months. On the other hand, those taught that reading is meaning attempt to maintain meaning when meeting an unknown word from the start; later, they learn to use graphic cues. Barr (1974; 1974–1975) found that children learning to read with a phonic emphasis tended to focus on the letter as a strategy for unlocking words; those taught with a sight-word strategy focused upon the word as the critical unit. However, there are exceptions; a few children begin with an alternate strategy that they maintain despite the mode of instruction. Children who are successful with whichever method is being presented appear to be able to combine their taught strategy with others. Thus, the reading-for-meaning children in the top quartile increasingly added graphic cue use to their reading at the end of the year, and the decoding top group increasingly attended to the context to maintain meaning.

In the years since method studies were conducted (Bond and Dykstra 1967; Chall 1967), basal programs in the United States have devoted more attention to phonics in their beginning reading programs. Differences in regard to how much phonics is included in the first grade programs still exist, but they are not as profound as earlier. Some programs have much more phonics than others. Some control vocabulary on the basis of decodability of the words; others select words in terms of the frequency of use. These factors appear to affect the extent of initial reading. Higher word recognition occurred for children who began reading in texts with vocabulary controlled by regularity and decodability than for those reading in texts with control based on word frequency in the language, even though both groups received the same phonics instruction (Juel and Roper-Schneider 1985).

The impact of method and instructional strategy is probably greater for those who do not have a successful start at reading than for those who find reading to be easy. While the children's initial success with reading may relate with their level of cognitive functioning, it also reflects their ease with the alphabetic principle and their confidence that text ought to make sense. Poor readers have greater difficulty in combining strategies, as evidenced in the difference Weber (1970b) found in self-correction. To self correct, readers reanalyze a word in light of contextual information and combine letter/sound information with context. Weber's poor readers were less successful in self correcting their serious errors; they were less sensitive to context and/or unable to synthesize cues.

Children who experience difficulty in reading also tend to have less ability in phonemic segmentation (Juel 1984; Vellutino 1977). It may be that they are unable to acquire the alphabetic principle to the point at which it can be used easily; only when it can be used easily are children able to combine decoding analysis with consideration of meaning. Alternatively, if children having problems are repeatedly told by their teachers to use graphic cues as it appears they are (Allington 1980; Pflaum et al. 1980), they are likely to focus on letters. These readers may conclude that reading is a matter of "sounding out" words. Obtaining meaning from reading may not be a goal they understand. I was involved with developing a program for disabled readers to teach them to recognize their own errors, to determine the significance of the errors for meaning, and to self correct. Those readers still at the beginning stages of reading were unable to profit from the lessons. Those at least at a second-grade level did use this information to read more effectively: they combined strategies (Pflaum and Pascarella 1980). These studies suggest that children who are not successful will profit from instruction in phonemic segmentation, materials with highly decodable words, and finally, after ease with decoding is established, direct instruction on how to maintain meaning through determination of error impact on meaning and self correction.

This section illustrates the range of issues in beginning reading instruction. There is an alphabetic principle, which beginners, if successful, gain control over; they do so in a variety of ways, including through the use of independently constructed induction. Direct instruction and material design will influence the initial stages of acquisition; continued progress requires attention to several strands. For the less successful beginner, the focus of instruction and materials has a greater impact. Several sources point to the need for several kinds of direct instruction; with insecure preparatory experiences, instruction needs to assure the acquisition of the alphabetic principle and the acquisition of strategies to maintain meaning.

As we turn to the beginnings of writing in school, several of the same questions relating to reading are also appropriate. How do reading and writing relate to one another? Are there clear developmental indices in spelling growth that would be helpful for teachers and that tie in with reading stages? What types of meaning do young writers express?

THE BEGINNINGS OF WRITING

As in the section on beginning reading instruction, we draw upon observations made of initial writing to find patterns of development. There are important differences in how the observations have been done in these two modes of literacy acquisition. When researchers observed first graders learning to read, they collected specific information about reading errors and synthesized the various types of behavior indices. This empirical approach is contrasted with a newer way of examining learning, the ethnographic approach, in which as much information as possible is gathered about the events, settings, and interactions occurring that might influence learning. The observations are synthesized, and apparent patterns are described. Ethnographic techniques apply a broader brush than empirical ones; as a result, types of relationships emerge. In writing, the relationships offer information about more events, but the information is less specific about the behavior than findings from empirical studies. Ultimately, both kinds of study help us understand the process of learning to read and write. Nevertheless, because of differences in method of observation, at this time it is difficult to establish specific points of influence between beginning reading and beginning writing.

Literacy acquisition is not universal, of course. But the observations of early writing and reading are beginning to have a serious impact upon school instruction. If children can acquire writing and reading skill by structuring systems out of their experiences with stories and writing at home, it is reasoned that the process of acquisition need not be directed so much from without, that perhaps all children can acquire writing in ways reminiscent of language acquisition. In this section, we contrast traditional writing instruction with how writing develops in informal settings.

Traditional Writing Instruction for Beginners

Common to most first grades has been the idea that writing grows rather slowly and that it follows the acquisition of reading, even though reading and writing appear to emerge simultaneously or at least in close proximity. The nearly simultaneous growth of initial reading and writing is not surprising to those who understand language growth; traditionally, however, there was little instruction in writing during the first year of reading instruction. Indeed, twenty years ago, we were told not to begin spelling instruction as a regular subject until the second grade.

Writing instruction in traditional kindergarten and/or first grade includes instruction on how to construct the letters. Children are taught particular movements and directions for each printed upper and lowercase letter so that optimum fluency will develop (Durkin 1976). In many cases, children copy over letters having arrows for directions and then copy the letters below on worksheets and in workbooks. Pupils write their names, single words, dates, and often in classes with *more* rather than less writing, they copy a "story for the day" from the board on their papers.

Recognizing the physical difficulty of writing for young children, thick pencils are used for the first two years of writing. Large, separate erasers are basic to the task of writing and vastly overused in classes where correctness rather than communication is the teacher's goal. The paper has wide spaces marked with a dotted line to show where to bring the halflines of lowercase letters. Children receive information about how to form letters, how to make spaces between words, and how to place the paper on the desk for ease (Durkin 1976). Children turn in papers to the teacher for her responses about the correctness of the writing and spelling. Success tends to be measured in terms of paper appearance, rather than the spontaneity of word use and the content.

Generally, the traditional approach requires that children learn the conventions of spelling and writing; "errors" must be corrected. Much of the writing consists of copying sentences and filling in the blanks with the correct word on worksheets and in workbooks. Such an approach is not very creative. However, there always have been some teachers who followed their own observations and theories about child development. For example, in language experience classrooms, beginning readers are encouraged to write their own pieces soon after they demonstrate the ability to read their dictated stories (Stauffer 1970). These teachers are able to help children acquire skill at tasks such as letter formation and still stimulate creative work.

Accepting a very different notion about children's writing requires viewing "errors" as immaturities, indicators of what children know rather than what they do not know. There are several reasons why attitudes toward early writing are changing. One has to do with our understanding that we can gain rich interpretations of children's functioning level through "errors." Even though some teachers always have interpreted writing this way, the study of reading miscues as indicators for children's reading has increased the number of teachers who understand that "errors" are messages from the learners. Moreover, recognition of invented spelling (Read 1971) has given educators a view of writing growth as a development from within the child. And descriptions of writing workshop instruction even for young writers suggest the medium for a very different approach to teaching (Calkins 1982; Graves 1983). As teachers begin to accept invented spellings and spontaneously composed writings as demonstrations of current phonological knowledge (spelling), and thinking (content), the instructors are in a position to encourage growth through interactive teaching.

The Relatedness of Reading and Writing

We have known for some time that reading and writing are correlated (e.g., Loban 1976). Once educators learned that invented spellings illustrated children's phonological knowledge (Read 1971), they began to question this relationship more closely. How, for example, does acquisition of knowledge about words and phonemes affect writing and reading? Does one follow the other? Since some children are able to represent the sequence of sounds heard in words with letters (first on the basis of letter name = syllable and then on the basis of letter name = phoneme), researchers wanted to discover how writing and reading draw upon and stimulate one another.

This really is not a chicken-and-egg question. Knowing if intensive writing helps young children who have little prior literacy experience to acquire knowledge of the alphabetic principle more easily than the decoding materials in reading programs may have an enormous influence upon how we introduce literacy instruction in schools. If the process of invented spelling were found to direct the process of phonemic analysis for reading, we would shift the instructional focus from initial reading acquisition to writing. Unfortunately, the answer is not yet available, but there are hypotheses that emerge from consideration of the question and from examination of early writing observations.

Many educators believe that writing stimulates reading and is preliminary to reading (Graves 1983). With this presumed relationship, it seems that one would urge children to write more than to read at the initial stages (Graves 1983). In fact, when these beliefs are realized, children are encouraged to read materials they choose and to figure out words independently, by asking for help from the teacher and peers and by developing a system for applying phonemic knowledge (Hansen 1984). Such an approach does parallel the natural learning of language. Children construct systems for reading and writing by using the elements of the environment they need and in an interactive process, as the teacher accepts the writings (and readings, too), comments on the meaning of the efforts, and provides scaffolding to encourage children to build new ways to generate production. As communications with language, reading and writing ought to emerge, it seems, much like oral communication does.

Some scholars define reading and writing as two forms of the same process. That is, writing is producing, and reading is reacting to print (Durkin 1976). But the relationship between reading and writing is more complex; at different points in development, the relationship changes (Shanahan 1984). Teaching writing is not sufficient for acquiring reading; the reverse is also true. The development of each skill is somewhat independent of the other (Shanahan, unpublished).

But applying the relationship question to the very start of reading and writing, when phonemic awareness appears, we might find a stronger tie between the idea of segmentation in one mode and the other than when regarding later developments of reading and writing. If children acquire writing with greater ease than reading, or vice versa, one would expect their language complexity to be greater in that mode, at least during the first months. However, evidence from one study suggests that by the middle of first grade (the period somewhat after the critical movement into the phonemic realization that we have found in reading), there is little language complexity difference evident in children's writings, dictations, and retellings of stories (Froese 1984). That is, there is little difference in the syntactic complexity of productions in the three modes. Fewer words are used in writing, however; this fact is not particularly surprising considering the physical effort required. While the three modes appear to draw equally upon the same competencies, the study does not inform us how the essential knowledge about word phonemic segmentation occurs in reading and writing.

Close examination of spelling demonstrates an orderly progression and suggests that an influence of reading on writing and writing on reading is attractive at the early acquisition stages. But, since, except for case studies, there is little observation of parallel and specific emergence of skill in both reading and writing, we cannot be sure if the alphabetic principle is equally or separately acquired. Through the examination of spelling development, we find the point at which the writing/reading relationship is strong. In any case, teachers are well-advised to have plenty of reading and writing opportunities for students to encourage the development of both skills.

The Stages of Spelling Development

When educators observe children's learning, stages of development emerge. Like children who construct meaning out of their experiences, observers of children need to find frameworks for the organization of information gathered. While they are continuously being examined by scholars and are, therefore, still tentative, developmental stages do offer teachers a way to shape their interactive teaching goals. With a schema for children's development in spelling in mind, a teacher can judge unconventional spellings as indicators of current functioning level and can determine how to provide the appropriate scaffolding in dialogue over writing. There are several versions of the invented spelling stages (e.g., Graves 1983; Sulzby 1981; Temple, Nathan, and Burris 1982). These different versions are based on the early spellings of children who invent or who are asked to write words in school or on tests. The stages of writing development that emerge have come from writing done in open, criticism-free settings. Since a particular piece of writing may include spellings from different stages, we must consider these stages as overlapping and descriptive.

The first "stage" includes those works children do when they pretend to write (Sulzby 1981) (see Chapter 3, page 66). We know from the discussion in Chapter 3 that children's early invented, spontaneous "writing" begins with strings of first markings like letters and, often, letters with some knowledge of printed form but not letter names (Sulzby 1981). Called "prephonemic spelling," this stage of development includes children who are not reading but who know that print represents words (Temple, Nathan, and Burris 1982).

The second stage is the point at which letters are used more consistently to represent words and initial letter names represent whole words (Graves' first stage, 1983). In this initial letter name stage, children use letters to represent a word's most prominent feature. The youngsters have acquired some knowledge of the alphabet and letter formation. Children use the point of articulation (where the tongue touches the mouth) when saying the word to find the consonant. A piece by Jocelyn combines letter strings with initial letter-name writing. Her first string was DMOLU to represent "Dear Mom, I love you." The D, M, L, and U each represent the names of the initial letter sound of *dear, mom, love,* and *you.* Following this string are several letters not translated (like the O of the first string) that represent *I'm going to give you a strawberry cake.* These last words are represented by SC. Although Jocelyn is only four, such letter-name writing is fairly common among kindergarten children. And during kindergarten, children also are learning the alphabet.

At the next stage, children represent more of the syllables they perceive; vowel names occasionally are used. Children identify the point of articulation and associate that point with letter names. (See Chapter 3.) We will call this "syllabic writing." Some examples from Graves' (1983) Stages II and III are KS for *kiss*, GM for *game*, and GRS for *grass*. A first grader in October wrote an entire piece of discourse with syllabic writing: VLTN DAL ISOMTHR "Valentine's Day is almost here" (Temple et al. 1982, 105). This interesting piece shows knowledge of the major consonant sounds of the words, one memorized spelling (IS), some knowledge of word boundaries the younger speller did not have, the ability to correctly associate points of articulation to several letter names, and a confusion of Halloween and Valentine's Day.

Less than two months after Jocelyn wrote to her mother about a strawberry cake, she wrote a birthday card to her father with several strings, including HAPPY BIRTA, CIS?, LOS UF PEPL, FMJOCELIYN. Perhaps by asking and copying, *happy* is conventionally spelled. The second string includes *kiss* (CIS); the next string contains *Lots of people*, and the last string conveys *From Jocelyn*. She has moved into syllabic spelling. Besides the awareness of more letters, including vowel names, she knows more about the syllabic segmentation of words. Moreover, spacing is beginning to appear, although it is not yet stable.

The next stage marks the movement from syllabic awareness noted in the reading section to phonemic knowledge—the alphabetic principle—called the "phonemic spelling" stage. This important shift occurs as children acquire a notion of word spelling stability. Probably, children concurrently change from the ability to read a few words to the beginning ability to use new phonemic awareness and visual letter groupings to read less familiar words. Temple et al. (1982) illustrate a story from this stage: HE HAD A BLUE CLTH. IT TRD IN TO A BRD. (p. 107) is the imaginative *He had a blue cloth. It turned into a bird.* This story represents considerable knowledge about writing, word formation, and stories; the word forms of the function words are clearly demarked and appear to be stable.

The next stage, the transition to conventional spelling, occurs as children become independent in reading and writing. That is, as children are able to read simple stories themselves and recognize most words in these stories, they attend more and more to printed words. When the youngsters recognize differences between their own invented spelling and the conventions of literacy, they begin to acquire the desire for reaching the conventional form. Those words that are not familiar (not *very* familiar) are represented with the prior, invented approach. Other words probably are part of the children's reading and are spelled conventionally. One first grader wrote

Susie
Can I go Play with Billey mom
I like to Play withe Billey.
We are goweg now. are You comeg
I like to go to grane's haws.
Dad is home mom I will be ther in a minit.

Can I Play With you.
Bill wont let me play mom. (Temple et al. 1982, 85)

This child demonstrates considerable knowledge of spelling and writing. First, she uses the conventional spelling of most words. In GOWEG and COMEG, the child reverts to syllabic spelling; otherwise, the unconventionally spelled words demonstrate phonemic knowledge. There is also evidence of the influence of formal school instruction. For example, starting most new sentences on new lines is reminiscent of how preprimers are printed. She places her name at the top as in a school paper. She uses lowercase lettering consistently, in contrast to early, invented spellings that are largely uppercase. She capitalizes the beginnings of sentences and uses punctuation more often than not. In short, this child spells, formats, and writes with the conventions of the written language.

English requires that we learn to spell many words in ways not predicted by sounds. We have spelling instruction in schools to help children learn patterns of letter combinations. In Spanish-speaking schools, however, one does not find that "orthografia" is a school subject. Written Spanish more closely resembles spoken Spanish than written English matches its oral counterpart. Because successful English spelling requires a rich store of the visual forms of various patterns of letter combinations and basic word units, learning reading and writing skills in English requires the development of a visual storehouse.

The Content of Early Writing

Just as the beginnings of reading were examined from two points of view, the technical aspects involved in analysis and the development of meaning, writing also may be studied for the emergence of spelling control and for its meaning. The glimpses we have had of children's writing suggest that youngsters write about themselves with directness and simplicity. We are charmed by the content as well as amazed by the inventiveness of the expression. In one study of middle-grade writing development, contrast was drawn between these qualities of first graders' writings with the dullness of the middle-grade vision (Calkins 1982). Some of this change has to do with the contrast of first-grade and middle-grade expectations. For our purposes, we need to know the possible types of writing used by young children, for such children have little experience in reading expository text and do not abstract.

Temple and his associates (1982) have categorized early writing into three types: purely expressive writing, transactional writing, and poetic writing (p. 134 ff.). The expressive voice directly involves the realization of one's ideas and feelings. It does not attempt to inform, persuade, or even be aesthetic. Children's expressive writings may be in the form of a letter, a list, a written dialogue, or a diary. Practice is essential to fluent writing, and expressive writing is ideal for practice. Indeed, many children participate in expressive writing on their own. Some teachers encourage daily diary writing. Even first-grade classes can do journal writing; in many classes, children are free to ask the teacher and peers to read their journals. Such decisions about private writing help children come to understand variations in audience.

Transactional writing is writing that informs, explains, persuades, argues, and describes. It requires a much greater distance between the writer and audience than expressive writing and is therefore more difficult. Temple and his associates (1982) suggest that teacher assignments encourage children into this form of writing; an example for a persuasive piece was: "Think of something you want to do and of someone who will not let you do it. Then write a letter to that person and try to persuade him or her to let you do it." (p. 137)

Poetic writing requires children to create through words a fictive world. Even very young children are quite capable of writing stories and poems. A short list of adjectives, for example, that represent feelings about an event or observations of a rainy day begins the writing of poetry. Daily readings from an anthology of children's poetry will stimulate children's writings.

Children with a lot of knowledge about stories will attempt to write them much earlier and with much greater success. Daily reading of good stories and talk about story parts will enable all children to gain a schema for story structure. But in the beginning, during the first two years of writing, children's stories are apt to diverge from expected structure: Characters may be confused; events leading to a consequence may not be logical, and, most likely, stories may end precipitously due to fatigue. Whatever happens in the production, children's work ought to be viewed as evidence of what they have learned about representing their ideas rather than as pieces with difficulties that need to be cleared up.

Educators examine children's spelling as more than scribbles and errors and their writing as more than the simple production of tyros. Thus, instructional changes are needed, and the instructional implications of the work on writing in the rest of this book must rely on the work that has examined both the more technical knowledge children are acquiring during the critical beginnings of literacy as well as on understanding both expression and the grasp of meaning of text. Because we must try to integrate reading and writing, the discussions of reading and writing in this chapter both summarize and foretell.

SUMMARY

This chapter is summarized in two tables. Table 7 represents the specific links between the reading and the spelling sound-letter-word knowledge beginning readers and writers learn. Table 8 turns to meaning. The material in the sections on reading and on writing is linked with these tables. These apparently concurrent developments are hypothetical; however, the juxtaposition of reading and writing developments serves as a suggestion of overall literacy acquisition.

These understandings of what children are learning about reading and writing must be considered in the classroom setting. How they are realized, given the comments earlier in this chapter about basals, grouping for instruction, the characteristics of first graders' reading, and differences between successful and less-successful beginners, is the content of Chapters 7 and 8.

TABLE 7. Technical knowledge of words, letters, segments, and sounds

Stage Model	Reading	Writing
Before literacy	Has story, print, letter knowledge	Is in the prephonemic stage, makes letter-like, unstable marks
Initial segmentation	Recognizes a few words. Knows the alphabet. Knows to segment by syllable. Has much experience with words and sounds. Expands set of known words	Is in the initial letter-name stage and letter-name stage. Selects letters on basis of place of articulation. Learns to write names
Phonemic segmentation	Analyzes words by phoneme. Knows common letter patterns. Manipulates patterns and sounds. Has growing confidence. Figures out words on own. Begins to use more semantic cues and self-correction	Uses phonemic spelling. Represents most sound elements. Can format papers, use spacing, and punctuate. Includes more memorized items in practice. Presents much individual expression
Synthesis	Combines use of graphic and meaning cues. Uses independent reading in sight as accuracy and rate expand. Sees practice as important	Makes transition to conventional spelling. Expands writing expression. Finds that practice helps

TABLE 8. Meaning knowledge in reading and writing

Variable	Reading	Writing
Problem solving	Searches for meaning in text	Expresses range of feeling and ideas, of information, and of poetic voice
Memorization of words for increased fluency	Recognizes words met often on sight	Uses useful words over and over
Use of linguistic cues	Uses redundancy of language. Uses function cues to suggest meaning	Generalizes rules to represent inflections in writing
Use of prior knowledge	Reads better when stimulated to use prior knowledge, including concepts	Is enriched by encouragement to use experience in writing and analysis
Interactions	Uses internal knowledge of written language and oral language interactively with external knowledge and text cues	Produces writing that informs and communicates

SELECTED ACTIVITIES

1. Would the following group of words most likely be found in a program with vocabulary based on high frequency or in a program with words based on regular sound/symbol correspondence?

top	mop	use	us
same	tame	feed	me

2. Imagine having to learn the following printed message:

$$\triangle\perp \ \text{T}\cup \ \square\triangleright \ \triangleright\square\sqcap$$

Prepare a list of the information and skills you need in order to read it. At what step along the way to reading it do you need this information?

$$\triangle \ /\eth/ \qquad \text{T} \ /b/ \qquad \square \ /i/$$

$$\sqcap \ /k/ \qquad \cup \ /oy/ \qquad \triangleright \ /s/ \qquad \perp \ /\partial/$$

3. A small child has taken a spelling test, with the following results: FID = *fish,* BND = *bend,* JUP = *jumped,* UL = *yell,* LRD = *learned,* DUV = *shove,* WEH = *which,* PES = *piece,* LAT = *late,* BNH = *bench,* and JIV = *drive.* Which spelling stage is the child functioning in? How would you support your answer for each item?

4. There were references in this chapter to word stability. Define it in terms of both reading and writing. How would you determine if a child had a stable concept of words?

5. Try to find a first grader who is willing to talk with you. Ask the child what reading is and what is needed for successful reading.

6. Ask a child who is not yet writing or reading much to try some simple reading and writing tasks. List the reading and writing concepts the child has acquired.

7 Teaching in the First Stages of Literacy

In these last two chapters, we continue to be concerned with initial reading and writing. But the focus changes to actual classroom practice and recommendations for the teaching of essential reading and writing concepts. The purpose of the discussion in these chapters is to establish a workable bridge between the view developed in previous chapters of the child's construction of literacy concepts and the real world of the classroom. It is not easy to teach beginning literacy in classrooms with pupils of very different experiences and to meet several other, sometimes conflicting, demands. Thus, it is not surprising that so many teachers have come to rely on commercially designed reading programs (basals). In these chapters, I have tried to describe how the use of these programs may be modified so that the bridge to a constructive approach to literacy attainment is truly established.

This chapter presents teaching principles and practices for the beginnings of literacy and the transition from prereading and writing to independence. The chapter examines aspects of the transition considered to be crucial to literacy acquisition. It begins with a description of the traditional readiness concept so that we may review how schools have viewed the transition to literacy stage at various times in the past. The second section is about letters: their perception singly and in combination, letter names, and the memorization of a set of initial words. As one might predict based on the previous chapter, we also discuss the teaching of phonemic analysis and letter-sound correspondences. There is a section on word meaning here, too; in spite of the comparatively little attention to word meaning acquisition heretofore, I have included this important part of language development in this chapter. The chapter also contains a brief description about writing in connection with beginning reading. How these complementary parts of beginning literacy are brought together is the topic of the final chapter.

One might wonder if the interactive teaching recommended for preschool education applies to literacy instruction. The question is: Will the idea of the metaphor—the extent and quality of language and literacy interactions determine academic preparedness—work in the teaching of reading and writing? The answer rests upon whether one views initial reading (and writing, too) as the acquisition of a whole new set of skills or whether one views it as a gradual accommodation of new ideas to existing structures. If one holds the former view, then the accordian idea will not work well, for instruction must include many new concepts that are directly taught to children. If one holds the latter opinion, however, the accordian idea is appropriate and will direct the form and kind of instruction. The metaphor also may work for part but not all of the instruction.

CLASSROOM TRANSITIONS TO BEGINNING LITERACY

The Traditional Concept of Reading Readiness

The term *reading readiness* was first used in the 1920s to describe the instructional period that prepared children for reading. From this time period until the end of the 1950s, research studies were undertaken to find answers to the questions:

170

When is the best time to begin reading instruction? and How can an individual's readiness be determined? Although it may appear that the following discussion applies only to instruction that occurs *before formal reading instruction*, many of the readiness skills described here continue to be useful to children *after they have begun to read*. In fact, it is often difficult to know whether training in the association of sounds and symbols, for example, is a readiness or a beginning reading activity. Thus, readiness instruction begins well before reading and continues afterwards.

Reading readiness instruction traditionally includes storytelling and listening activities as well as auditory training in sounds of letters, visual training, and the naming of letters. It sometimes includes eye movement training and practice in writing letters. While *testing* to determine if children are ready to learn to read has consistently been a part of the application of the readiness concept to classrooms, *training* to prepare children for reading has varied greatly. To illustrate, two different trends in early childhood education have led to very different concepts about readiness.

One important trend in early childhood education dates back to work begun in the 1930s. During this period, Gesell (1940) examined in detail the motor, cognitive, and social development of children from birth through adolescence. From the observational records of children seen at various chronologically determined intervals, the researchers searched for common growth patterns which they then combined into descriptions of typical behavior of children at each interval. As a result of this study, childhood was described as a period of natural movement from one discernible stage to another. Children would be "ready" to learn new skills when genetically determined growth developments allowed new learning to take place. Gesell's work influenced educators for many years and still is considered important; however, researchers and educators alike accepted this approach, particularly in reference to reading readiness, more than empirical study and classroom experience justified.

During the 1950s—especially at the end of the decade when the launch of Sputnik redirected their attention—educators began to look more closely at environmental influences on learning. As a result, educators and psychologists outlined alternate approaches to curricula matters during the late 1950s and 1960s. For example, Bruner (1960) stated that by closely analyzing the conceptual framework of a field, it was possible to find hierarchically arranged material which could be adapted appropriately to the learning level of all students. In other words, the new thinking required analysis to find, first, the components of prereading; these components were ordered as a series of steps. Second, the topics were specified, or operationalized, in hierarchical fashion so that each step presumably was dependent on mastery of the previous one. Theoretically, any preliterate child then could be tested and assigned lessons on the skills he needed. A major implication of this approach was that schools began to prepare young children for reading and to teach reading as children appeared to be ready.

Bradley (1956) delayed instruction up to a half year for some children and studied the effects in comparison to a control group. Her conclusions, based on tests made at the start of third grade, were that the children whose instruction had been delayed were better readers. Spache et al. (1966), using a better research design, found that at the end of first grade, the children in the experimental groups, where reading instruction had been delayed if warranted, were not significantly superior to the children of the control groups who were all taught reading at the beginning of first grade. The experimental children with low readiness in this study, though, showed gains over the controls as a result of delayed reading and extended readiness. It would be difficult to measure the effect of a more extended delay in reading given societal expectations. Few parents and children would be willing to agree to a planned delay of a year or more.

One feature of the traditional approach to reading readiness is the use of tests to determine when children are ready for reading. Educators in the 1920s, 1930s, and later used standard methods to determine achievement levels of groups of children. During the twenties, large-scale testing of school achievement and of intelligence uncovered reading problems among American children. Since the thesis that stressed natural ripening within the child influenced how these test findings were interpreted, it was thought that failure to read well in first grade must be due to the imposition of reading instruction before children were ready (Ilg and Ames 1965).

In order to prevent further reading problems, researchers believed that they should find a Mental Age (MA) at which reading would be most effectively taught. Morphett and Washburne's 1931 study supplied an answer, but not conclusive evidence, to this question. Based on the first-grade reading achievement in one school system taught with one approach, this study found that those children who had achieved a mental age of 6.6 were more successful than those whose MA was below this point. Morphett and Washburne stated that teachers should wait until children had a mental age of 6.6 before beginning reading instruction. This one study influenced reading instruction more than was warranted, particularly since Gates (1937) reported that postponing reading for all children who did not have a mental age of 6.6 was not necessary. In a later study, the effectiveness of the teacher and the method he used was found to be far more crucial to reading success than was a 6.6 MA (Gates and Bond 1935–1936). The Gates and Bond studies were virtually ignored, though, while textbooks (Harrison 1936; Micucci 1964) continued to inform readers that reading instruction should be delayed until children achieved a mental age of 6.6. Fortunately, educators today are quite willing to accept the idea that teacher skill does matter in developing successful beginning readers. In fact, Bond and Dykstra (1967) found that instruction is a major factor in determining first-grade reading success.

Nevertheless, the use of tests to determine reading readiness continues to be common. The *Metropolitan Readiness Test* (Harcourt Brace Jovanovich) has been used in many schools since the 1950s; like the others, this test is a group-administered paper-and-pencil test. There are, as noted in Chapter 5, newer tests of reading preparation, such as Clay's (1979). Special tests of reading subskills also are used (e.g., Goldman, Fristoe, and Woodcock 1970). These tests predict reading success for the most part. That is, more children who do well on the tests are children who are good at beginning reading than otherwise. Even in instances of statistical reliability in prediction, though, teachers are advised to also use their own judgment about children's preparation for reading, tempered, of course, by knowledge of development and the ability to make objective observations.

Experienced kindergarten teachers are also generally good at predicting which children will do well in primary grade reading (e.g., Koppman and Lapray 1969). In fact, teachers using an observation checklist were found to be more successful than standardized tests at identifying children who would later experience success in reading. Nevertheless, the teachers were unable to predict more than half of the individual children who experienced difficulty (Feshbach, Adelman, and Fuller 1974). While it makes good instructional sense to try to identify children who appear to be at risk so they may receive special help from the beginning, for the most part children's reading success is best measured by how well they read. Since some children will surprise even the most skilled teacher by doing well when they did not appear to be really ready (or the reverse), it is far more important to observe how children are progressing in class and to finetune instruction to maintain progress than to rely solely on tests.

However, the content of readiness measures suggests what types of learning have been the focus of school readiness instruction. We have known for a long time that success in beginning reading is predicted by ability to name letters in kindergarten (Durrell 1958). This makes perfect sense; knowing letters is like learning to read, and children who have acquired this knowledge before school probably also will acquire reading in school with some ease. Since children use letter names for writing, for talking about school tasks, and for remembering their first set of words (Ehri 1985), they should learn letter names. Children who learn a few common words begin reading with greater speed than those who have few letter names and words (Mason 1984). And, as we know from Chapter 6, children who can segment words into phonemic elements have greater success (Juel 1984).

These, then, are some of the elements of reading readiness instruction. They are also the elements of beginning reading instruction. One of the most productive changes in beginning reading during the last few years (which is undoubtedly the result of increased awareness and acceptance of preschool emergent literacy) is the blurring of the line between reading readiness and reading. Indeed, taking the descriptions of reading and writing from Chapters 3 and 6, we are comfortable with such a position. Hence, readiness for reading and writing is considered to be essential to children before and during the initial stages.

Early Readers at School

Early readers fare better these days when they come to school than early readers did a decade ago. Teachers used to be advised to warn parents against teaching their children to read before school (Micucci 1964). It was felt that early reading would introduce children to incorrect notions about reading, that it would interfere with important play activities, and that it would limit visual development. However, we have learned not to be so concerned; beginning reading is not a mystifying process, and early reading has a positive influence on later success. Two decades ago, the early readers Durkin (1966) followed appeared to be superior achievers through elementary school, compared with equivalent non-early readers. Retrospective interviews with parents confirm what we learned in Chapter 3: The parents supplied specific answers to children's questions. As was true of the children Hall, Moretz, and Statom (1976) studied, Durkin's early readers began with lots of questions about and interest in writing.

When early readers enter school, teachers make arrangements for these children to continue to progress, either in an individualized program or in a small group with other independent readers. Children who read comfortably in a first-reader level, normally, at the end of the first year of instruction, have a reading vocabulary of several hundred words. If they have acquired reading without formal instruction, teachers can assume the children have induced a system for figuring out single-syllable words based on recognizable patterns. These pupils need to acquire more advanced skills: for example, skills to help them analyze longer, multisyllabic words, dictionary skills, and more complex narrative and expository text. Wide reading in texts and tradebooks is recommended as are group reading experiences so the children begin to perceive how others interpret. Finally, the youngsters should be encouraged to write: to write in response to reading, to write their observations, to write about their experiences, to write their expressive stories, and to write in journals.

It is difficult to establish good reading programs for one or two more advanced readers, for those who are at the point of reading independence, and for children who have not had many preliteracy experiences. Managing this breadth of instructional need is not easy. Reliance on commercial materials may help but certainly is not a total solution. So that good readers are not bored by unnecessary instruction and skill practice, it is very important for teachers to assess their pupils' knowledge of reading. For, if some children read well, simple phonics is not only unnecessary, but it also may cause confusion. Overly simple text certainly will not provide the challenge needed for growth. Early readers who have constructed their own system for understanding the alphabetic principle probably require an instructional program emphasizing vocabulary growth and comprehension of different types of text. They certainly should receive a modified instructional program with a great deal of writing instruction. To turn back to the *preparation* for reading, however, we must examine how schooling helps children who have not learned the rudiments of letter discrimination and naming to prepare for this part of literacy acquisition.

LETTERS AND WORDS

Letters and Letter Combinations

The ability to discriminate letters from one another, an *a* from a *d*, for example, is normally tested on traditional readiness tests. However, many children appear to develop the ability to discriminate single letters naturally. Gibson and Levin (1975) reviewed studies of visual discrimination and found preliterate children had difficulty with few letters except for the mirror reversed letters (*b* and *d*) and, to a lesser extent, rotated letters (*n* and *u, p* and *d*). As Gibson and Levin explain, when children learn to discriminate objects in the real world, it does not matter if an object is reversed or rotated. A key turned around is still a key. Only in the two-dimensional world of print do reversal and rotation discriminate.

On the other hand, preliterate children have considerable difficulty in matching a string of letter combinations to a stimulus: CQ–OQ OC QC CQ CO (Calfee, Chapman, and Venezky 1972). The difficulty lies in the perception of letter order, not the letters themselves. Similarly, when the sequence of assessment instruments (to be described shortly) has been used with prereading children, many children who cannot discriminate real words can discriminate single letters easily.

Nevertheless, some children have problems discriminating single letters and need to learn this skill. Most of the children tested in the published studies of discrimination were from middle-class homes where familial prereading experiences may have prepared them more than experiences in lower-class homes. According to Gibson and Levin's (1975) suggestion, children learn to discriminate as they practice writing letters; perhaps some children are encouraged more than others to learn to write letters. Research indicates successful discrimination training includes learning the distinguishing features of letters (Samuels 1971). Stallard's (1977) first-grade children benefitted from experiences in discriminating single and combined letter-like forms.

As we know from Chapter 3, most children learn the names of at least some letters before formal schooling. And for centuries, learning the names of letters was considered the essential first step in acquiring literacy. In fact, spelling words—saying the letter names—was used as the link to figuring out words, a somewhat dubious method. In recent decades, educators recognized that while the correlations between naming letters and reading were strong, these associations did not assure that the naming of letters caused reading learning. Taking this point further, the authors of one reading program (*DISTAR,* 1968) had children learn letter sounds before they learned letter names. However, because letters are mnemonics for words, letter naming may be helpful. That is, because knowing letter names is likely to help children notice and talk about letters in word contexts, letter name knowledge may facilitate word learning. And, to step back a bit, to know letter names requires that children discriminate letters and letter sequences. Although basal materials and readiness materials have activities intended for letter work, users must be careful that the actual tasks lead to the expected learning. The suggestions in Chart 7 are progressive; that is, they should be expanded with similar activities as they are suitable for the period of transition into literacy.

Learning Words

Children can learn to recognize a few words as memorized items even before the youngsters can segment words into elements of sound (Ehri and Wilce 1985). Teachers provide opportunities for children to acquire useful words from the very start of reading (through readiness instruction and transition to independent reading) so that through repeated, direct experiences with printed words, children will remember them. Athough the number of experiences needed for recall varies (Gates and Russell 1938), the more children see words, the greater the chance the words will be remembered. In the absence of analysis skills to figure out unknown words, repeated experiences are necessary.

CHART 7.   Discriminating letters and words: naming letters

Skill	Activity
Testing letter discrimination	*Directions:* Ask the children to circle the letter that does not belong. (Be sure they know *letter.*) Practice with *m m m a* together.
	1. L O L L 10. E E E F
	2. b b b n 11. i j j j
	3. s t t t 12. p p d p
	4. f p f f 13. u n u u
	5. c o o o 14. h h n h
	6. A H A A 15. B B R B
	7. k k k h 16. z s s s
	8. M M N M 17. b d b b
	9. g a g g 18. q q g q
Teaching single-letter discrimination	(Only for those who have difficulty with the test.) Create indented letter puzzles by cutting letters from cardboard; have the children place the letters within outlines so they learn differentiating features. Begin with easy letters (c and o), and move progressively to harder letters (p and d).
	Have the children match magnetic letters on a board.
	Ask the children to match paper and cardboard letters.
	Have the children find magnetic letters for matching letters on the chalkboard, on charts, in books, etc. as they learn directional, two-dimensional features of letters.
Helping to discriminate letter combinations	Use the children's names and common real words for possible acquisition; ask the children to find letters to match a friend's name.
	Ask the children to find letters to make important words such as PAPER, BOOK, and TABLE.
	Have children talk about differences between words like CAB and TAB, CALL and TALL (beginnings) and CAT and CAP (endings) when the words are placed in vertical pairs.
	Ask the children to find the one of four words that is different; begin with easy items such as TREE, TREE, APPLE, TREE and progress to harder items such as BIG, DIG, BIG, BIG.

CHART 7, *continued*

Skill	Activity
Developing letter naming	Fill the room with letter names and use them in talk whenever possible.
	Help the children associate lower and uppercase letters when the letters are taught together (b and B).
	Include letter naming with sequence placement in the alphabet.
	Have a letter bank for each child; when the letters in their names are recognized elsewhere, ask the children to write each letter in lower and uppercase for their own letter bank.
	Encourage children to identify letters they know in printed material.
	Use workbooks with letter learning activities; let children move through the activities as quickly as possible, adding daily to the letter bank.
	Have children play letter identification games such as bingo, fish and memory. (Use many sets of letter cards.)

Children experiencing the transition from prereading to reading, who have a full array of preliterate story, book, word, letter, and, importantly, writing experiences, are perforce learning the most common words of the language (such as *the, of,* and *is*). Reading programs provide lots of practice with these high-frequency words, especially those that do not stress word-analysis skills like phonics. For those children who do not learn these highly frequent words through materials and text exposures, additional practice and use are needed. A few of the ways to extend vocabulary practice are illustrated in Chart 8. (An excellent source for planning activities on word learning and other reading topics is Fry, Polk, and Fountoukidis, *The Reading Teacher's Book of Lists,* 1984.)

Classroom experiences in letters, letter combinations, and words are not necessary for all young children; many youngsters already will have advanced sufficiently beyond the stage of first-word learning, the stage of transition from nonreading to first starts. At this point, children may be said to read because they recall the common words to which they have been exposed. According to the argument of Chapter 6, it is also important for the children to learn ways to independently figure out unknown words. Helping children develop a structure for understanding and using the alphabetic principle and for associating letters and their patterns with sounds will enable the youngsters to develop that skill. Readers who figure out unknown words through the application of principles and who focus on text meaning are strategic, active readers. The process of learning these principles ought to occur jointly with and immediately follow word learning.

CHART 8.   Teaching initial sight words

Become very familiar with a list of frequent words, such as in Fry et al. (1984) so you can select meaningful words for classroom activities that are common and therefore useful. (MAKE, PEOPLE, BOY)

Keeping in mind that children learn words when they focus directly on them repeatedly, plan activities so that words are brought to children's attention. Make several sets of word cards for use by groups in games.

Plan to introduce one or two words each school day. New words need to be incorporated into word experiences on successive days for review. Each week, the cumulative set of words needs to be reviewed. This review does not mean a test; rather, children need to have little stories with the taught words (Mason 1984). Careful observation will indicate when individual pupils do not remember a taught word.

Highlight "words for the day" in several places.

Make games so that words are answers to win: "Go Fish," "Memory," etc.

Use words in the daily story.

Ask children to say a sentence using several of the words being learned. Write the sentence on the board, and show how function words are necessary to complete it: THE *boy makes* A *picture.*

Encourage pairs of children to use the new word cards to make their own sentences. Give the youngsters a set of common function words to help: THE, OF, AND, A, TO, IN, etc.

When talking with children about words, have different children identify the words in different settings: in their sentences, in a list on the board, in magazines and newspapers, in children's books, etc.

Use the letter bank idea for words, according to Stauffer's (1970) technique. When a word is known in and out of context, it is written on a card and becomes part of the child's word bank. The bank is then the source for writing. If the cards are small, they may be rearranged easily to make sentences.

Send a list of new words (or the bank) home with the child. If sentences have been made, or a longer piece written, they also should be sent home with requests for practice.

Find preprimers or tradebooks with several of the known words, and have the children read those words as you read the rest. Select further words from favorite books as the next words to study.

Continue to focus upon words for banks even after the beginning of the preprimer program by including new words from the program until the banks are so large as to be unwieldy.

Keep in mind that the reading program may not have enough word practice for some children. Whenever possible, children who are not acquiring words well should be asked to look, point to, underline, find, and match the new words.

PHONEMIC SEGMENTATION AND PHONICS INSTRUCTION

Instruction in two aspects of the sounds of language are thought to be particularly helpful in learning to read. This section presents a rationale and ideas about the teaching of phonemic segmentation and phonics skills. They are both of transitory importance as aids to children moving into independent reading. Unlike the ability to comprehend text, the skills in the area of language sounds in relation to reading, once learned, apply thenceforth to all reading and do not require additional instructional attention. The purpose of the instruction in the sound elements of the language is to stimulate the start of this process in the beginning reader.

Segmentation

Instruction in how to discriminate and segment words into smaller sound elements should occur, ideally, only for those who need it during kindergarten and the beginning months of first grade. (The material in Chart 9 indicates how need may be determined.) The activities are oral and ought to be presented as sound and word games. There are a number of reasons why phonemic segmentation instruction is recommended. For one thing, the ability to segment is related with successful reading acquisition (Juel 1984). For another, the teaching of this ability influences reading acquisition positively (Bradley and Bryant 1983). Thus, unless children indicate they already understand phonemic components in words, the instruction is needed.

Segmenting words into component parts requires the ability to perceive the different sounds. That is, children who are unable to perceive the differences between HAT and HOT or BUG and RUG will not be able to acquire the skill to manipulate the sounds within words. If the children cannot manipulate the sounds, then they will not be as able to use grapheme-phoneme relationships to figure out difficult words. Whatever the background, teachers should determine if children can segment words into phonemic elements and should provide instruction for those who cannot. This recommendation is manifest in the suggestions of Chart 9. As several "lessons," the phonemic segmentation suggestions are not sufficient; children need to have a lot of alliteration and rhyming experiences in talk, games, stories, and word play. Chart 9 merely provides a "tip of the iceberg" experience.

Beginning Phonics

Principles of Phonics Instruction

No area of beginning reading instruction has historically attracted more attention than phonics instruction. The controversy about the role of phonics in learning to read has evolved around whether instruction in beginning reading should include phonics and, if so, how much and what kind, but, as other concerns about instruction in beginning reading emerge (Barr 1984), the controversy is abating. Most beginning reading programs include some attention to phonics for phonics provides rule-based ways for children to apply knowledge of sound segments to letters and letter combinations in unfamiliar words. Moreover, phonics instruction is associated with greater beginning reading achievement (Bond and Dykstra 1967), especially phonics instruction that teaches children how to synthesize phonic elements (Chall 1967; Pflaum et al. 1980). Of course, there is plenty of evidence that children learn to read without phonics instruction; they apparently induce a system for analyzing the sound patterns of words based on prior experience (Bissex 1980). But many children do not induce such a system, and they need phonics.

Phonics is the term used to describe the formal instruction of sound and letter or letter pattern associations. Appendix B lists recommended essential consonant and vowel principles common to programs in beginning reading. Terms used in phonics such as *clusters, digraphs,* and *diphthongs* are defined through illustration in those lists. Many beginning reading programs include more phonic elements than on the lists. I have included only those that work for a large number of words and are sufficiently reliable. It is important for teachers to become familiar with the content of phonics; a good source is Ives, Bursak, and Ives (1979).

CHART 9. Developing auditory discrimination and phonemic segmentation

Task	Activity
Test auditory discrimination	Use a formal test (Goldman, Fristoe, and Woodcock 1970).
	Using the word pairs below, pronounce the words, and have the child, who cannot see you, tell if the words are the same or different.
	man/nan sip/ship lamb/lamb pan/pan fat/vat top/dop ran/rin dig/dig pin/pen shin/chin bad/pad sat/zat gap/cap tag/tag
Practice auditory discrimination	Practice with word pairs as in the test above. Exaggerate differences, and use very obvious items (box/box; rattle/mop). Move toward less obvious ones (ramp/ramp; flack/flick).
	Consider the auditory discrimination when pupils' dialects predict certain items are not differentiated, as described in Chapter 4. It is best to avoid these potentially confusing experiences.
Test phonemic segmentation	Determine if children can segment words in one of these ways: (1) Have the children say which of 3 words has a different beginning sound (hill, pin, pig), a different medial sound (bun, gun, pin), or a different ending sound (hop, top, doll) (Bradley and Bryant 1983). (2) Have the children state the phonogram of words (the -op of mop, for example) and the initial sounds, too.
Teach phonemic segmentation	Fill the classroom with opportunities for alliteration and rhyming, out of which children will learn about sounds in words.
	Say silly alliteration sentences: "Did Donny dump the dolls? Jerry jumped on the jungle gym. Martha made a merry mark." Encourage the children to do the same.
	Ask the children for words that begin like . . . Billy, Mary, etc. Accept offerings, and add to them without evaluation.
	Say rhymes every day until children learn a few favorites. Then, say the rhymes leaving off a rhyming word for them to add: "Hey, diddle, diddle. The cat and the _____."

CHART 9, *continued*

Task	Activity
	Begin to use the terms, *beginning sound, ending sound, rhyming,* and *same sounds* when playing word and sound games.
	Begin to note silently the children who do not seem to be participating, and focus emphasis and attention on them, thereby encouraging them to enter games easily. But keep an eye on them for later transfer to reading.
	Incorporate questions about beginning sounds in everyday talk. At this point, children should supply similar examples in a systematic way. Children's names are an appropriate place to begin. The teacher can hold up a ball, ask for it to be named, and then ask everyone whose name begins in the same way "ball" does to stand up. He can refer later to the "ball" boys and girls (Bobby, Bill, and Betty) and the "sock" boys and girls (Sammy, Sally, and Sue).
	Do the same with rhyming: Encourage children to supply an item in a rhyming sequence. Say FAT, CAT, and ask for another.
	Have individual children provide rhymes. The children should begin to use the terms correctly. ("Do you know a word that rhymes with POOL?")
	With pictures and objects, children learn when words have the same beginning sound (hat, hen), the same middle sounds (hen, pet), and the same ends (man, hen). Have children group pictures of objects in the appropriate category (Bradley and Bryant 1983).
	Have the children find pictures to use in asking the same questions of their classmates about words with similar beginning, medial, and ending sounds.
	Have children learn to say words slowly so they can identify the beginning, the medial, and the ending sounds, as in their names (JEAN: J . . . . E . . . . N). Have them do the same with other names and words.
	Ask children to combine knowledge of sound segments with letter-sound combinations as the youngsters watch and then themselves find the letter that is used for the same beginning sound (hen, hat /H) (Bradley and Bryant 1983).

The purpose of phonics instruction is to enable children to develop a system of internally generated rules to unlock new words. A typical way to reach this goal is to help children learn how to perceive known letters and letter sequences in unknown words and to try out the analysis until it fits with a word known in the oral lexicon. When a child meets a new word such as *fold*, which contains a recognizable initial letter and the letter pattern, the phonogram -old known from *sold*, and *cold*, he or she ought to be able to blend /f/ with /ōld/ and thereby recognize the new word. Several levels of learning are involved: (1) Children need to recognize the initial letter and the phonogram in the new word as familiar. (2) They need to know that the sounds of these two elements are predictable and what those sounds are. (3) They must join these oral segments and try the new word. (4) They next have to adjust that pronunciation to a known word in their oral lexicon. To accomplish this rather complex analysis, children must have understood the significance of the process and have found that it works.

The extent and type of phonics teaching provided to beginners is determined largely by the basals. Teachers' guides contain directions on how to teach phonic skills; the workbooks and worksheets have practice materials for pupils. Because there are several potential problems with basal materials, teachers must be quite critical in their selection. Many of the practice activities do not, in fact, fulfill the stated objectives; blending is seldom taught, and there are too many complicated jumps from one point to another (Stein 1985).

There are several features common in most basal programs. My review of six popular basal programs indicates that common to all (first-grade programs) are: a study of letter(s) and sounds in word context; an analysis of letter-sound patterns within words (/f/ and /ĭg/ in /fĭg/) without instruction on how to combine them and little blending of single letter/sound associations (/f/ . . . /ĭ/ . . . /g/ to make /fĭg/); an introduction to single consonant letter/sounds in the initial position; a study of consonant clusters (such as cl, st, and br); a review of consonant digraphs (th, sh, and ch); a study of short vowel sounds (as in *can, hen, fit, hop,* and *cup*); and a review of some long vowel patterns (as in *cape, be,* and *week*). In several programs, children are introduced to phonograms, common letter combinations including consonants and vowels (-old, -ape, and -ick, as in *fold, bold; cape, shape; sick, pick,* respectively).

Variations exist in the extent of attention to phonics in these programs. For example, the *American Book Reading Program* (1977) had more phonics instruction than the Scott-Foresman *Reading Unlimited* program (1976). Most programs currently begin the study of phonics as part of the readiness materials. Indeed, a decade ago, Popp (1975) noted that phonics was taught earlier and more intensively through the early 1970s than had been true the previous decade. That pattern has continued.

With these principles in mind, we may examine how phonics is typically presented in basal programs. Many children learn to use phonics effectively, as we know from the observational studies of beginners (Biemiller 1970; Cohen 1974–1975; Weber 1970a). But, as the observation studies have also shown, many children are not sufficiently strategic to apply the process described earlier. Perhaps if initial phonics instruction helped children apply the skills, some children would be less confused. In other words, it is proposed that direct instruction on the *use* of skills will produce more active readers and fewer passive ones. We know that instruction for poor readers on how to integrate phonics with context helped them read (Pflaum and Pascarella 1980; Samuels, Dahl, and Archwamety 1974). With these experiences, I recommend the following as add-ons to the basal materials for teaching phonics:

1. All lessons on phonics skills should begin with remarks about how the particular skill will be used so children understand the real purpose. Teachers

may do this with statements like: "Today the lesson on the phonogram -old will help you when you are reading and come to a word you don't know that has OLD in it" or, "Sometimes you pronounce the C in words one way and sometimes another. Today you will learn a way to figure out which way to pronounce C in words you don't know."

2. Whenever a lesson on a particular skill is presented, children should be asked to use the skill right away. Using a word list such as in Fry, Polk, and Fountoukidis (1984), the teacher should select an unknown word (even a nonsense word may be used) or two. She asks all the pupils to figure it out. Children who do not read these new words successfully need additional instruction, modelling of the process of using the principles, and practice. (I used to ask each child to come up to me and read two words with the new phonic element. If successful, they returned to their seats; if not, the lesson resumed until success occurred.)

3. When children are reading continuous prose and miss a word that contains a phonic element that had been taught, it should be noted and brought to the child's attention after his or her turn at reading. The child then should be shown how to combine understanding of the sentence meaning and the phonic element. For example, the teacher might say, "You missed this word. Read the sentence again, think what would make sense here, look at the beginning of the word and for other parts that you know, and try to figure it out. I'll help if you can't get it then."

Another feature of basal phonics programs deserves consideration. Most introduce a particular phonic element in pieces. That is, a phonic skill is initially introduced in one lesson (perhaps detailing the auditory features) and referred to and expanded in a later lesson (perhaps describing the visual form in known words). Not only are the parts spread out, but the lessons also may conclude without any application to new words. And interspersed with these presentations may be information about several other skills. Since the important thing is for children to use each phonic element on their own in their reading, it seems more appropriate to me to learn a particular element as a whole. That is, instead of learning a little bit about the long vowel pattern in consonant-vowel-consonant-"silent" e words, such as *cape, make,* and *use,* in a series of separate steps, I propose that entire sets of the pattern be learned in consecutive lessons and immediately be put to use.

Examples of Phonics Instruction

Typically and appropriately, learning the associations between initial consonants and their sounds is the first phonic feature commonly taught. Several important teaching steps are incorporated into the demonstrated lesson of Chart 10. Teachers find sequential lessons on initial letter-sound associations in many materials; the skills need to be practiced, applied to new words, and reviewed. If the text material contains words involving the new skills, word learning is likely to be enhanced (Juel 1984). If not, the teacher may develop additional methods of practice.

CHART 10.   A demonstration lesson on initial consonants

Instructional Steps	Lesson for p-/p/
1. Review the sound of the initial position.	1. Ask the children to listen to "pat," "pick," "Peter," and "Patty"; then, ask how these words are alike.
2. Recognize the letter in the initial position.	2. Write "pat," "pick," "Peter," and "Patty" on a chart; then, ask if the words are alike and, if so, where and how.
3. Have the children supply new examples.	3. Ask the children to look in their word banks for words that begin like "pat."
4. Differentiate which words belong and which do not.	4. Have the children write *P* on a work-sheet for each picture that has the phoneme /p/ in the initial position.
5. Apply a new concept to new words. Nonsense words can be used to test the application if children understand that the words are *not real ones*.	5. Write sentences on a chart with new words beginning with *p* (e.g., "Bobby *put* the toy away").

The instructional steps in Chart 10 form a framework that should be amplified in creative ways. Planning may include a new single consonant sound/symbol correspondence each day for three days. The fourth day can be used for review. Common practice materials are workbooks, or children can create their own. Each page of the child-made book can contain the target letter on which children paste pictures representing the sound; these pictures then can be labeled accordingly.

The sequence of letters introduced needs to be attended to since confusion may arise. For example, since /p/ and /b/, /t/ and /d/, /g/ and /k/, and /f/ and /v/ differ only by the presence or absence of *voicing* (caused by vibrations of the vocal cords), these elements should not be presented next to each other. Furthermore, the instances when two graphemes make one sound should follow the single grapheme/phoneme correspondences. A recommended order is: p/p/, s/s/, m/m/, t/t/, f/f/, g/g/, b/b/, l/l/, n/n/, d/d/, j/j/, c/c/, and k/k/, v/v/, r/r/, w/w/, h/h/, z/z/.

The next important *consonant* feature concerns learning about consonant clusters. This area includes situations in which *two consonant graphemes* are heard as *two consonant phonemes*: for example, *st* in "stop" and *cl* in "cluster." (The word "cluster" also has the *st* cluster in the middle.) Study of phonograms will include final consonant clusters, but we are concerned first only with initial clusters. The instructional steps are similar to those already presented, but they also include a review of each single consonant. Chart 11 includes a demonstration lesson.

The study of phonograms expands the number of words children can decode on the basis of predictable English letter patterns. As soon as the children are relatively familiar with the initial single consonants, they can be exposed to

CHART 11. A demonstration lesson on initial consonant clusters

Instructional Steps	Lesson for *cl-/cl/*
1. Review the initial sound.	1. Ask the children to identify the initial sound in "can" and "cup."
2. Review the other phoneme.	2. Ask the children to identify the initial sound in "loud" and "lap."
3. Provide auditory experiences having combined consonant phonemes.	3. Ask the children to listen to the combined sound in "cloud," "clam," "close," etc.
4. Provide visual identification.	4. Present the children with the written words "cloud," "clam," "close," etc., and have the youngsters identify graphic similarities.
5. Ask the children to find *cl* words in their word banks.	5. Have children supply new examples.
6. Present new *cl* words in sentence context.	6. Apply new concepts to new words.

some familiar phonograms. At first, teachers should help children substitute a single consonant in a phonogram to make a new word; later, the children should be encouraged to make their own substitutions with these phonograms so that many new words can be formed (see Appendix B for examples.) Chart 12 illustrates how sets of word families may be combined to extend the number of words beginning readers may decode.

With prior rhyming experiences and practice with phonogram patterns, children begin to develop a sense of letter patterns to predict both consonant and vowel sounds. However, because the phonogram patterns include both vowel

CHART 12. Phonograms

Sample word families with single consonant phonograms	pan	bed	big	pay	cat	
	man	Ted	dig	may	bat	
	tan	fed	fig	day	mat	
	fan	red	jig	bay	sat	
	can	Ned	pig	say	fat	
New words added	span	bled	stay	flat	stop	
	plan	sled	play	skat	flop	
		Fred				
Phonograms with final consonant clusters	pest	past	hand	sold	sent	melt
	test	fast	sand	told	tent	felt
	best	last	land	fold	bent	belt
	nest	vast	band	gold	dent	
	vest		stand	bold		
				cold		
				hold		

sounds and final word consonant elements, there are likely to be variations in pronunciations due to dialect differences. Moreover, as described in Chapter 4, speakers who do not produce a difference in the pronunciation of, for example, *meant* and *men* or between *pin* and *pen* as in black English, are not likely to hear differences either. The set of words in one pattern will resemble those in another. Thus, the phonogram sets will not operate with some dialects as they do with others. In the case of black English speakers, for example, the sets of words that rhyme with /pĭn/ and /pĕn/ would be merged. Since the goal is to help pupils pronounce unknown reading words that are known in the oral lexicon, the separation of these sets is not critical as long as the students figure out a system that works. Chart 13 illustrates a way of teaching these important phonic elements.

When children can blend initial single consonant sounds and the sounds of initial clusters with common phonogram patterns, their ability to uncover unknown reading words is vastly expanded. It is critical that teachers model and establish practice at blending. For example, the teacher demonstrates that when she says /pl/ and adds /ăn/, she has a word they know. Booklets and card sets with common phonograms and a variety of initial letters and clusters provide good practice materials as children build sets of words that rhyme and contain the same letter sequence. Learning about the initial letters and about the phonograms will not help in reading unknown words unless the children know how to blend the elements together.

In regard to vowels, many programs introduce short vowel sounds early, even though study of these sounds in the context of phonograms may be more sensible. Some short vowel sound words are *hand, hen, long, fun,* and *fin*; each may be attached to phonograms. Yet, awareness of these individual phonic elements may help. Study of the pattern that predicts a vowel will have a short (lax) sound illustrates a very important and universal feature of phonics instruc-

CHART 13.   A demonstration lesson for phonograms

Instructional Steps	Lesson for -an
1. Present known words in a pattern.	1. Remind children that they know the words "pan" and "Dan."
2. Recognize rhyme and graphic similarity.	2. Encourage children to identify two common elements of -an: rhyme and letters.
3. Make a new word.	3. Write "fan"; have the children identify graphic similarity; have them use rhyming and pronounce the word.
4. Supply new and additional words.	4. Let the children suggest another word like "man," and then have them search for more examples from their word banks.
5. Make application to new words.	5. Have each child pronounce new words: for example, "ran" and "tan."

tion. There are reliable rules upon which guesses about words may be made. Children need to have sufficient experiences and instruction with the patterns to generalize the knowledge to new instances. The pattern that predicts short vowels is consonant-vowel-consonant (CVC), a closed syllable. As is true with phonics instruction in general, the instruction may be directive and take a deductive direction or it may be less didactic and encourage induction. That is, teachers may *tell* children the general rule, or the instructors may encourage children to figure out the general rule through the careful introduction of salient points. The following list illustrates the inductive approach to short vowel sound generalizations:

1. Having become familiar with certain phonograms, such as the following:

sat, fat	bed, fed	pig, rig	rob, sob	run, sun
rag, lag	den, hen	kid, lid	hog, fog	cut, hut

   the teacher may help children identify the vowel sounds associated with each set.
2. Once children have identified the sounds, the youngsters should learn a name for the sounds so the children can talk about their new concepts.
3. Then, referring to short vowel sounds in these and like patterns, the teacher should ask the children to examine the sequence of letter types in each set. With careful probing, the teacher should encourage the pupils to identify the CVC pattern.
4. The pupils then should state a rule in their own words for what kind of vowel sound they would expect in the CVC pattern.
5. Practice and application to many words is needed next.
6. It also might be a good idea for teachers to ask pupils to predict what vowel sound they might expect in the pattern CVCC with these examples: *cash, bend, sill, song,* and *bump.*

Although the steps of acquiring the complex concepts of this phonic generalization are highly compressed, the illustration demonstrates that the sequence of letters in the unknown words is the primary stimulation for phonic analysis.

One reason that the long, or tense, vowels normally are focused upon after short vowels is, of course, because they are predicted by several letter sequences. To illustrate, the long vowel sounds are predicted in the consonant-vowel (CV) pattern (as in *be* and *so*), called the open syllable; they are predicted in the consonant-vowel-consonant-silent e (CVCe) pattern (as in *make, dice,* and *use*), and they are predicted in some combinations of medial vowels CVVC (as in *sleep* and *coat*). As with short vowels, children's analysis of unfamiliar words containing one of these patterns begins with the perception of a familiar pattern. Thus, the instruction would be like that of the short vowel pattern; it would begin with review of the phonogram patterns the pupils know. It would, like learning the generalization of short vowel sounds, focus on the recognition of the sequence of letters and the associated vowel sound.

There is an aspect of learning to use long vowel patterns in unfamiliar words that requires care so that children are not confused: Several highly frequent words represent exceptions to the common pattern. For example, an exception to the CV pattern is *to,* and an exception to the CVCe rule is *some.* While words containing the vowel pairs *oa* and *ee* usually contain long vowel sounds, other vowel pairs are not so predictable, as in *head, build,* and *again* (Mazurkiewicz 1976). (Appendix B contains a list of common vowel generalizations and their utility.) My suggestion is to teach children to use the term "exception" and to learn a way to handle the possibility that an unknown word is an exception. It will be less confusing if the teacher models the process in instances with words that follow the rule and in instances with exceptions, as illustrated in the following:

1. The teacher ackowledges the children's statements of the generalization that usually words of the pattern CVCe produce long vowels.
2. She sets the modelling process, "Now, watch me use the rule on some words. We will pretend that I don't know the words. See these: *fake* and *some.*"
3. She then says, "Let's see. This word (*fake*) begins, of course, with the sound I know, /f/; it ends like words I know. It ends like *make.* I'll use /f/ and add /āk/; let's see . . . /fāk/."
4. The teacher shows how to determine if process produces a known word. "Oh, I know the word /fāk/; it's something not real."
1, 2. Teacher works with *some.*
3. She says, "This word is like the word *home,* so I'll take the /ōm/ and add /s/ and try /sōm/."
4. She adds, "What might this be: /sōm/? I don't know the word. Maybe this is an exception. I'll try another sound. It has to have /s/ and /m/. Maybe it's /sŏm/. Oh, yes, I know *some,* like in, 'I'd like some grapes.' "

In summary, several underlying principles of instruction in phonics have been described. Teachers may need to make several kinds of adjustments when using basal materials for phonics instruction. First, some phonic elements in the materials may not be useful and therefore should be skipped. Second, teachers may want to consider rearranging the skills of phonics that are being taught in order to compress the learning into massed rather than spaced lessons. Next, since the only critical part of phonics instruction is its use in beginning reading (in writing, too), practice and tests that examine only at the discrimination, matching level need to be amplified by tests that have children pronounce new words. Moreover, children need to learn how to blend the sounds of letters and word parts together. I also have recommended that instruction be constructed to help children induce a workable system. The instruction ranges from the initial experience with the auditory aspect of the element and concludes with applications. Inductive experiences, modelling, practice with supportive materials, and illustrations of how to combine elements together are included. Finally, there has been a hint that children who are familiar with the terminology of reading, writing, and the classroom (for example, the term "exception") are able to thereby gain perspective. This feature of beginning literacy is the focus of the next section.

CONCEPTUAL DEVELOPMENT
The Words of Literacy

We are increasingly aware that children who have a perspective on their cognitive activities have greater control and are therefore more strategic. This is called "metacognition" and is roughly described as "knowing about knowing." Much of the examination of metacognition has involved pupils beyond the initial stages (Brown 1984), but some indications from the materials we already have reviewed and from others suggest that some children have a strong start on knowing about reading. During early storybook experiences, children talk about the stories using the technical terms used later in instruction. Thus, the youngsters not only are familiar with the terms, but they also are beginning to acquire a perspective about reading (Olson 1984).

When they begin to read, knowledgeable children are strategic; for example, they self correct only those errors that cause meaning change (Weber 1970b). These children understand what reading, writing, and paperwork entail because they know the words used to explain the activity and they have the ability to do the required tasks. Less knowledgeable children may not be able to complete task demands, and unless careful, teachers may infer that they did not understand the literacy task when, in fact, they did not understand the language used to describe the tasks.

Not knowing the language of instruction is likely to result in confusion (Downing 1975). Several studies indicate that first graders do not have precise understanding of the terms used daily in reading instruction (Downing and Oliver 1973–1974; Meltzer and Herse 1969). For example, a child who does not know *circle* as a verb may not know what to do when directed to "circle all the words that begin like apple." As we know, quite a number of five- or six-year-olds do not know the meaning of *word* as we do. They do not know how many words are in the oral sentence, "I'm gonna run down to the store for it." Furthermore, it's odd, for example, from our point of view to think that a big person ought to have a "big" name, and a small person the reverse. Yet, some children believe that idea (Ferreiro and Teberosky 1982). And, when children who do not understand *word* are asked "find the words which . . . ," "which words rhyme with . . . ," and "underline the words which . . . ," they are likely to become confused. Many children who are confused simply will figure out what to do by following a neighbor; others may respond randomly. These pupils thus have no sense of control over their learning. Thus, for a positive context for learning literacy, children need to understand the language of literacy instruction.

Two questions follow from the conclusion that children need to learn the language of literacy instruction: What words should be taught, and how should they be taught? There are several types of words to be included: words used in reading group activities, words in written and spoken discourse, and the important function words of the language, especially prepositions. Some samples of each type are in Chart 14.

These words (and others) are commonplace. While most children will use them accurately eventually, the words are needed in the very beginning of

CHART 14.   Technical words in reading and writing instruction

Words Used in Group Instruction

Beginning, capital letters, clue words, compound words, consonant, different, end, endings, ending sounds, first, first sound, last, long (a) sound, mean (the meaning), middle, names, next, pairs, pattern, punctuation words, rhyme, same, sentence, short (a) sound, sound, and word

Words for Directions

Check mark, answer the question, circle (verb), color (verb), draw, end the sentence, do not go with, find, names begin with, finish, finish the sentence, list, match, missing (letter), put (in a box), read, ring (the word), say the word, sentence, show, silly words, stand for, underline, word, write, and X on the (word)

Important Prepositions

In, in front of, next to, on, over, through, under, with, and which (as well as at, by, from, into, of, and off)

instruction, during the time when important new concepts about reading, words for reading, and the first skills for reaching independence are being introduced. It is extremely unfortunate if some children fail to learn the basic concepts of reading and writing for failure to know the words.

The first task is for teachers to become conscious of the language of literacy; this consciousness will help them provide a good context for teaching about the terms. They will stop and explain, illustrate, model, repeat, ask for children's definitions, and ask for children's examples. The terms will be acquired in these ways.

One explicit instructional practice in addition to these daily features of talk with children is to include direct explanation of the most critical terms (e.g., *word, sentence,* and *sound*). An example follows.

1. The target term is analyzed in regard to how it must be understood by the pupils. To understand *word,* for example, is to understand its use in many ways and at many levels. Children learning literacy need to know: words are the elements of written prose; words in print are bounded by spaces; and there are words that make speech. When using this knowledge in school study, children learn that words may be short or long, may have more than one syllable, and have beginning, middle, and end sounds and letters.
2. Sensitive assessment is needed to know which aspects of knowing the term are confusing to the pupils. Sample techniques include having children point to words in prose, cut words apart when printed on a card, point to words in their own writing, explain the relationship between oral and printed words, match oral with written words and the reverse, and identify the sequence of sounds in oral and written form.
3. The instruction has two parts, the informal talk in interaction over school tasks and the more formal clarification through study of "what's in a word?" Interactive talk takes place regarding words in speech. Children and the teacher identify the words in oral sentences. The youngsters identify the

words in a written sentence on the chalkboard, and the children are each asked to find a written word in the room.

4. A worksheet with several words on the top and a sentence at the bottom is used as children count the words at the top, find the words at the bottom, and circle each word. One or two words on the sheet are used for the teacher to model how oral sequences of sounds are matched by the sequence of letters.

5. The concept of "word" is expanded as the teacher asks more difficult questions: "Are both *a* and *grandfather* words? Why do you think *a* is not a word and *grandfather* is? Is your name a word? How is it like the word *bear* or *girl*?"

In conclusion, it is asserted that awareness of the technical language of literacy needs to be accompanied by explanatory use so that inability to understand the terminology will not interfere with acquiring the content. I have additionally suggested that the acquisition of these terms will encourage the development of independence.

General Vocabulary Development

The technical language of instruction does not constitute the only attention to word meaning needed in reading and writing. Throughout the preschool and elementary years, children need to be continuously adding to their store of general lexical knowledge, the store which is the source for reading, writing, talking, and listening. Typically, in the preschool years, educators encourage conceptual development; increasingly, in the instruction for middle-grade pupils, vocabulary development is encouraged. And though the goals of the primary grades emphasize words in regard to reading and writing, hence word recognition over meaning, I strongly recommend that some time be devoted to deliberate vocabulary extension, for, indeed, it underlies all school verbal work.

Using material from the semantic feature theory (Clark 1973; Chapter 2), words are thought to be loosely clustered according to the attributes they share. I propose that children will learn more about individual words, about related words, and about the process of word learning when they learn about words within the set of clustered words. For example, the rather complicated relational term, *more*, may be studied with the other members of the set: *less* and *some*. Since knowing complex terms is a process over time rather than something that occurs at once, I also propose that words already used in language be examined in greater depth in class work. Moreover, because learning about words involves knowing when they *do not apply* as well as when they do (Carroll 1970), this study of words means that children will learn more about a partially known word (*bucket*, for example) when they learn when it is not used and when a new, related word is (*jug*, for example). Finally, I propose that the study of a set of partially known words is an excellent context for introducing a new term, one related yet distinct. The context will suggest the attributes that are alike and those that are unique (Pflaum 1973).

As before, there are two questions to consider: What words will be the focus, and how will they be studied? Concerning the selection of words, there is no difficulty in identifying words to study; nearly any set of words is the beginning of possible activity. What governs the selection is the grouping of words by semantic attributes, submeanings that are shared. As children learn to sort out the differences among words that share attributes, the youngsters acquire what we hope for them: greater precision. Greater precision in understanding words met in reading and in using words in talk and writing leads to greater specific knowledge and experience. Chart 15 includes sets of words taken from knowledge of the interests of five- and six-year-olds, from lists of beginning reading words, and texts. (It is not scientific.)

There are several ways to talk about words in sets so that both in-depth study and the introduction of new words occurs. As children study the terms they know, the youngsters identify the shared attributes. When a new term is brought in, they understand that it, too, shares those attributes; the children know it somewhat already. They then learn the unique features of the new word and thereby enrich their understanding of the terms they knew somewhat from the start. For example, if children know *make* and *build*, it will be relatively easy to fit in *construct*; knowing about the latter will enhance understanding of the

CHART 15.   Groups of words for study within clusters

cat, dog, cow, goat, pig, burro
park, playground, field, lot
seats, chairs, benches
smart, wise, clever
leave, exit
song, music, tune
watch, see, look, stare
later, after
morning, evening, afternoon, night
below, underneath, behind
different, unlike, not alike
land, earth, dirt, world
made, built, constructed, created
months, days, hours, weeks, years, eras
some, a lot, most, much
great, wonderful, extraordinary
man, woman, lady, gentleman
man, boy, male
too, also, as well as
same, similar, alike
ask, tell, insist, relate, answer, question
river, lake, stream, ocean, brook, bay, sea
city, town, village, country, nation
large, wide, huge, great, fat
little, small, narrow, thin
kind, nice, sweet, generous

first two. In the examples that follow, teachers are urged to let their pupils use their own knowledge and language to talk about the clusters. The purpose is clear; we hope that systematic construction of vocabulary clusters will result. This development is less likely when didactic means are used to support personal lexical development. Reference material, including the expert knowledge of the teacher, may be used to check on progress.

In addition to the suggestions in Chart 16, there are many fine methods for working with word meaning in other sources. Although intended for older pupils, the activities in Johnson and Pearson (1978) and McNeil (1984) may be adapted for younger pupils.

CHART 16. Helping children experience semantic clusters

Informal Talk about Clusters

Introduce a well-known member of a cluster—*town*—and discuss and list its features as follows:

> *town:* people living close to one another in a number of dwellings and having different jobs and functions

Next, enter another well-known member, and identify its similar and dissimilar attributes.

> *city: same:* people living close to one another in a number of dwellings and having different jobs and roles;
> *dissimilar:* many more people, dwellings, and jobs

Bring in a new term. The previous attributive discussion enables it to be established easily.

> *village: same:* people living close to one another in a number of dwellings and having different jobs;
> *dissimilar:* fewer people, dwellings, jobs, and roles than town, a lot fewer than city

Using Cluster Members to Describe a Story Character

After reading a story, list the familiar cluster members, *kind* and *nice* and the less-familiar one (in this sense), *sweet* on the board. Discuss the match (or mismatch) of story characters and all cluster members. (One may be thought to be *kind*, perhaps, but not *sweet*.)

Working from the Attributes Rather Than the Terms

Children should be expected to supply through class talk the term to fit one of several sets of attributes. For example, working with attribute sets, students may be asked to "figure out which of the terms (*bench, throne, seat,* and *chair*) fit the following sets of attributes. . . ."

Shared			
-piece of furniture	-piece of furniture	-piece of furniture	-piece of furniture
-to sit on	-to sit on	-to sit on	-to sit on
Unique			
-all kinds	-to fit under tables and to move	-long, for lots of people	-for kings and queens

---

CHART 16, *continued*

Relationships

For example, compare morning to afternoon and afternoon to _____ .

Family Relationships

Draw family chart of story characters.

Predictions about New Word Meaning

Say, for example, "You know what it is to carry. Show me what you would look like while you were carrying a heavy pail. Now, what if I said your pail was heavy and you had to *lug* it a long way. Show us how that would look."

Using a Dictionary to Confirm

Say, for example, "You do look like you are lugging that pail. What do you think is the difference between *carry* and *lug*? Let's look *lug* up in the dictionary."

Keeping Track of Good Words

Give each child a small notebook for his or her favorite words. To keep it active, ask the children to share it. Encourage the children to use these words in talk and in writing.

Learning Single Words Have More Than
One Definition through the Study of Clusters

For example, ask for words with which *sweet* might be clustered. Probe, too. Put the following possibilities on one side of the board: *nice, gentle, warm,* and *kind.* Put these elsewhere: *sugary* and *creamy.* Discuss how words may be in more than one cluster, and ask children to find another example.

There are three major points to this section: Conceptual development ought to be part of the curriculum at each grade level; interactive talk about word meaning will enhance the store of general lexical items, and since children need to know words more precisely, the study of words as collections of related terms provides both the opportunity to learn more about partially known items and the opportunity to more easily learn about new items.

WRITING AT THE TRANSITION

As children move in their reading through the period in which they "read" with a few memorized items to the point where they begin to figure out new words independently, those who have been writing are going through changes. The question of this section is how teaching may encourage writing. This section pays attention to the development of spelling skill as well as to experiences that enhance beginning writing.

Some Thoughts about Spelling and Other Writing Conventions

Specialists in the area of writing attest to children's natural desires to use conventional spelling and to give up inventions once reading begins (Graves 1983). For some children, this skill is a matter of recognizing differences easily between the way they have spelled a word and its common form. These children then adjust their own spelling to the printed form, especially with words they meet often. Other youngsters, however, do not so easily recognize differences between their own and printed words for these children do not have the perspective. For them, special direction on how to realize the sound-symbol patterns of English in spelling and how to memorize exceptions is needed. And for a few others whose visual memory for words is weak, conventional spelling is not easily achieved.

Study of phonics may enhance the transition from invented spellings and early attempts with memorized words into freer writing. To achieve that smoother transition, children learn to say the target words they want and to listen to themselves (their "mind's ear") to realize the corresponding letters and patterns needed. This is the opposite process from reading, of course. For example, in reading, the child who meets *plate* for the first time recognizes the beginning through consonant cluster study and the ending as the phonogram *ate*. She puts the parts together through synthesis skills modelled in class and says /plāt/. Now, imagine another child who does not have a spelling response to the word in writing. He says /plāt/ to himself, knows the first two letters, writes *pl*, thinks about the final sound sequence /āt/ and its letter pattern, and writes *ate*.

Because children are able to construct workable systems, reminders of how the various phonic elements might help in writing should be part of the phonic lessons. Teachers also should model how the phonic knowledge may be applied in writing, as follows:

1. "Remember that yesterday you learned how words with a vowel, then a consonant, then an *e* at the end usually meant that the vowel sound would be long? You know a lot about the words *gate, wise,* and *hope.* What do you do when you see a word that has the vowel-consonant-e combination that you do not know: for example, *flame?* Yes, you look at the *fl* and know that the beginning *fl* makes /fl/; then, you look at *ame* and know it by the pattern and because of words you know like *game.* You then put them together as /flām/ and decide whether it makes sense."
2. "Now, what about the opposite? What if you are writing along and want to write the word, /blām/? First, you can figure out the beginning of the word from words and sounds you know and write *bl* like this. Then, you would do the same with the ending, /ām/, remember *came,* and write the *ame* at the end."

In addition to the application of all the major phonic elements to the writing/ spelling process, there is another feature of the reading and writing relationship that has reciprocal influence. And it has to do with inflections. While study of inflections as a *reading* tool comes later, it is needed right away for writing. Several rules will generate large numbers of conventionally spelled words if learned to the level of application. These rules are

1. With closed syllables (short vowels), the final consonant is doubled when adding inflections that begin with a vowel: for example, stop, stopped, stopping; pat, patted, patting.
2. The *e* in final position in CVCe-patterned words is dropped before the inflection *-ing:* make, making; bike, biking.

3. The *y* in final position (if it is preceded by a consonant) must be changed to *i* before the addition of the inflections *-es* and *-ed.*

Recent interest in spelling has brought about a change in how teachers may view "errors." Just as in the study of oral reading development in the first grade, spelling growth may be examined by looking at the patterns of errors in children's writing across time. For example, a young child who writes *stoping* for *stopping, spined* for *spinned,* or *makeing* for *making* has not acquired understanding of the inflections and their role in maintaining consistent patterns. Analysis of errors for patterns of understanding helps suggest the role for instruction. Just as the preschoolers' invention of spelling demonstrates their phonemic understanding, so, too, school children's errors while attempting conventional spelling illustrate their knowledge.

As well as helping children become conventional spellers by the middle grades, the spelling goal in the primary years is to encourage children to strive for the goal of conventional spelling for themselves and to seek independence in fulfilling it. But, of course, conventional spelling is not the only goal in writing; indeed, it is less important than aspects of the expression put forth on paper. Therefore, the place of spelling should be kept in perspective. Children ought to learn that often, a piece is rewritten, and, in the rewriting, the spelling is edited and improved. Thus, we have the following three concerns:

1. During first draft writing, children need to practice using knowledge of sounds and letters to figure out how to spell as the teacher has modelled. Also, children can be taught to put just the first letter or two and a space—if they cannot figure out the spelling—for later consideration. As another method during the writing of the first draft, children may use an accessible source for difficult words such as a personal list, a dictionary, or a knowledgeable and accessible friend.
2. During the first part of the editing stage, children can read for meaning and for impressions about spelling and punctuation. Children learn to read carefully, to find problems in the hard words, and to mark them with a dot. In later editing, the dot will remind them to check these words.
3. The checking stage is also part of editing. Children learn to go back to all the words marked with a dot and to the words with spaces. As sources to determine the correct spelling, the youngsters ought to have: their own word banks, picture dictionaries they know how to use, personal booklets with special words they have needed in the past alphabetized by first letter, and the direct help of another pupil or the teacher.

When young children invent their own writing, they deal with the conventions of spacing and punctuation rather idiosyncratically, as we saw in Chapter 3. Like spelling, in formal school writing, children should be challenged to use writing conventions. Punctuation in writing is parallel to the intonation and suprasegmentals of oral language. That resource in children's experience and the fact that *they like to punctuate* facilitate instruction.

The essence of punctuation is to make markings in writing that will signal some of the boundaries that are marked in oral language by intonation. Since children have strong understanding of English grammar and mark their talk quite clearly, it is proposed that punctuation talk begin with this relationship. I like to use an example from *Curious George* (Rey 1941). The teacher should read these sentences aloud (not the first reading, of course):

> George wanted to get out.
> He climbed up to the window
> to try the bars.
> Just then the watchman came in. (p. 40)

The teacher should point out the beginnings and ends of the sentences and exaggerate the intonation. After reading, he should make these boundaries explicit by calling attention to and naming periods and capital letters. Following this introduction, the teacher may redo the activity on a worksheet, show where he punctuates as he writes on the board, and encourage the pupils to figure out why the period is used in some instances and the question mark in others. Finally, the teacher should show children how to use knowledge about punctuation in editing their work.

Until the last two decades, learning to print was considered a very important matter. Penmanship is considered less important today; much of the practice with letter forms takes place through workbooks. The quality of printing is a matter of concern especially when papers are rewritten. Precision and discipline are not altogether negative things, and the challenge to reach high goals in regard to paper formatting, neatness, and careful consistent printing is worthy.

Writing Experiences

What children write about and how they do so is of far greater importance than their spelling, punctuation, and penmanship. Following the logic of the book to this point, and buttressed by the work on writing processes by Graves (1983) and his associates (Calkins 1982), several recommendations may be made.

The process of writing is emphasized in Graves' (1983) work and that of his associates. The process encourages children to act as professional writers do. In some ways, this format is like the holistic approach to reading; the idea is that children who learn skills as they need them in the course of writing will learn them more thoroughly and will understand their purpose.

Among the innovative features of Graves' work is the emphasis on the child as writer whose work must be taken seriously. As an example, one of five pieces written by the beginners is selected (by the child) for publication in the class. And the preparation of the piece is an excellent context in which to learn several skills and thereby the important process of editing one's own work. In rewriting and checking, children become more precise and gain independence.

The teacher's role is critical. The teacher, in Graves' approach, does not suggest topics; instead, in interviews that occur privately and regularly, the teacher probes in the areas of a child's interests and encourages writing from that talk. Similarly, the teacher helps the young writer find ways to improve expression rather than to demand it. The teacher presents skills that an individual or group needs when the need does arise *and the children are aware of the need.* The teacher keeps track of individual progress in several ways: by keeping children's writing in folders they have access to; by jotting notes after conferences; by writing topics of pieces on the fronts of folders; by developing a list of *known,* not unknown, skills for sharing with the pupil and parents; and by utilizing periodic dictation to measure use of skills. In the Graves approach, children are not compared; the progress of each individual is traced through these measures. Thus, the process of development in writing is the main concern, and teachers are advised of ways to become increasingly adept at bringing out productive change in their pupils.

The form classroom writing may take is limited only by the teacher's classroom originality and the children's experiences. As we learned in Chapter 3, untutored writers make their own, quite varied writing experiences. The youngsters write lists, news items, notes for the family, birthday cards, advertisements, special messages to relatives, and pure expression. Similarly, children in school may have a wide range of writing experiences, if we stimulate and support the process.

Daily writing is recommended. If the writing workshop notion is not completely adapted, there are ways in which writing experiences may fit with reading instruction. Even during the transition period, children can start a journal. Since so much of their work is expected to fit into the lines and spaces of worksheets and workbooks, what better offer could you make to young writers than to ask them to format and devise a personal scheme for notebook writing? Instead of being right or wrong in their responses, the journal writing is not evaluated; it is merely read by the teacher and classmates upon request. Beginners may make pictures and label them, write lists, and begin expressive writing. When unusual writing appears in a child's journal, the teacher may inform others that "someone used their journal to write a list of what they had to do."

There are also ways to bypass the workbooks and extend a reading experience. Children may be asked to: write a new ending; explain why characters said what they did; write the important parts of the story; write what would happen if some feature of the plot were changed; or write why a character's life was the same or different from the child's. Class projects, such as a book of poems or a newsletter for parents, also encourage good writing.

Among the ways in which teachers have organized the reading and editing portions of the writing process is to have children help one another edit. Since we all have experienced the need for outside readers to enhance our perspective on what we write, this is a good, natural process for children to learn. Several years ago, Moffett (1968) suggested that children act as intermediary editors of their peers' works in order to teach editing and to enlarge the sense of audience. Indeed, the concept that the teacher is the sole audience is limiting. When children find that their peers do not understand, they are involved more actively in figuring out what is missing. With young children, the sharing of editing must be done quite carefully. Children need to be taught how to edit others' works. Teachers who find ways to stress skill items as points to discover will have modelled a good way for the children to help one another.

When writing is a major activity of a classroom concerned with initial literacy, children learn to integrate ideas learned in reading with those learned during writing. The emphasis should be on personal development and expression. But growth will not occur without careful guidance to support the progress of each child. Growth cannot occur all at once. But excellence in early writing is achievable, and it is compatible with a structured program that includes lessons in word learning and phonics.

SUMMARY

This chapter has discussed a series of separate issues that are of concern at the transition between prereading and beginning writing experiences to the real start of independent reading and writing. The traditional notion about reading readiness contrasted with what we know of reading at the start from early readers, emergent literacy, and the gradual acquisition of the application of the alphabetic principle suggests that this transitional stage is quite important to young children and should be treated carefully by their teachers.

For one thing, children need to be carefully helped so that they do learn the names of letters and can identify a few words that are of high frequency. The development of this ability requires straight memorization, and teachers must make it possible by repeated experiences with words. These experiences will give youngsters confidence about reading. Children also need to have sufficient experiences so they can identify the phonemes in words they hear and begin to apply knowledge of sounds to letter-sound correspondences. This instruction must neither consume the entire reading program nor be ignored. What is important, however, is that teachers make certain that their pupils *apply* major, productive notions about letters and sounds to unfamiliar words successfully.

We have examined how the terminology of instruction matter might be taught during children's initial literacy experiences. Such word experiences have immediate application to learning to read. But word learning should not stop with technical terms. As is true before and later, the primary grades are also a period when attention to general vocabulary development is important. While there are many ways to enhance conceptual development, in this chapter we examined words through the relatedness among words.

Writing is the reverse process of reading, it is stated. While this statement is not entirely true (since both writers and readers construct meaning with words), in regard to spelling words, it is. At this point, it is proposed, instruction in the one area meets the needs of another. Writing is a very personal process, and the instructional recommendations reflect that.

The instruction features at the transition point have not been integrated; this is the topic of the next and final chapter. We need to find how the study of words, phonemes, phonics, the terms of direction, concept development, spelling, and writing may be combined in a coherent program. More importantly, we need to know how children come to construct meaning out of their reading and to use skills in support of that endeavor.

SELECTED ACTIVITIES

1. Find a readiness or preprimer workbook. Search through it to locate instances of activities claimed to be experiences in auditory discrimination. Examine the real pupil task, and decide if the task supports discrimination of sounds. Describe a good example and a poor one.
2. Find examples of practice on high frequency words in the teacher's guides. Evaluate if the examples are sufficient for a group of youngsters who are not having an easy time learning to read. If there are not enough examples, add ideas that you think are appropriate to the list.
3. It was asserted that children can write in response to a story. Examine a first-grade level, basal program teacher's guidebook and find how many free writing activities are suggested. Develop a substitute writing activity from a story you think is appropriate.
4. Imagine that your first-grade pupils are confused about the verbs used to provide directions (*match, underline, cross out, fill in,* and *circle*). Plan a lesson to help the youngsters use these direction words.
5. To do a good job in teaching phonics, teachers, themselves, need to be able to analyze sounds and segments within words and to label them correctly. Complete the following:
   • Choose the correct one:

_____	cluster	so	cc	ph	th	sw
_____	digraph	th	rh	st	psy	ft
_____	long vowel	pup	use	toy	crew	stumble
_____	short vowel	nest	wipe	fold	proof	plow

   • Explain what these terms are: phonogram, CVCe pattern.
6. Talk with a six-year-old about his or her writing. Ask the child to write a story for you on any topic he or she prefers. Talk with the child first, and see if the topic emerges from your talk.
7. Try to get a child or a group of children to ask *you* questions about something they have written or read. Do this activity in a school and in a nonschool setting.

8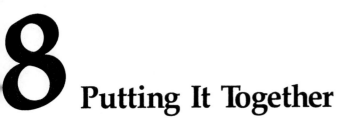
Putting It Together

A coherent beginning literacy program consists of far more than the disparate segments described in Chapter 7. Not only would it be incorrect to teach lessons on phonics separate from lessons about the technical words of instruction, but it also would be impossible to speak of sounds without proper preparation using the terms. There are other reasons to discuss the unification of elements in the beginning reading program, as well. The reading instruction components discussed in Chapter 7, while important, do not form the basis of the program; processing prose for meaning is reading. Thus, the purpose of Chapter 8 is to consider how instruction may support young readers' construction of meaning from prose. The chapter describes where and how the strands described in Chapter 7 are integrated.

Chapter 8 discusses the total literacy program. The first section outlines the structure of literacy lessons, a structure that is sufficiently general to allow for recommended modifications. The second section describes the Language Experience Method; the third section reveals how classrooms may be organized. Oral (and silent) reading instruction is the topic of the next section, which includes comments on how oral reading may be used as the medium for instruction and good feedback to enhance pupils' reading strategies. A discussion of reading assessment using oral reading also is present in this section. The period of transition from the primacy of oral to silent reading, also discussed in this section, demonstrates how instruction in reading supports growing independence in primary-grade pupils' reading. Finally, the chapter concludes with a word on writing and a reference to the accordian metaphor in beginning literacy instruction.

SCHOOL LITERACY LESSONS

The Directed Reading Lesson

The Directed Reading Lesson (DRL) has several common components. The main unit is the text story, and the first segment of the DRL involves the introduction to the story: teaching new vocabulary and providing purposes for reading. The second part of the DRL is initial story reading, which is either oral or silent depending on the students' proficiency levels and teacher goals. For beginners, the reading is teacher guided; components of the story are sequentially read and discussed. The next part of the DRL is the rereading, which is usually oral, and the final part of the DRL is the skills segment. While referred to as a single lesson, the DRL is, in fact, a series of lessons across two or more days. In short, the DRL consists of the following:

The introduction of vocabulary and story theme presented as reading purpose
Initial reading and discussion of meaning
Rereading to solidify story meaning and skills
Skills lessons and practice

As described in Chapter 6, reading instruction normally develops out of the basal reading program and its teacher's guides, the pupil reading texts, and the

202

workbooks. There are several, usually three, small reading groups, and each contains children of like reading achievement ranging in number from about four (usually the children of lower ability) to larger groups of twelve to fifteen.

Teachers may control the pace through which the pupils experience the stories of the basals; pace is strongly associated with reading achievement (Barr and Dreeben 1983). That is, one teacher may complete a DRL in two days while another with a similar group may take four days. A group that moves quickly through the stories of the first grade program, reading a new story every other day, for example, will experience more new vocabulary, more stories, and more skills development than those children whose teachers take a more leisurely pace. Of course, instructional pace is influenced by how well the pupils are acquiring the new concepts, but Barr and Dreeben (1983) found critical variations in instructional pace among teachers who had like ability pupils. Because the prose, skills development, word introduction, and practice provision in the basals are tightly woven together, a teacher's decision about a group's acquisition of any part of these aspects of reading will affect the acquisition pace of the rest. Use of the basals for initial reading is a topic that deserves attention.

A Historical Perspective

A review of the changes in the American basals in the twentieth century helps our understanding of current practice (Woodward 1985), including decisions about pacing. This review also raises good questions about instructional practice. Children ought to be given every opportunity to advance at a pace commensurate with their potential rate of learning. With wide diversity in student achievement, it is not appropriate to teach reading to a group of twenty-eight first-grade pupils without some kind of individualization. While other, more closely individualized programs might appear more appropriate still, in reality it is quite difficult to manage even the three groups common to first-grade classes. The basal materials ease the difficulty somewhat, and, as a result, there is widespread dependence on the basals. Given the features of the modern basal, however, unquestioned reliance raises concern.

The modern basal differs in important ways from its predecessors. McGuffey's readers, an early progenitor of the modern basal in America, were sets of graded readers used in most schools during the last half of the nineteenth century. Except for the inclusion of some minor advice to teachers, these books were just for schoolchildren. It was assumed that teachers knew how to use the readers, which contained poems, moralistic essays, patriotic stories, and some skill practice exercises. During the first half of the twentieth century, publishing houses produced more inclusive sets of readers for American schoolchildren. Not only did the newer materials include fewer moralistic essays, more fiction, and a much more gradual rate of introduction to new vocabulary, but they also began to be addressed to teaching and teachers. By the 1940s, there were special teachers' editions with advice about practice, information from reading research, and sample instructional segments. The authors of the basals included essays to teachers about instruction with bibliographies of professional sources. The basal authors assumed that teachers could and would design appropriate instruction.

Beginning in the 1960s and increasingly in the 1970s, the teacher's guides grew in size and variety. In most programs today, teachers are given complete scripts to use in teaching; the instructors are told what to say to the pupils about each part of the DRL, such as the words to use when introducing a story and the questions to ask when talking about the skills. Now, essays for teachers to draw upon and extend their professional knowledge have been substituted with introductory materials to introduce the teacher to the complex program management system. No bibliographies of professional reading are included. The modern teacher's guides even include summaries of the pupil stories. Teachers are told which questions to ask and the answers. Special editions of the workbooks include the answers to all activities. Woodward (1985) concluded from his review of the changes in the basal programs that now teachers are assumed to administer reading instruction that the authors, staff writers, and editors design. To me, these changes illustrate many of the problems in American education.

Relevant to the question at hand, however, the shifts in the basals have produced several new problems for the teacher of beginning literacy. The teacher may rely totally on the materials and realize that in her interactions with pupils and her decisions about pacing, the real effects of the program are taking place. Better yet, well-informed teachers who have read widely in professional literature (including this book) will make wise decisions about which parts of the basals will and will not be used and which parts need expansion or reduction. And, indeed, no informed rule specifies that the basals must be followed closely. To my knowledge, no data reveal that teachers who follow basal programs closely have pupils with greater reading success than teachers who do not. While the reverse is also not verified with research data, logic argues against the need for such a prescription. Literacy education was at least as productive in past decades as today in spite of a steady increase in teacher direction in the materials (and a concomitant increase in cost). This author believes teachers' pride in their professional accomplishments has been undermined as teachers steadily have lost freedom to compose and invent instruction and have had to conform to prescriptive materials designed to fulfill commercial goals.

We do know that good teaching is characterized by teacher responsiveness to pupil needs, by sensible movement through graded materials, by an appropriate inclusion of systematic phonics instruction, and by processes that enhance children's ability to comprehend. Modifying the basal programs is likely to improve instruction, and there are several ways to modify the programs.

Comprehension-based Modification of the Basal DRL

This section emphasizes how teachers may design instruction independently of the directions in the guide. The intent is to construct coherent, meaningful lessons that are planned according to the particular group of pupils: their backgrounds, needs, and interests.

The first step in the process is to select the words to introduce. There are three types of words to consider. One type includes those undecodable, high frequency words listed in the indexes of the pupil books and in the teacher's guides. In planning the teaching, teachers should think of ways to help pupils focus repeatedly on these words. The second type includes decodable words that are presented in sentences that the pupils read to practice new skills and review old ones. The third type of words may pose *meaning* difficulty. Although most words of the first and second grade reading programs are believed to be known by most pupils, some words may pose problems. For example, rural children may not have a very clear concept of a *city park*. Midwestern children may not understand *sea* and *ocean*. And the word *scrub* may not be familiar to some youngsters. Concepts that need sharpening may be taught as described in Chapter 7.

The basal DRL may be strengthened by emphasizing one or two basic themes from each story. While it is not always easy to find an important theme in many of the beginning stories, the first step in this modification is for the teacher to carefully read the pupil story in order to locate one or two central points that can serve as the thematic emphases for the entire DRL. An example from a primer story (American Book Company 1977) about a boy's foot race might be: "Friendship is more important than winning a race." In planning, the theme or themes are used to initiate talk about the children's prior experiences with the story content and to set purposes for the reading. For the race story, the teacher may use the following as ways to encourage children to use their previous experiences to focus on the story theme: "We are going to read a story about a foot race. Have you ever run in a race? Have you seen a real race that grown-ups run in? Do the runners want to win? When you read this story, you will find that Peter does something different in the race. I want you to decide if what Peter does in the story is what you would want your friend to do . . . As you read, try to think about whether the race is like races you have run."

The guided reading portion of the story is planned next. Actually, it takes little planning, merely the writing of several good questions that will help pupils focus on the purpose questions and the theme of the story. In practice, however, the guided reading portion is quite important. (The next section describes the guided reading part of the lesson in detail.)

Rereading the story, which is planned next, should be considered in light of its overall role in reading acquisition. Rereading provides practice with the prose and the new words in order to increase accuracy and fluency. For most first and second graders, rereading is a necessary step. For those progressing very well, rereading may not be needed. If used, the pupils need a meaningful purpose for the rereading. Alternatives to the common round-robin reading (taking consecutive turns reading aloud) include asking the children to reread in order: to prepare a list of all the reasons why the race in the story is not like a race at school (such reasons could include that only five children were in the story's race, that the story's racers were all boys, and that the story's racers wore special racing clothes), to write their own experiences about races, to read to other children, to find specific information, to answer a specific question ("Would you ask your friend the same thing Peter did?"), and to draw a picture.

In contrast to the DRL outline above (and much current practice), another activity may solidify the story theme experience. An excellent opportunity for integrating reading and writing, since beginners may write about a story, the teacher may plan for the pupils to answer a question: "If you were Peter, what would you have done? . . . List all the ways that the race in the story is not like school races. . . . Write about a time you wanted to win something and didn't." If the teacher has many written responses to stories, story logs for written responses may be developed for each pupil.

The final part of the planning includes the skills lesson. If the basal vocabulary includes carefully controlled, decodable words that are included in the story texts, then the sequence of skills in the teacher's guides ought to govern the selection of skills to be taught. If not, teachers may follow the recommendations of Chapter 7. Some unreliable skills such as the -ea combination (as in *head* and *beam*) may be ignored with no harm to pupils. The segments of skills lessons may be rearranged to achieve massed learning. Modelling of skills is important in lesson planning, as is preparation of ways that pupils may apply the skills. Although Stein (1985) found many instances in which skills practice activities were poorly related to the desired learning, if the workbook materials are appropriate, they will be a planned part of the skills lessons.

Thus, the planning portion of the instruction involves a lengthy process that is not part of the much more conventionally used teacher's guides. The planning time needed is a problem for novices, but it is time spent well. Having initiated this process with preservice teachers and having observed the comparisons of their work with the basal recommendations, I expect teachers will find their own lessons to be more coherent and more fun to teach than following the scripts in the teacher's guides. As they become more expert, teachers do not need much time for planning; they read the story, jot down the themes and words, think about questions, organize rereading activities, develop writing experiences, and plan skills to teach. This approach helps teachers develop the ability to select among the commercial materials at their disposal. With greater experience, the instruction that takes place in guided reading increasingly becomes the core of reading instruction.

Guided Reading Techniques in the DRL

Good questioning engages children in the critical meaning of the prose they are reading, in the thinking proposed during the initial talk about the children's prior knowledge, and in the purpose-setting questions. Children need to be led to the major ideas through the evidence of the text's details. The teacher should ask about the details and concepts that are critical to understanding the story theme(s). Questions that ask pupils to read a sentence showing, for example, that a character wants to win the race engage the youngsters in the meaning of the story. One or perhaps two good questions for each page accomplish the dual goals of maintaining the reading and focusing on meaning. Great emphasis should not be placed on word recognition; however, feedback on errors is a concern and is addressed in the last section.

Another way to guide reading is to use story grammar, referred to in Chapter 7. Prior to the guided reading, the teacher writes the following on the board: *characters, the story problem* (the question of winner versus friendship, for example), *plans,* and *solution.* As the pupils read the assigned segments and as information emerges from the pupils' discussion about the story constituents, the teacher fills in the spaces on the board. At the end of the reading and discussion, the story grammar components are reviewed and summarized. This format has the advantage of focusing on essential story structure and building pupils' expectations for stories.

Yet another way to guide reading is the Directed-Reading-Thinking-Activity (Stauffer 1970). The DRTA is a version of the DRL usually used with pupils beyond the initial stages. In the DRTA, after the introduction (which consists only of the *vocabulary* portion), the pupils are asked, based only on the story title and pictures, to predict the story content. Using questions that elicit predictions, the teacher writes the predictions on the board. Then, after a short reading segment, the predictions are reviewed. Those that still hold are kept; those that do not are erased, and new predictions are added. The process continues through each story segment, and as the process continues, the pupils increasingly are involved in the story. Progressing through the guided reading, the pupils discuss the characters, relationships, and story events. The DRTA is quite popular with many teachers, but it is recommended that teachers do not expect enthusiastic predictions from pupils at first.

In the search for effective ways to help children having difficulty, Hoffman and Crone (1984) described ways for altering the essential structure of the DRL to increase fluency. Second graders who were not reading successfully at the first-grade level were involved in a program that included much teacher modelling of fluent reading, practice, high expectations for performance, and planned repetition. In their program, the children initially *heard* the teacher read the new story. Subsequent discussion used story grammar to enhance the pupils' comprehension. Then, guided oral reading used several techniques including group reading (choral reading) reminiscent of an earlier reading practice, echoic reading whereby pupils read just after the teachers, and much repeated reading. Hoffman and Crone believe these changes in the DRL for slow readers help the youngsters gain greater fluency and accuracy. It is noteworthy that the pupils' reading only began after they had become familiar with story content; thus, they were able to use their expectations about meaning as a framework for the difficult demands of word recognition.

There are almost no limits to how the basal-defined DRL structure may be modified. In addition to the suggested comprehension-based modification of the present teacher's guides, several other methods enhance the guided reading portion of the lessons, including the use of story grammar, the DRTA, and planned repeated practice after modelling for slower readers. It is hoped that this discussion clarifies that teachers may modify basal programs without harming their pupils' progress; indeed, modification may improve progress. The DRL lesson structure based on the story unit, however, is not the only way in which to direct beginning reading acquisition.

THE LANGUAGE EXPERIENCE APPROACH

For many years, a group of teachers and reading experts has promoted a most interesting approach to beginning reading. The Language Experience Method (LEA) has been viewed by these professionals as an example of how apparently natural means for constructing understanding of literacy may be incorporated into classroom practice. The LEA integrates reading and writing in strong ways.

The most salient features of LEA include

1. Use of children's oral language for reading material; the child's written language therefore parallels his spoken language.
2. Built-in provision for dialect and experiential variation.
3. A personalized instructional approach; the teacher and child share important thoughts, experiences, and observations.
4. A natural means for an integrated language arts program; reading, writing, listening (to others' stories), and speaking (dictating) are all involved in the production of language-experience stories.
5. An open system to encourage creativity in children and in teaching.
6. Ease in combining the system with other methods of teaching reading.

In practice, the LEA becomes either a part of the reading program, blended with a basal program, or the central reading and writing program for beginners. The following LEA sequence is slightly amended from one by Stauffer (1970).

Day 1: On the first day of the sequence, the child dictates a story to the teacher, who reads it back immediately to see if it is *correct*. The child then is asked to identify any words she knows in the story, and those words are underlined. Then, the teacher and child reread the story; the teacher reads and hesitates before each underlined word so that the child can respond.

When taking children's dictation, the teacher should observe a number of conditions. She should encourage free-flowing language as much as possible. That is, the teacher should not interrupt or slow down the story dictation process unless necessary. For the unresponsive child, some prodding may be needed, but even in these circumstances, the child's words only are recorded—even if these words are not in complete sentences. For a long-winded child, the teacher may need to suggest alternatives because of time constraints. At a good stopping point, she might suggest that they discontinue dictation and continue the following day. She also might suggest that the child's parents complete the story that night. Under no circumstances should the exuberant child be discouraged.

If the teacher has a primary typewriter or computer available, the dictation process is facilitated. The typed words and spacing are more consistent than in hand-printed stories and are, therefore, perceptually clearer. If there is no primary typewriter, the teacher should have a *very neat, consistent* manuscript form and should use a black pen for clarity.

Whether a typewriter or pen is used, a carbon should be made of each story and filed in the child's folder. The files then are used for informal progress assessment. The file of dictated stories contains data about the size of a child's reading vocabulary (underlined words), the span of his interests (the variation of story content), his ability to observe the world around him, the complexity of his sentence structures, the development of his conceptual understanding, and the extent of his oral vocabulary.

Teachers often are perplexed about taking dictation from nonstandard-speaking children; however, since the goal of this technique is to preserve each child's language and unique experiences for reading acquisition, I think the solution is clear. The child's sentence structure should be preserved as the teacher writes the story, but conventional spelling should be used. I would not hesitate to write double negatives, insert a subject pronoun after a topic name, use nonstandard pronouns or immature or nonstandard past-tense verbs, but I would spell each word in the traditional manner. Just as children will learn later new ideas and new ways of expressing ideas from reading others' writings, so too will they learn to understand alternative sentence structures.

Day 2: The previous day's story is reread and, again, the teacher hesitates before each underlined word. If the words underlined previously are identified again, they are underlined again. The reading activity is followed by more sight practice with these words. Twice-underlined words are listed in random order or isolated from the story context by a window card so that clues are minimized and the newly underlined words are practiced.

Day 3: On rereading, those words still recognized in and out of context are printed on small cards by the teacher (so as to maintain model print) and are placed in the child's word bank. A new story can be produced on the second or third day for the active, excited learner, and the sequence begins again.

Organizing LEA Activities

Teachers using language experience need to be creative in stimulating both the dictated and the self-written stories and observations. The more the teacher relates the language experiences with ongoing classroom units and other activities, the more relevant the program will become. The general categories of stimulants discussed here are personal experiences, scientific observations and learning, nature, picture storytelling, role-playing through words, and folk and family stories. Stauffer (1970), Lee and Allen (1963), Herrick and Nerbourg (1964), Hall (1976), and Allen and Allen (1968) offer many more such possible stimulants.

Personal Experiences

Sharing personal experience should be handled with care. The teacher should never expose a child's personal difficulties, but she and the others in the class should delight in a child's joy. The following are some suggestions for sharing personal experiences in the context of classroom writing and dictation:

1. Introduction of the word "me" on the first day of first grade. The teacher, from that beginning, can carry out introductions in dictated stories that can be collected later into a book of self-portraits (see *A Day Dream I Had at Night* [1971] for ideas on how to make books).

2. Illustrated and accompanying stories about the family.
3. Personal lists of "Things to do."
4. Stories beginning with the following titles: "My Favorite Animal," "What I Hate to Do at Home," "My Favorite Relative," "The Most Beautiful Place I've Seen," "My Favorite TV Program," "My New Baby Sister," "What I Look Like," "My Mother," and "Our Trip."

Many teachers and scholars (e.g., Graves 1983) believe children should *not* be given story topics. When their stories are read carefully by their teacher as the topic of conferences, the children's dictations and writing increasingly become their own creations. Story topic ceases to be an issue.

Scientific Observations and Learnings

Any simple experiment performed by the children can be translated into an experience story. Ongoing notes of observations are a good idea. Some suggestions in this area are

1. Asking for descriptions of how an electrical circuit is made.
2. Asking, "Which objects floated and which did not?"
3. Keeping a weather chart to record seasonal change.
4. Asking, "Which objects are attracted by magnets and which are not?"
5. Asking, "Which of these foods have seeds inside and which do not?"
6. Asking, "What would have happened to our plants without water . . . without sun . . . with water . . . with sun (etc.)?"
7. Developing the concept of measurement of size determined by strings, of weight determined by a simple frame, of temperature, and of measurement of liquids.
8. Requesting descriptions of what happens when oil and water, sugar and water, and detergent and water are mixed.
9. Asking for descriptions of the effect of freezing and boiling water.

Nature

The world around the school environment is available to stimulate language experience no matter where the school is located. A few items that can be related to language experience follow.

1. The difference between how people move around outside on a snowy day and on a warm day. The teacher can ask for descriptions of how grown-ups and children differ in the way they move.
2. The construction (or demolition) of a nearby building.
3. Comparison of the school neighborhood with a contrasting one.
4. All of the foods eaten by the class gerbil or guinea pig. The teacher can ask the children to make a list of these items.
5. How the class animal cares for her young.

Picture Storytelling

This activity is an almost too common way of eliciting stories from the children. Therefore, the teacher must take care in selecting the pictures. As a criterion for choice, she might think of what story she could tell from any given picture. A few suggestions to develop this activity follow.

1. Asking, "How would the children in the picture live differently from the children in the class?"
2. Telling what tools each worker uses by looking at pictures.
3. Beginning to develop a sense of people's diversity by looking at pictures of people from different cultures.
4. Drawing pictures of a classmate, describing him in writing without naming him, and participating in a classroom guessing game to name him.
5. Dictating a story to accompany picture books without words.

Role-Playing through Words

In order to maximize the development of abstract language, the teacher should encourage the children to imagine themselves in a new situation. Much motivational introduction is needed before asking the following questions:

1. What would it be like to be an inchworm on the stem of a plant?
2. What would it be like to be a pencil?
3. What would it be like to be the school secretary?
4. What would it be like to be a mother?
5. What would it be like to be a Christmas tree?
6. What would it be like to be a worm in an apple?

Folk and Family Stories

In *A Day Dream I Had at Night* (1971), Landrum describes how older children of diverse backgrounds collected family stories to use as reading materials. Some suggestions for similar activities follow.

1. Each child asks for a special story about his family to be retold and written at school. In a class of children having immigrant parents, the move to America would be a productive source of story material. Each family's celebration of Christmas also might provide material, as might the family's move to a new area.
2. Each child thinks up a folktale after hearing the teacher read a number of folktales. Each child discusses with the teacher the stories' common characteristics.
3. The class plans to write fables after listening to *Aesop's Fables*.

Whatever techniques are used to stimulate writing and dictation, the teacher should be sure to allow interests to develop naturally from the stimulation that children bring to these programs. Although language experience is important to beginning literacy, other components also are needed.

ORGANIZING READING GROUPS

References have been made to reading groups, the classroom organizational structure used in most primary-grade classes. The purpose for dividing twenty-five children or more into smaller instructional units (more often than not into three groups) is to match children's ability to learn with the difficulty levels of the materials and instruction. As one might infer from previous discussions on language and literacy development, there are wide variations in how much experience children from the same community bring to formal reading instruction. Moreover, there are variations in the extent of literacy knowlege depending on the socioeconomic values of the community and the kind of instruction in the kindergartens. Considering the complexity that many novices face in learning to read, the division of a class of children into more "teachable" groups is sensible. But, as pointed out by Barr and Dreeben (1983) in their description of instructional effects on reading learning, some cost accompanies grouping decisions.

One may imagine a homogenous group of children who have had similarly effective experiences with literacy. Such a class would form one instructional group to allow the teacher to provide more time for direct instruction and more supervision of seatwork than would occur if she had to manage three instructional groups. Indeed, some schools with several classes of each group regroup across the classes to obtain homogeneity in reading instruction. Even in these instances, the decision to instruct the whole group as a unit means that several pupils will be working at such a level of frustration that little will be accomplished; others who are quite independent will not be challenged and will have to continue to learn on their own. (I remember the agony of whole-class oral recitation in my own schooling; I tried to figure out whether the risk of losing the place in the book by reading ahead and being interested in the story was worse than listening to my classmates who painfully read word-by-word.)

The alternative grouping arrangements described in these pages result in cost, too. For as the teacher attends more closely to individual progress in one smaller reading group, the other children will have less time for direct teacher interaction, and they will receive less supervision of their work. There are several effects associated with grouping. Barr and Dreeben (1983) demonstrated that the more children are able to read successfully, the more complicated their reading materials became. Thus, mean group aptitude predicted the amount of basal coverage; because of the interwoven character of the basals, basal coverage predicted how many words and phonics concepts were learned. Moreover, and somewhat worrisome, Barr and Dreeben also found that teacher instructional time was correlated with the extent of phonics instruction so that those learning the more advanced phonics skills were also the pupils receiving more direct teacher instruction. Barr and Dreeben explained this phenomenon was due to the greater complexity of the instruction at the higher levels.

The message from this work, for me at least, is: Due to the nearly inevitable character of the aptitude associations with initial reading acquisition, the teacher needs to do two things to encourage learning among the lower-aptitude children in regard to organization. First, the teacher must maintain higher expectations than may feel comfortable. When such children are unable to cope with a fast rate of new-word introduction and new phonics embedded in the basals, modifications are needed. These modifications can include practice with word cards, repeated readings, writing using a word bank, prepared oral reading presentations, and the application of phonics in text. Thus, the slower beginning readers receive appropriately designed experiences at a fast pace. It is also critical that these slower-learning children receive a fair share of the teacher's instructional time. I would suggest that if any group ought to have more teacher time than others, it is the low group.

When the adverse costs of grouping are diminished in these ways, grouping children for reading (but not for writing, language, or literature experiences) makes sense. The question, then, is when and how to determine group membership. Some teachers delay organizing groups for two or three months into the first grade; most, however, form groups in the first month. Early group formation is quite common in schools with mandated competency programs. Assignment of pupils to groups usually is determined by scores on aptitude and reading readiness tests. If there are no such tests, or, indeed, to supplement these tests, informal assessment of literacy skills is highly recommended.

During the first two weeks, several major literacy skills may be assessed in test parts administered to individuals and groups. For example, group tests may be used to assess the recognition of letters and words, the writing of letters and words, and the associations of letters and sounds as shown in Chart 17.

Because the pupils may not understand the directions in Chart 17 or be so unfamiliar with testing that their real knowledge is not being properly assessed and because further knowledge is needed, individual testing of each child on the several parts of this assessment also is recommended. Children who appear to know a few words should be asked to read segments of the first preprimer;

CHART 17. Sample test items for group assessment

Teacher Direction	Test Form			
Letter and word recognition				
• Draw a circle around the *A*.	b	d	a	o
• Draw a circle around the word *boy*.	the	boy	man	is
Letter and word writing				
• On the space next to the ball, make a *b*.	O _____			
• On the next line, write the word *come*.	_____			
Sound and letter associations				
• I will say some words that all begin with the same sound: *small, sun, snake*. Draw a circle around the letter for that sound.	m	s	l	t

those youngsters who make very few errors should read in the next, and so on. Teachers may want to find pupils' knowledge of high-frequency words as well (Fry et al. 1984).

The next step is to gather all the materials of the group and individual assessments, assign a scoring system to each, and rank the children by total scores. This ranking provides data for the first tentative group assignment as well as information about the instructional needs of each group. It is important to note the word "tentative"; further observation of pupil progress undoubtedly will require several shifts. Among the first grade teachers Barr and Dreeben (1983) studied, many moved pupils from one to another group in the course of the year.

The informal test data may be at variance with normed test scores. In such cases, my recommendation is to rely on the informal data, especially if the teacher believes the child was uncomfortable in the test-taking sessions. It is important that such children are monitored carefully for possible misunderstanding of their potential to learn to read and write.

Once groups are formed, the teacher matches each to the appropriate level of the materials. Children who read a few words may be placed in the second of several preprimers. Children who have the prereading skills but who know only one or two words are placed at the first preprimer. Children needing more letter recognition and phonemic analysis skills require readiness work and initial, firm learning of several high-frequency words prior to movement into the preprimers. Those pupils who are independent at the first reader or above level, as determined by oral reading with word recognition rates of 95% accuracy or above and reasonable comprehension, must be placed in more challenging materials, even if this placement requires another instructional group.

For continued review of progress, and in addition to the close observation of pupils within groups, informal individual assessment should be included as part of the instructional time during January and at the end of the academic year. At these sessions, reading group instruction is brief, seatwork is given out, and the teacher asks individuals to read current and more advanced materials aloud. Keeping track of errors in oral reading (see the last section) as well as the extent and kind of comprehension response, a teacher may determine (in midyear) the appropriateness of group assignments, particular difficulties that require change in approach, and the overall effects of instruction.

Beginning teachers find management of reading groups quite a challenge, for the instruction must not only be appropriate to each level, but children must also learn from the teacher how to behave to conform to the goals of instruction. The tensions that occur as at least two-thirds of the pupils work at their seats while the teacher attends closely to the reading of a small group must be overcome. It is especially important that all pupils become independent in solving work problems and in overcoming other difficulties by drawing upon class regulations, their own resources, and the help of others. Uncontrolled access to teachers during reading is disruptive and potentially harmful to progress in reading.

The seatwork assigned to children during the time the reading groups meet should occupy the pupils well; the exercises should provide good practice and even challenge, and they should be simple enough to be completed independently. It is difficult for young children to understand the specific directions of one worksheet; often, the youngsters must understand how to complete several. For this reason, instruction on how to follow directions, including reading written directions, is essential. To cope with the demands to provide enough seatwork to occupy the children during the reading group time and to ensure that the work is profitable, the considerable reliance on commercial materials is not surprising.

Workbook activities may provide good practice for children when their group is not meeting. And it is sometimes appropriate for teachers to provide more practice by developing special worksheets for groups and individuals. When pupils have learned good work habits, the youngsters may be able to engage in more free-time activities in work centers. But probably the most important addition to seatwork is pupil writing exercises. As suggested in the previous discussion and in Chapter 7, children may write on many topics: Some writing may be directed by the class activities, including the stories being read; some may be personal expressions, and some may be part of a daily journal. For writing activities to work well and to free the teacher to concentrate on the reading groups, the children must be able to independently spell the words they need. Thus, for very practical reasons, the teacher ought to support the use of word banks, individual spelling books, dictionaries, and the freedom to figure out words on their own.

Within the reading groups, teachers often are bothered by pupil callouts, the intrusion of one child's "help" as another is reading. Children must learn that their own errors help them learn; each time a child self corrects and is praised, this point becomes clearer. Teachers need to make their disapproval of callouts clear by clarifying comments and by ignoring any which do occur. Interruptions of connected reading constitute a threat to desired goals of fluency and meaningfulness.

In all, the whole point of grouping for reading instruction is to enable teachers to reach each pupil's needs and interests effectively. This purpose can direct self-assessment of teaching. For example, teachers can determine whether their time allocations are in line with student needs. Since slower students need supervised learning more than the others, they deserve more teacher time. And teacher time can be provided to the slower pupils if the more-advanced pupils experience sequentially and carefully planned independent activities. It is not an easy matter to provide good practice through seatwork, but it is possible with careful selection among the commercial materials, the development of further materials, and the encouragement of writing.

ORAL AND SILENT READING MODES

Although teachers and parents of young children, clerics, and poets are exceptions, most adults seldom read aloud. Those who do develop techniques for oral reading delivery to enhance listener comprehension; good oral reading is performance-based. By contrast, silent reading among skilled readers is internal and seldom directed by conscious effort. If conscious effort is applied to silent reading, it is usually effort directed toward increased comprehension (for example, an effort to read for an examination). With beginning readers, oral and silent reading do not differ so much, but the preferred mode for instruction was a hotly debated issue among educators for many years.

Until the late nineteenth century, reading instruction was essentially oral. Pupils read chorally in groups; individual recitations of prepared materials were common. When examined from his comprehension perspective, Huey (1908) found such practice limited, and he urged that teachers use the silent reading mode. Other educators agreed that oral reading put too much emphasis upon performance and thereby detracted from the development of good comprehension. In 1920, several professors of education published papers in a volume from the National Society for the Study of Education which decried the superficiality of recitation reading in the schools. Subsequent to this publication, the pendulum of instructional change shifted (as it often does), and silent reading became the advocated mode (in some cases, to the exclusion of oral reading). By the 1940s, authorities in reading were recommending a balanced use of both modes (Allington 1984).

Today, much of the reading in primary-grade instructional groups is still oral. The extent of the oral mode depends in some measure on the reading level of the group. For example, in first grades, low reader groups read orally about 90% of the time; high groups read orally about 40% of the time. Group differences were found through the fifth grade (Allington 1984). Such data raise a difficult question, and one that is not easily answered: Is this difference due to reading ability, or does it contribute to reading problems? Probably both parts of this question are true to some extent. The discussion to follow suggests that instructional practice during oral reading may modify some of the group differences.

The Purpose and Practice of Oral Reading

Imagining a beginning reading event with a teacher and several children, we may understand why initial reading instruction is so often oral. In a DRL with beginners at the preprimer level, for example, imagine the following page of text read silently:

> Can I go with you?
> Get in.
> Then we will go up. (American Book Company 1977)
> (Each new line/sentence is preceded by a picture of a story character to indicate the person speaking.)

Using the silent reading mode, the teacher may ask pupils to read the page and then may ask comprehension questions to guide further reading. But to ask questions about this page that would demonstrate strictly reading comprehension is nearly impossible since the meaning depends, to a large extent, on the illustrations; pupils who are falling behind in word learning may be able to answer questions without actually reading. Given the limitations of a beginning reader's vocabulary, it is very difficult to produce text that does not rely on the pictures. Thus, the teacher is unable to assess reading growth when using the silent mode during the crucial transition period. Therefore, it becomes difficult for teachers to make sound instructional decisions.

During this period, the oral mode is preferred. Oral reading enables the teacher to determine student progress and to draw upon children's story comprehension knowledge. And because oral reading produces language that resembles storybook experiences and talk, it provides a familiar means toward literacy acquisition. Oral reading, moreover, has the potential of being an excellent medium for learning about reading. Because fluent reading is particularly difficult for slow beginners to achieve, teachers may use various oral reading methods to help the youngsters develop greater fluency.

Unfortunately, as described in Chapter 6, some instructional practices experienced by slower readers may limit their progress. Not only do teachers tend to focus poor readers on sound/symbol cues and good readers on meaning cues (Chapter 6), but also more pupil callouts and teacher prompts occur in low-reader groups (Allington 1980). Disruptions of oral reading prevent children from learning about fluent expression. While these phenomena have been perceived as teacher produced (Allington 1980), we found teacher behavior related with pupil reading skill more than with low pupil status (Pflaum, Pascarella, Boswick, and Auer 1980). It seems that as teachers try to maintain attention on the reading, and as pupils in the low group make many errors and hesitations, the prompts are the teachers' way of trying to keep the reading flowing (Hoffman and Clements 1983).

A common oral reading structure is for children to read segments of text in turn and aloud. There is some evidence that in the higher reading groups, these turns take place according to seating arrangements; movements from one reader to another occur smoothly. In low groups, however, the turns are open to bid, and time taken to assign reading is much greater (McDermott 1977). Again, we see a pattern of disruption, which perhaps is caused by teachers' desire to gain the interest and attention of the low readers.

This conflict between the teaching goal—fluent reading—and teaching behavior—interruptions—may be understood through yet another observation. Many teachers of beginners feel obligated to bring all their pupils to the most advanced level as possible in an academic year. Indeed, the study of instructional pace by Barr and Dreeben (1983) suggests this desire is in line with improved learning. The teacher is torn between expectations that all children complete the first-grade reading program and the difficulty of achieving these expectations. Teachers try to move the low groups into successively more difficult material, often before pupils are ready. But children who require many repetitive experiences to remember words, who have difficulty applying phonic skills to reading, and who have not yet become fluent may not benefit from situations in which they are reading at their frustration level (accuracy rates below 85 to 90%). To increase instructional pace for slower readers and to provide experiences at a level where learning may occur may be accomplished by having slower readers read several texts at the same level (simple tradebooks or several preprimers from different basal programs). In this way, the youngsters have more material to read, and they experience practice toward fluency with restricted vocabularies. The *Laidlaw Reading Program* (1980) provides for some appropriate practice with its prebasic readers at each level and expansion texts for those needing greater challenge.

Oral reading appears to have an important place in the beginning of reading instruction. However, differences in how oral reading experiences occur by achievement groups suggest that we may not be taking full advantage of oral reading as a medium for instruction.

Oral Reading Instruction

We have seen that oral reading is a preferred mode for reading instruction, at least at the start. Not only does oral reading allow the teacher to make informed decisions about instruction and pupil progress, but it also provides a medium for direct instruction in reading. Chart 18 outlines several ways in which oral reading can be appropriate for reading instruction.

Storybook experiences ought to continue into the primary grades. The teacher models fluent oral reading in this way. But for many pupils, further modelling is required. The initial oral reading by the teacher of text stories was mentioned previously as an alternative to the DRL. When children understand that they, too, will be expected to produce fluent oral rendering of the story the teacher reads, a different kind of attention may be expected (Hoffman and Crone 1984). By having several sets of tapes and book copies of stories available, children may listen and read. The most important form of modelling may be during the initial, guided reading. When pupils have difficulty putting their word-by-word reading into coherent language, the teacher may, once the reading is over, praise the success of the word reading and provide a model of how those words sound when read fluently. That is, after the halting reading of "The . . . pe . . . people on my st . . . str . . . eet . . . street go to work . . . in the m . . . morn . . . But . . . not what . . . man, th . . . that man." the teacher says, "good reading. Listen now as I read it, "The people . . ." In this context, several rereadings may occur and, as fluency increases, the focus turns to comprehension.

Practice is a major way to learn, and reading is no exception. It is important to provide plenty of opportunities for beginning readers to read and reread. To

CHART 18. Recommended oral reading instructional strategies

Modelling of oral reading

Rereading for fluency

Reading as a search for sentence constituents

Rereading to find supportive details and other story information

Learning self-correction skills

Using teacher-prompting behaviors to support fluency, word attack skills, and comprehension apply this principle to beginning reading, let us recall Vygotsky's (1978) zone of proximal development. The level at which a child may perform when reading independently contrasts with the level possible when reading with guidance from the teacher. Ideally, a similar contrast exists with the DRL guided reading lesson. That is, during initial reading, the teacher provides a framework for success at a challenging level. This framework is developed through the initial introduction of difficult new words and concepts, guidance about story content and prior knowledge, and (minimal) prompts and aids when reading falters. When the difficulty level between the group's independent level and their instructional level is not great, the children will be able to incorporate the prompted help and reread successfully. On the other hand, if the distance is great, fluent reading will not occur, and adjustments are required.

Not only does the oral reading mode provide opportunities for the teacher to model fluent reading and to give pupils the chance for good practice through rereading, specific opportunities are needed to demonstrate how the oral language the youngsters know is helpful to their reading. For example, after a first or second story reading, once the pupils have demonstrated comprehension of a story, the teacher may direct them to particularly difficult points in the story and, through an interactive discussion, show them how their language knowledge will help them predict what is to come. Observe the following text:

> Big Fish was grumpy.
> He was grumpy because he was hungry.
> He was hungry because there was nothing to eat.
> Why was there nothing to eat?
> This is why. (Allyn and Bacon 1977)

The teacher uses this text to lead readers to use their language knowledge. For example,

> *Teacher:* Turn to the beginning of the story, and look at the first sentence. I want to help you see how your reading is very much like talking and listening. So look away from the book. And . . . Michael, please read the first sentence.
> *Pupil:* Big Fish was grumpy.
> *Teacher:* If you just heard that and didn't know a thing about the story, *Big Fish Was Grumpy,* what do you suppose would come next?
> *Pupil:* We would find out why he was grumpy.
> *Teacher:* Right, and that's what happens. And what word do you use when you are explaining something to someone, when you have said something that needs more information? Don't you use *because*? Joan, read the next sentence, and see if *because* is there.
> *Pupil:* ———
> *Teacher:* Now we have another statement about Big Fish. What would you want to know if you were listening to someone who said this?
> *Pupil:* We would want to know why he was hungry.
> *Teacher:* And what word is used to answer *why*?
> *Pupil:* Because.

Teacher: And what do you already know about why someone might be hungry?
Pupil: ———
Teacher: Do you see how reading is like listening? When you expect something—and we expected a *because*—you often find it. Just knowing how to listen helps reading.

During oral rereading, an alternative to round-robin repetitive reading practice is to ask pupils to reread to answer specific questions of a story, questions that require a search through the story. Pupils are asked to read aloud the portion of the story that answers a question or adds to the discussion, such as "Find the paragraph that tells why . . . ," or "Joan, you thought the girl in the story was brave. Would you find a sentence that shows that is so. And since there are several sentences, everyone else should also look for these sentences."

Oral reading is also the medium for instruction in self-correction, the strategy that we found was more common among good than poor readers, but something the poor readers could learn (Pflaum and Pascarella 1980). The instruction we used with poor readers involved regular classroom reading materials (Pascarella and Pflaum 1981). First, the pupils learned to find their own reading errors. Because it is difficult for children to initially think about their mistakes, we asked the teachers to read sentences and paragraphs with deliberate "errors" the children were to find. When they were good at finding those errors, the children taped their own reading and, while reading along, identified where their reading did not make sense. The next step was to learn the difference between an important error—the kind that made the text impossible to understand—and little errors—those errors on function words, for example, that did not disrupt the meaning. Once the children could determine the serious errors in their oral reading, they then learned how to self correct. Because this method required that pupils read with sufficient context for self-correction, it was crucial that the children read with reasonable accuracy while yet with sufficient challenge to err for practice self correcting (between 90 and 94% accuracy). The pupils first learned the meaning of self-correction and how the reading of an entire sentence or just a few words helped in self-correction. The pupils were taught to think about what word would make sense according to the letter cues. With worksheets used interactively with the teacher, these principles were applied to real errors. And children who were reading above the first-grade level learned to use the sense of the text better; their achievement improved.

The final recommendation for using oral reading as the medium for instruction has to do with teacher prompts. Fortunately, we know more about the effects of teacher prompts than we have before. Using the findings from work by Hoffman and his colleagues (1984) and unpublished work by myself and my colleagues, the following guidelines are strongly recommended for all readers:

Delay interruptions and prompts until at least the end of the sentence.
Eliminate pupil callouts by making it plain that one learns better reading by figuring out one's own errors.

Ignore errors that do not change the meaning of the text.

Focus on the meaningfulness of the sentence and the difficult word(s).

Use comments such as the following to help pupils recover, and use the comments in this order: "You had trouble with this word." (point) "Go back to the beginning of the sentence, read it again, and figure out what word would be a sensible one there that begins with *D*." . . . "Yes, good self correcting. Now, read the whole sentence." Or say, "No, almost. The word is *grumpy.*"

The point of these exchanges about difficult words is that the teacher guides the reader to independence. The reading guidance is an example of the teacher leading the pupil in areas of challenge and growth. Thus, oral reading serves as a medium through which to accomplish many important aspects of learning at the initial stage. In the next discussion, how oral reading helps the teacher assess progress and plan instructional strategy is described.

Oral Reading Assessment

By observing how children read aloud, teachers and researchers have learned a lot about individual performance and how reading skill develops. We found in Chapter 6 that observations of the errors first-grade readers make have led to several understandings of the process of beginning reading growth: how children come to integrate different cues, how the progress experienced by good and poor beginners differs, and how teacher feedback appears to partially influence that growth.

Oral reading analysis is based on assessing the deviations from text and the type and significance of the deviations each reader makes. Although early oral reading tests did not differentiate meaning—and nonmeaning—change errors, self-corrections versus errors, and different dialect pronunciations and errors, most oral reading measures follow the procedures, the scoring system, and, to a much lesser extent, the analysis of the earlier tests (e.g., Spache 1963). That is, the examiner follows the pupil reading closely and marks in his or her copy of the test those words on which the reader substituted another word, those which were mispronounced (often the same), reversals of letters, insertions of new words, and omissions of text words. The number of errors proportional to the number of words in the passage determines the accuracy. The number of correct responses to subsequent comprehension questions determines comprehension. The new informal reading inventories (IRI's) include more than one form of the test so that it is possible to compare comprehension of passages at different levels in the oral and the silent mode.

Oral reading analysis is intended to help classroom and remedial teachers determine a pupil's reading progress and level for instruction. Drawn from standardized measures of oral reading, the many popular IRI's on the market today typically contain several sequential, rather short prose passages; each passage purports to measure a specific reading level. According to the level at which pupils perform well in accuracy and comprehension, pupils are placed in reading texts that presumably correspond to their achievement. Teachers search for each pupil's independent level, instructional level, and frustration level to find out where an individual may be challenged and may experience growth through teacher guidance.

The criteria to determine these levels originally were established by Betts (1954) based on work by his student, Kilgallon. The independent level was determined on *oral rereading* after initial silent reading by only fourth graders as 99% word accuracy and 90% comprehension; the instructional level was where a pupil had 95% accuracy and 75% comprehension; the frustration level, never well-operationalized, was below 95% accuracy and 50% comprehension. Amazingly, considering the unscientific origin of these criteria, they continue to be used in IRI's, with some small adjustments here and there.

While some IRI's have materials at only one first-grade-reader level, my favorite IRI, that by Woods and Moe (1981), includes both a primer and first-reader level. The directions are clear, and the material is long enough to be relatively reliable but short enough for teachers to complete in 15 to 20 minutes. However, like other IRI's, the Woods and Moe test assumes that a single oral reading is a reliable source for determining placement, perhaps an unwarranted assumption (Riske 1982). Moreover, since it is quite difficult for several users of a particular test to agree with one another about the scoring and interpretation of errors (Pflaum 1979), the results of these tests may be too idiosyncratic to be meaningful.

A more valid way to use oral reading to assess progress is periodic assessment of oral reading behaviors during day-to-day reading. Based on miscue analysis by Goodman (1976), the work in the first-grade observation studies, and from my own research, there are specific oral reading behaviors in unskilled readers that help determine progress. These behaviors are described in Chart 19.

As teachers take an assessment of pupils' reading once or twice during the first year with individual readings from the class texts, they can assess if current placements are correct. If not, further analysis will be needed in other texts. It is relatively easy to do this assessment if a selection is copied and if these copies are used to score each reader. These records are a good source for deciding on instructional direction. For example, if a teacher were to find that several members of a group, while correctly placed, were not self correcting well, it would be a good idea to extend that aspect of oral reading. If the pupils of a group are not using the phonogram knowledge tests suggest they have, then further practice on application is needed, perhaps with the teacher modelling.

While oral reading is believed to be the better mode for initial reading than silent reading, once progress is underway, oral reading is of limited value to young readers.

The Transition to Silent Reading

By the time children are reading at the primer or first-reader levels, silent reading should be introduced. There are obvious reasons to encourage early silent reading. Independent readers are, of course, silent readers. When reading silently, children do not need to perform; the emphasis begins to be where it ought to

CHART 19. Oral reading indices of beginning readers

Error or Miscue	Illustration
Types	*Substitution:* "county" for country, deviation written over text word. *(county written above country)*
	Insertion: "I am coming" for I come, written with a carat over text word. *(am, ing written above)*
	Omission: "girls" for boys and girls. Omission is circled. *(boys and circled)*
	Reversals: "Says the cow" for The cow says as marked. *(marked with reversal lines)*
Interpretation	*Meaning change:* Does the miscue change the meaning of the sentence/passage?
	Correction: Is the miscue corrected? If so, mark a small *c* next to the miscue.
	Graphic cue use: Does the miscue show use of initial, medial, and final letter of text word? Use a different color to circle the miscue.
	Dialect influence: Mark this miscue with a small *d*, and ignore it.
Scoring	Determine the error rate by comparing the proportion of noncorrected errors to total words.
	Count the meaning change and nonmeaning-change errors as proportional to miscues (all deviations).
	Count self-corrected miscues as proportional to noncorrected miscues.
	Count miscues with use of graphic cues (by position).
Significance	Pupils are in correct placement and doing well at that level when they have
	• Error rates above 95%
	• Self-corrections close to 30%
	• Meaning-change rates lower than 50%
	• Most miscues showing use of graphic cues

be: on reading for meaning. After much practice, silent reading is faster than oral reading; therefore, more can be read in a school day. Silent reading frees instructional time in the reading groups for the other essential parts of the DRL, for focus on understanding stories for their themes, and for extending reading from one story to another. During silent reading, all readers are expected to attend to reading, something that cannot be assured when one child is reading orally. In short, silent reading is a necessary condition to the acquisition of skilled reading behavior.

Pupils vary in their attitudes toward silent reading. For many, reading silently is a very natural outgrowth of strong reading beginnings. Some children, however, resist silent reading; often, those who resist silent reading have not yet experienced fluent reading. They need the experience of easy reading material. Moreover, in contrast to the natural silent readers, they need help through the transition to silent reading.

In keeping with other instructional practice, the teacher can ask children to describe adults who are reading. Being assured that they are ready to begin to do some reading like older children and adults, youngsters can begin by whispering small segments of a story during reading group. After the children have had several "whispering" sessions, the teacher asks the readers to take another step toward mature reading by having them read without making a sound. After a time, the teacher asks the children to try to read without moving their lips at all. In addition, as teachers assure that pupils have many opportunities for easy reading, make these reading suggestions during group reading, and develop other fix-up strategies, silent reading will emerge.

Once silent reading has begun in this way, the first reading in the DRL may be guided reading with each story segment read silently. As the pupils demonstrate good comprehension, the story segments read in each part are lengthened. In this way, pupils are prepared to read an entire story by themselves, silently. Rereading becomes necessary with difficult material, for new expository reading experiences, and when occasional assessment of progress is needed. But as reading experiences continue, the pace of reading quickens, and independence is achieved.

WRITING EXPERIENCES IN THE TRANSITION TO INDEPENDENCE

This chapter contains several references to the use of writing as a means to enhance the reading program. In the first section, writing was recommended as a good way to encourage children to reflect on story theme. Writing is a critical component of the language experience approach. Writing also must be considered for its independent contribution to literacy growth, the topic of this section.

Instruction contributes to the development of independence in writing. Not only should young children have daily experiences writing materials they compose themselves, but certain practices that come out of the observations of the writing process also contribute to independence. Like skilled writers, children benefit when they experience the following steps in creating writings: preparation for writing; planning; drafting—writing; rereading and rethinking; and rewriting (optional) (adapted from Temple, Nathan, and Burris 1982).

Teachers often prepare their whole class for a writing experience through some kind of stimulation and direction such as described in the section on LEA. Once a writing program is underway, group writings on common topics may continue; however, individual preparation may be appropriate (Graves 1983). If journal writing, for example, has begun and is understood, the preparation comes through reflection about what has been written, teacher responses, and the experiences that precede the writing and that lead to new ideas and comments. In the workshop approach to writing, preparation for writing comes out of teacher-pupil consultations about current writing and the stimulation of classroom and personal activities (Calkins 1982; Graves 1983).

When teachers select the topics for group writings, they are able to help children move into new forms of writing. For example, teachers may establish an unusual object which is described, thereby encouraging beginnings of expository, transactional writing. If the experience is to describe a flower, for example, the teacher might prepare the writing by asking children to tell what they see, to reveal words they might need, and to read a short description. If the focus is on the poetic, the preparation would be more open, with talk about words, sensations, and rhythms suggested by the flower.

When children experience the effects of planning on writing, they begin to understand its usefulness. It is possible for children to learn to use scraps of paper to jot down ideas they want to include in a piece before the actual draft begins. I used to ask students to spend a few minutes writing words to use before the papers were distributed. For good planning, children learn they can start over several times. As teachers emphasize the *thinking* that is involved in composing, the children will begin to do what more experienced writers do: They will scratch out material they reject. For their work to be successful, in other words, children who are in first and second grades should understand that there are two key segments to the development of a piece for others to read: the draft and the final form.

Drafting begins once the plans are made. Just as skilled writers need uninterrupted times for writing, the teacher might establish the drafting times as the time when children may only consult with the teacher, not each other; interruptions may damage the composing of others.

The next step is to reread and to reconsider. Of all the parts of the writing process, this step is probably the most critical in teaching writing. Consultation with individual writers or groups of pupils about a *draft* emphasizes the work in progress, not the finished piece. (See Calkins 1982; Graves 1984 for full descriptions of the consultations over drafts.) Children gain the ability to examine their expression as they read their piece to the teacher and explain where changes might be made. Good, probing questions engage the pupils in identifying how their original ideas had changed in the course of the drafting. Since it is common for children to inadvertently leave out some of their ideas, talk with classmates who act as critical readers also may improve the rethinking and may help formulate plans for rewriting. One way for teachers to help beginning writers express themselves is to engage the whole group in a review of one sample piece. Of course, to select one pupil's work for group criticism is risky, and teachers must be careful to select one of the more mature pieces, to obtain agreement of the author, and to rewrite the piece anonymously. After identifying the positive elements, the rereading process is demonstrated as pupils read the sample draft. Initially, the teacher indicates how he might read the material critically, examining the sequence of ideas, the use of words used in expression, the logic and coherence, and the use of punctuation and spelling. With greater experience, the children take on this task for themselves. Finally, the rereading and rethinking about a draft leads to plans for rewriting.

The final step in the process of writing is the rewriting, the step which may be considered optional for young writers. Considering the physical demands of writing on young children, to fulfill the expectations identified for rewriting may be sufficiently difficult that only the most important writings are brought to conclusion. In this way, children learn that the thinking involved in good writing is at least as important as appearance. Less negative response to the process of thinking and writing is likely when the writers, themselves, are allowed to make decisions about which of their work deserves a rewriting to a finished product.

When children are beginning to enjoy writing, they enjoy writing in different modes (not only the expressive and expository modes); they write simple stories and poetry. Either as a direct stimulant to new writing or as an indirect influence on pupils' writing, good stories and poems that are read to the class expand children's writing options. Talk about the structure, words, ideas, expression of feelings, sensations expressed, and the rhythms of poetry encourages new exploration. Teacher acceptance and pleasure in even a short string of words that express a new idea begin an outpouring of poems. And when that expression is realized through preservation of children's work in collections for all to read, the message is clear: Their writing is important and valued.

When children gather in a group to read and discuss a story, each individual learns that there are several ways to respond. These group discussions, especially in the kinds of interactions described above as modifications of the DRL, provide young readers with opportunities to experience a little distance from their own interpretations of reading. Comparing their ideas with the ideas of others expands children's thinking. In writing, too, reading the work of classmates is a fruitful way for children to think about their own writing, about different ways of expression, and about different ways people think about a particular topic. The process of reading the work of others is enhanced when children's writings are preserved and collected. Chart 20 describes alternatives for collecting and preserving children's work.

CHART 20.   Collecting and transforming children's writings

Type	Procedure
Individual folders	Give each pupil a folder for drafts and work-in-progress, drafts not to be rewritten, and rewritten work. (This procedure is useful for the facilitation of pupil decisions and for teacher, parent, and pupil assessment of progress.)
Blank notebooks	Use blank notebooks for ongoing journal writing, responses to stories, and storing good ideas, good words, etc.
Content for class books	Create individual pupils' books containing the best rewritten materials of all sorts.
	Use class books: poems, stories, descriptions, family stories, fantasies, etc.
Construction of books	Have writing in cloth-bound books.
	Create books with illustrations, cover the pages with clear plastic, and bind the pages with staples, tape, large yarn, metal rings, etc.
	Make covers class activity projects; have the children create books from all sorts of sized papers, including tiny books from a reduced-copy machine.

The preservation and collection of children's writings expand the audience for reading and for writing to parallel that of the publishing world. Children in classrooms that encourage the sharing of individual work profit from one another.

THE ACCORDIAN METAPHOR EXTENDED—A SUMMARY

The accordian metaphor of Chapter 5 has not been part of the discussion in these last chapters of formal school literacy instruction. If an interactive teaching style that understands and expands children's language and initial literacy concepts is appropriate at home and in preschools, we can ask why it is not also appropriate after formal instruction begins. One explanation may be that the skills of reading such as new phonic skills, for example, constitute new material for children; as a result, teaching is not so much a matter of interaction as it is a matter for direct presentation of new material. Direct didactic teaching of new material would not suit the interactive teaching mode of the accordian metaphor.

On the other hand, reading and writing growth also can be seen as the product of internally constructed systems of understanding. We have seen how many children, in fact, construct a system for reading and writing with relatively little new direct instruction. We also have noted that many children learn to read and write without much difficulty in the first and second grades. These children have not read before school but have had a sufficiently enriched preparation for reading and writing so that the increasing vocabularies, the application of new word analysis skills, the increasingly complex prose, and, importantly, the teacher guidance that helps them read in a context like that of the zone of proximal development create a situation much like the picture presented in the accordian metaphor of Chapter 5.

For those children who do not easily acquire initial reading and writing, however, it may appear that an interactive teaching style that expands upon current knowledge is not sufficient. Teaching accommodations for children who experience a slow beginning with literacy have been emphasized in these pages. For one example, children who do not apply skills for reading independence may need to observe the modelling of that application, considerable practice, and careful use of skills in texts. For another, when self-correction is not naturally acquired, direct explanation of each part of that process can be presented, practiced, and applied to actual reading. These teaching episodes do not appear to be like the interactive teaching of the metaphor. Yet, it can be argued that the modelling and practice involved in the teaching of effective strategies is, indeed, part of this view of instruction.

When a teacher determines that some children are not applying phonogram knowledge, for example, to new words containing familiar parts, the review of the application process which will ensue is based upon a reanalysis of the pupils' current knowledge. To return to the phonograms and review them is to assure the base for which the interactive teaching will emerge. Subsequent experiences include explanation, modelling, application, and discussion of how to approach such new words in text. These experiences, in fact, are based on current knowledge and occur in a context in which the talk, modelling, practice, etc. take the pupils from one level of understanding to the next. Thus, while it may appear that some of the technical skills of reading (phonics instruction in particular) do not fit into an instructional metaphor that emphasizes children's internal construction of systematic knowledge, we may argue that the failure to learn well is partially the result of *not* using such an interactive approach. Let us conclude, then, by applying the accordian metaphor in this instance to the acquisition of reading and writing in general. (See Figure 4.)

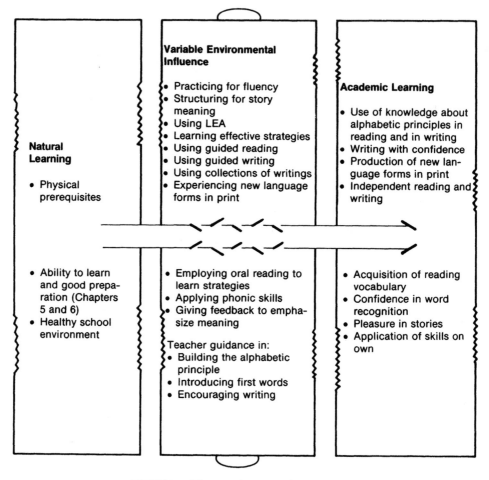

FIGURE 4. *The accordian metaphor and literacy*

SELECTED ACTIVITIES

1. Select an unfamiliar primer or first reader. Read one story carefully. Choose a major idea (one or two) that you think exemplifies the story significance for young children. Jot the idea(s) down. Check the back of the book for the new words introduced in the story. Identify any words you think will pose meaning difficulty. Plan how to introduce the new words so that pupils will have to respond to them several times (singly, in sentences, on cards, etc.). How might you relate the meaning words to words the children know? Write down how you would introduce the story by drawing on prior experiences and focusing on the main ideas. Then, write several questions you would use to guide the reading toward these ideas. Decide upon a follow-up activity that extends these ideas.

   Now, compare your plan with the teacher's guide: Were your ways of introducing the new words good? Did the guide direct the teacher to the meaning difficult words? How does your introduction differ from the guide? Does the guide focus on the same main ideas? How do your questions for guided reading differ? Is there a follow-up activity for the story like yours? Which plan would you prefer to follow?

2. Try the DRTA using a story you like with a small group of pupils.

3. Examine a first-grade reading program to find the references to transitions from oral to silent reading.

4. Using the information of Chart 19, have a child read a selection aloud, and score the reading on a copy of the passage. Then, using the total words, determine the proportion of meaning-change, self-corrections, and graphic cues used. Decide, based on the accuracy rate and the proportional error types, if this is an appropriate instruction level for the child, keeping in mind the traditional criteria and your own sense of whether the child may be challenged—but not frustrated—at this level.

5. Observe a teacher (or tape yourself) conducting an oral reading lesson with a low reading group. Determine how many interruptions there are per paragraph read. Then, find where the interruptions occur (at the time of the error, at the end of the sentence). Then, note whether the prompts given direct the readers to graphic cues or to meaning. Do the same for the same teacher (yourself) guiding a high group. Compare the results.

6. Observe a morning's series of reading groups, and count the number of pupil callouts. Are there more callouts in the low than in the high groups?

Appendix A

Concepts for Instruction

Test items used are listed under each concept.

At 2.0

On top of
   favorite object, one
   table
On top of
   wood and dog
On top of
   horse, fence
Into
   box and animals
Close
   containers
Into
   box and chips
On top of
   hands and table
Open
   puppets
Out of
   box and chips
Open
   containers
Soft
   block versus felt
Many
   apples
Closed
   puppets
Up
   doll

Dirty
   socks
Big
   shoes
Fast
   car
Dirty
   paper
Loud
   sticks
Under
   bridge and car
Out of
   box and animals
Wet
   moisteners
Form
   circle insets
Down
   dolls
Through
   tunnel and train
Wet
   cloths
Over
   bridge and car
Full
   container of water
Down
   stairs

Through
   box and dog
Soft
   rock versus cotton
Form
   circle, blocks
One
   apples
Black
   horse
Form
   square, blocks
Empty
   container of water
High
   planes
Hard
   block versus felt
Light
   bean bag
White
   thread
Dry
   cloths
Short
   cylinders
Loud
   salt shakers
Big
   horse

230

Little
  horse
Form
  square insets
Full
  jar of beans
Over
  bridge and plane
Clean
  paper
Up
  stairs
Low
  windows
Empty
  jar of beans
Heavy
  bean bags
Clean
  socks
Low
  planes
Skinny
  blocks
Skinny
  crayons
Soft
  sticks
Short
  trains
Soft
  salt shakers

Long
  cylinders
Smooth
  paper
Slow
  car
Black
  thread
Fat
  crayons
Dry
  moisteners
Fast
  xylophone and stick
Under
  bridge and plane
Over
  wood and dog
Hard
  rock versus cotton
Long
  train
High
  windows
Rough
  paper
Little
  shoes
Littlest
  cups
Fat
  blocks

White
  horse
Light
  box and rocks
Littlest
  cylinders
Over
  horse and fence
Heavy
  box
Biggest
  cylinders
Biggest
  cups
One
  dot
Smooth
  burlap versus cotton
Many
  dots
Rough
  burlap versus satin
Under
  hands and table
Under
  favorite object and table
Slow
  xylophone and stick
Around
  box and dog
Around
  tunnel and train

At 3.0
Into
  box and animals
Out of
  box and animals
On top of
  wood and dog
Little
  horse
Black
  horse
Next to
  cowboy and horse
Down
  doll
Wet
  cloths

Open
  containers
Dirty
  napkin
Up
  doll
Top
  truck
Move
  sparklers
Under
  bridge and car
Big
  horse
Littlest
  cup

Closed
  puppets
Full
  jar of beans
One
  apples
Clean
  napkins
Form
  2-piece puzzle
Hard
  block and felt
Through
  box and dog
Many
  dots

Not move
  sparklers
Dry
  moisteners
Biggest
  cup
Forward
  doll
Soft
  block and felt
Under
  table and favorite object
Short
  train
Empty
  jar of beans
White
  thread

Rough
  paper
One
  dot
More
  chips
Long
  cylinders
Form
  square
Over
  wood and dog
Light
  bean bags
Many
  apples
Heavy
  bean bags

Smooth
  paper
Far away
  cowboy and horse
Around
  box and dog
Form
  insert puzzle
Side
  truck
Backward
  doll
Bottom
  truck
Form
  3-piece puzzle

From F. H. Palmer and R. J. Siegel. "Minimal Intervention at Ages Two and Three and Subsequent Intellective Changes." In *The Preschool in Action: Exploring Early Childhood Programs,* edited by M. C. Day and R. K. Parker, © 1977 by Allyn and Bacon, Inc. Reprinted with permission.

Appendix B

Essential Phonics Concepts

CONSONANTS

Skill and Definition	Example Grapheme	Phoneme	Word
Single consonant, symbol/sound relationships in initial position: A relationship between each beginning single consonant letter and sound exists, is relatively consistent, and helps one pronounce unknown words.	b	/b/	boy
	d	/d/	dog
	f	/f/	fog
	h	/h/	how
	j, g	/j/	just, George
	k, c	/k/	kitten, cat
	l	/l/	loud
	m	/m/	mitten
	n	/n/	now
	p	/p/	pig
	qu	/kw/	quit
	r	/r/	row
	s, c	/s/	sit, city
	t	/t/	Ted
	v	/v/	very
	w	/w/	was
	y	/y/	yes
	z	/z/	zombie
Single consonant, symbol/sound relationships in final position: A relationship between ending single consonant letters and sounds exists, is relatively consistent, and helps one pronounce words.	b	/b/	dab
	d	/d/	sad
	f	/f/	ruff
	g/	/g/	pig
	j, g	/j/	fudge, George
	k, c	/k/	dark, like, black
	l	/l/	rail
	m	/m/	ham
	n	/n/	ban
	p	/p/	zip
	r	/r/	roar
	s	/s/	boss
	t	/t/	wit, stopped
	v	/v/	save
	x	/ks/	fix
	z, s	/z/	fizz, has

233

Skill and Definition	Example Grapheme	Phoneme	Word
Single consonant relationships between c and g and variant sounds: The single letters c and g have soft sounds and hard sounds. The soft sounds of c and g are predicted by the letters which follow. E, i, and y predict soft sounds. Others predict hard sounds.	c	/s/	city, cent, chance
	c	/k/	cat, cup, mimic
	g	/j/	judge, gist
	g	/g/	gap, God, guppy
Initial two-letter consonant blends or clusters: Some consonants are combined with the sounds blended together.	br	/br/	break
	bl	/bl/	black
	cl	/kl/	club
	cr	/kr/	crate
	dr	/dr/	dram
	dw	/dw/	dwell
	fl	/fl/	flat
	fr	/fr/	freight
	gl	/gl/	glad
	gr	/gr/	growl
	pl	/pl/	please
	pr	/pr/	pray
	sl	/sl/	slay
	sc	/sk/	scant
	sk	/sk/	skate
	sm	/sm/	small
	sn	/sn/	snear
	sp	/sp/	speak
	st	/st/	state
	sv	/sv/	svelte
	sw	/sw/	swim
	tr	/tr/	train
	tw	/tw/	twin
Initial three-letter consonant blends or clusters: Three consonants are combined with three sounds blended together.	spl	/spl/	splash
	scr	/skr/	scratch
	spr	/spr/	spread
	str	/str/	string
	squ	/skw/	square
Final consonant clusters: Some consonants when combined at the ends of words have sounds blended together. There are two-letter final word clusters.	-nt	/nt/	ant
	-nd	/nd/	hand
	-lt	/lt/	dealt
	-mp	/mp/	damp
	-st	/st/	fist
	-ft	/ft/	bereft
	-ct	/kt/	act
	-pt	/pt/	apt
	-lf	/lf/	elf
	-lk	/lk/	ilk
	-lm	/lm/	helm
	-lp	/lp/	help
	-sk	/sk/	desk
	-sp	/sp/	rasp

Skill and Definition	Example Grapheme	Phoneme	Word
Initial consonant digraphs: Consonant digraphs are formed with two written consonants that represent one new sound. There are some in initial position.	th	/θ/	think
	th	/ð/	then
	sh	/š/	shed, sure
	ch	/Č/	church
	ph	/f/	phone
	wh	/hw/	when
Final consonant digraphs: Consonant digraphs have two written letters and one sound. Some are in final position only.	-ng	/ŋ/	wing
	-nk	/nk/	thank
Some are in either final or initial position.	th	/θ/	worth
	sh	/š/	wish
	ch	/Č/	church
Double consonants: When consonants are doubled in writing, they still represent only one sound.	-mm-	/m/	hammer
Silent consonants: Certain letter patterns predict silent consonants.	gh-	/g/	ghost
	wr-	/r/	wren
	gn-	/n/	gnash
	kn-	/n/	know
	-dge	/j/	bridge
	-gn	/n/	malign
	-tch	/Č/	blotch
	-mn	/m/	hymn
	-mb	/m/	lamb
	-sten	/sən/	fasten
	ps-	/s/	psalm

GENERALIZATIONS ABOUT CONSONANTS

Generalization	Clymer	Bailey	Emans
1. When *c* is followed by *e* or *i*, the sound of *s* is likely to be heard.	96%	92%	90%
2. When the letter *c* is followed by *o* or *a*, the sound of *k* is likely to be heard.	100	100	100
3. The letter *g* often has a sound similar to that of *j* in *jump* when it precedes the letters *i* or *e*.	64	78	80
4. When *c* and *h* are next to each other, they make only one sound.	100	100	100
5. When a word ends in *ck*, it has the same last sound as in *look*.	100	100	100
6. When two of the same consonants are side by side, only one is heard.	99	98	91

Generalization	Clymer	Bailey	Emans
7. When a word begins *kn*, the *k* is silent.	100	100	100
8. When a word begins with *wr*, the *w* is silent.	100	100	100
9. When *ght* is seen in a word, *gh* is silent.	100	100	100

Adapted from *Teaching about Phonics* by Albert J. Mazurkiewicz. Copyright © 1976 by Albert J. Mazurkiewicz and used with permission of St. Martin's Press, Inc.

VOWELS

Skill and Definition	Example Grapheme	Phoneme	Words
Short vowel sounds: Short vowels occur commonly in this pattern: C-V-C	a	/ae/	bat
	e	/e/	bet
	i	/i/	fit
	o	/o/	cob
	u	/ə/	sun
Long vowel sounds: Long vowel sounds are those that sound like the respective letter name. (Each generalization is listed below)	a	/ey/	ray
	e	/iy/	feat
	i	/ay/	ice
	o	/ow/	toe
	u	/uyw/	use
Another vowel pattern predicts long vowel sounds. One long vowel pattern is this: C-V-C-silent *e*	a	/ey/	mate
	e	/iy/	scene
	i	/ay/	ice
	o	/ow/	hope
	u	/uyw/	use
Another vowel pattern which predicts long vowel sounds is the combination of two vowel letters together, especially *oa*, *ee*, and *ea*.	oa	/ow/	goat
	ee	/iy/	week
	ea	/iy/	meat
	ai	/ey/	wait
Another vowel pattern which predicts long vowel sounds is C-V.	-e	/iy/	bee
	-o	/ow/	go
R-controlled words: When a vowel is followed by *r*, the *r* affects and changes the vowel sound.	-ir	/ər/	bird
	-er	/ər/	her
	-ur	/ər/	curd
	-ar	/aer/	car
	-or	/or/	for
L-controlled words: When *a* is followed by *l*, the *l* affects the sound.	-al	/al/	call
Diphthongs: A diphthong is a combination of two vowels that forms a new vowel sound representing a blending of two vowel sounds.	oy	/oy/	toy
	oi	/oy/	oil
	ou	/aw/	ouch
	ow	/aw/	how
	ew	/yuw/	new

Skill and Definition	Example Grapheme	Phoneme	Words
Others: There are a number of other vowel symbol/sound combinations discussed in various programs. These are listed separately and include:			
-oo- patterns. Sometimes *-oo-* represents a sound like the short /*u*/.	*-oo-*	/u/	book
	-oo-	/uw/	m*oo*se
	-ue	/uw/	bl*ue*
	-aw	/ə/	a*w*ful
	-au	/ə/	a*u*dit

GENERALIZATIONS ABOUT VOWELS

Generalization	Clymer	Bailey	Emans
1. When a vowel is in the middle of a one-syllable word, the vowel is short.	62%	71%	73%
2. When a word has only one vowel letter, the vowel sound is likely to be short.	57	69	70
3. When there are two vowels, one of which is final *e*, the first vowel is long, and the *e* silent.	45	34	18
4. When words end with silent *e*, the preceding *a* or *i* is long.	60	50	48
5. In many two- and three-syllable words, the final *e* lengthens the vowel in the last syllable.	46	46	42
6. When there are two vowels side by side, the long sound of the first one is heard, and the second is usually silent.	63	57	63
7. The first vowel is usually long and the second silent in the digraphs *ai, ea, oa,* and *ui*.	66	60	58
ai	64	72	83
ea	66	55	62
oa	97	95	86
ui	6	10	0
8. In the phonogram *ie*, the *i* is silent, and the *e* is a long sound.	17	31	23
9. Words having double *e* usually have the long *e* sound.	98	87	100
10. If the only vowel letter is at the end of a word, the letter usually stands for a long sound.	74	76	33
11. When *a* is followed by *r* and final *e*, we expect to hear the sound heard in *care*.	90	96	100

Generalization	Clymer	Bailey	Emans
12. The *r* gives the preceding vowel a sound that is neither long nor short.	48	34	24
13. The letter *a* has the same sound (o) when followed by *l*, *w*, and *u*.	84	89	98

Adapted from *Teaching about Phonics* by Albert J. Mazurkiewicz. Copyright © 1976 by Albert J. Mazurkiewicz and used with permission of St. Martin's Press, Inc.

SOME PHONOGRAMS

Phonogram	Examples
-ab	cab, dab, crab, stab
-ad	bad, dad, had, lad, mad, pad, sad, glad
-ag	bag, gag, rag, tag, wag, drag, flag
-am	dam, jam, clam, cram
-an	an, can, man, pan, ran, tan, bran, plan, than
-ap	cap, gap, lap, map, nap, sap, tap, rap, trap, wrap
-ar	bar, car, far, tar, star
-at	at, bat, cat, fat, hat, mat, pat, rat, sat, flat, that
-aw	law, paw, raw, draw, straw
-ay	day, gay, jay, lay, may, pay, ray, say, stay, clay
-ace	ace, lace, race, face, brace, place, space
-ack	back, lack, pack, rack, tack, black, crack, stack, shack
-ail	hail, mail, nail, pail, rail, sail, tail, snail, trail
-ain	gain, main, pain, rain, brain, grain, plain, train
-air	air, fair, hair, pair, chair
-ake	bake, cake, fake, lake, make, rake, sake, take, snake
-ale	male, pale, sale, tale, scale, whale
-all	all, ball, call, fall, hall, tall, wall, small
-ame	came, game, name, same, flame, shame
-and	and, hand, land, sand, stand, grand
-ank	bank, tank, drank, thank
-ape	ape, cape, tape, shape
-are	bare, care, dare, share, stare
-ark	ark, bark, dark, mark, park, shark
-art	art, cart, part, start, smart
-ash	cash, dash, hash, mash, smash, trash, flash
-ave	cave, gave, pave, save, wave, shave, brave
-ed	bed, fed, led, wed, shed
-ee	bee, see, tree, free
-en	den, hen, men, then, when
-et	bet, get, met, net, pet, set, wet, yet
-ew	few, new, flew, grew, knew
-ell	bell, cell, fell, hell, sell, tell, well, yell, shell
-end	end, bend, lend, mend, send, spend
-ent	bent, cent, dent, sent, tent, went
-est	best, nest, pest, rest, test, west
-ib	fib, crib, rib
-id	bid, did, hid, kid, lid, rid, skid
-ig	big, dig, fig, pig, twig

Phonogram	Examples
-im	dim, him, slim
-in	in, bin, din, pin, sin, tin, twin, spin
-ip	dip, hip, lip, nip, rip, sip, clip, grip, skip
-it	bit, fit, hit, lit, mit, pit, sit, knit
-ice	ice, lice, nice, rice, slice, twice
-ick	kick, lick, pick, sick, brick, quick, trick
-ide	hide, ride, side, tide, wide, bride
-ight	fight, light, might, night, flight
-ill	bill, dill, fill, hill, ill, skill, will, still, spill
-ind	bind, find, kind, mind, blind
-ine	fine, line, mine, nine, pine, vine, shine, wine
-ing	king, ring, sing, wing, bring, thing
-ink	ink, pink, wink, think, drink
-ive	dive, five, hive, live, arrive
-ob	job, mob, rob, sob, knob
-od	nod, pod, rod, sod, God
-og	dog, fog, frog, hog, log
-on	son, ton, won
-ot	cot, dot, got, hot, lot, not, pot, rot, knot, trot
-ow	low, mow, row, show, snow, throw
-ow	how, cow, vow, wow
-oy	boy, coy, toy
-oat	boat, coat, goat, gloat
-ock	dock, lock, rock, sock, block
-oil	boil, coil, oil, soil, toil
-oke	coke, joke, poke, broke, smoke
-old	old, bold, cold, fold, gold, hold, sold, told
-ole	hole, mole, pole, stole, whole
-one	bone, cone, lone, tone, alone, stone
-ong	long, song, strong, wrong, along
-oom	boom, room, bloom, broom, gloom
-oon	moon, noon, soon, croon
-ore	core, sore, tore, wore, score, shore, snore
-ough	rough, tough, enough
-ought	bought, ought, brought, fought, thought
-ound	found, hound, pound, round, sound, ground
-ouse	house, louse, mouse, blouse
-out	out, stout, trout, scout
-ub	cub, hub, tub, club, scrub
-ug	bug, dug, hug, mug, rug, drug, snug
-um	gum, rum, sum, drum
-un	bun, dun, fun, gun, run, sun, spun
-up	cup, pup, sup, up
-ut	but, cut, hut, rut, shut
-uck	duck, luck, puck, suck, stuck
-ump	bump, dump, jump, lump, rump, thump
-ung	hung, rung, sung, stung, clung
-urn	burn, turn, return
-ush	hush, rush, brush
-ust	dust, just, must, trust

Bibliography

Abrahams, R. (1971). *Welding communication breaks.* Paper presented at the conference on language and cultural diversity of the Trainers of Teacher Trainers, St. Cloud, MN.

Allen, R. V., & Allen, C. (1968). *Language experience in reading.* Chicago: Encyclopedia Britannica.

Allington, R. L. (1980). Teacher interruption behaviors during primary grade oral reading. *Journal of Educational Psychology, 72,* 371–377.

Allington, R. L. (1984). Oral reading. In P. D. Pearson, R. Barr, M. L. Kamil, & P. Mosenthal (Eds.), *Handbook of reading research.* New York: Longman.

American Book Reading Program (1977). New York: American Book Company.

American Readers (1980). New York: American Book Company.

Ammon, P. R., & Ammon, M. S. (1972). Effects of training black preschool children in vocabulary or sentence construction. *Journal of Educational Psychology, 63,* 421–426.

Anderson, A. B., & Stokes, S. J. (1984). Social and institutional influences on the development and practice of literacy. In H. Goelman, A. A. Oberg, & F. Smith (Eds.), *Awakening to literacy.* Exeter, NH: Heinemann.

Anderson, R. C., & Pearson, P. C. (1984). A schema-theoretic view of basic processes of reading. In P. D. Pearson, R. Barr, M. L. Kamil, & P. Mosenthal (Eds.), *Handbook of reading research.* New York: Longman.

Anderson, R. D., Osborn, J., & Tierney, R. J. (1984). *Learning to read in American schools: Basal readers and content texts.* Hillside, NJ: Erlbaum.

Athey, J. (1976). Reading research in the affective domain. In H. Singer, & R. B. Ruddell, *Theoretical models and processes of reading,* second edition. Newark, DE: International Reading Association.

Baratz, J. C. (1969). Teaching reading in an urban negro school system. In J. C. Baratz, & R. W. Shuy (Eds.), *Teaching black children to read.* Washington, D.C.: Center for Applied Linguistics.

Baratz, J. C. (1973). The relationship of black English to reading. A review of research. In J. L. Laffey, & R. W. Shuy (Eds.), *Language differences: Do they interfere?* Newark, DE: International Reading Association.

Baratz, S. S., & Baratz, J. C. (1970). Early childhood intervention: The social science base of institutional racism. *Harvard Educational Review, 40,* 29–50.

Barr, R. (1974). Influence of instruction on early reading. *Interchange, 5,* 13–22.

Barr, R. (1974–1975). The effect of instruction on pupil reading strategies. *Reading Research Quarterly, 10,* 555–582.

240

Barr, R. (1984). Beginning reading instruction: From debate to reformation. In P. D. Pearson, R. Barr, M. L. Kamil, & P. Mosenthal (Eds.), *Handbook of reading research.* New York: Longman.

Barr, R., & Dreeben, R. (1983). *How schools work.* Chicago: University of Chicago Press.

Beck, J. L., & McKeown, M. G. (1984). Application of theories of reading to instruction. *American Journal of Education, 93,* 61–81.

Berko, J. (1958). The child's learning of English morphology. *Word, 14,* 150–177.

Berko-Gleason, J. & Weintraub, S. (1978). Input language and the acquisition of communicative competence. In K. Nelson (Ed.), *Children's language* (Vol. 1). New York: Gardner Press.

Bernstein, B. (1970). A sociolinguistic approach to socialization. In F. Williams (Ed.), *Language and poverty: Perspectives on a theme.* Chicago: Markham.

Bernstein, B. (1971). *Class, codes, and control* (Vol. 1). London: Routledge.

Berreuta-Clement, J. R., Schweinhart, L. J., Barnett, W. S., Epstein, A. S., & Weikart, D. P. (1984). *Changed lives: The effects of the Perry Preschool program on youths through age 19.* Ypsilanti, MI: High Scope Press.

Betts, E. A. (1954). *Foundations of reading instruction.* New York: American Book Company.

Biber, B. (1977). A developmental-interactive approach: Bank Street College of Education. In M. C. Day, & R. K. Parker (Eds.), *The preschool in action: Exploring early childhood programs* (2nd ed.). Boston: Allyn and Bacon.

Biemiller, A. (1970). The development of the use of graphic and contextual information as children learn to read. *Reading Research Quarterly, 6,* 75–96.

Bissex, G. L. (1980). *GNYS at work: A child learns to write and read.* Cambridge: Harvard University Press.

Black, R. (1979). Crib talk and mother-child interaction: A comparison of form and function. *Paper and Reports on Child Language Acquisition, 17,* 90–97.

Blank, M. (1982). Moving beyond the difference. In L. Feagans, & D. C. Farron (Eds.), *The language of children reared in poverty.* New York: Academic Press.

Bloom, L. (1970). *Language development: Form and function in emerging grammars.* Cambridge: The M.I.T. Press.

Bloom, L. (1983). Of continuity and discontinuity and the magic of language development. In R. M. Golinkoff (Ed.), *The transition from prelinguistic to linguistic communication.* Hillside, NJ: Erlbaum.

Bloom, L., Lightboom, P., & Hood, L. (1975). Structure and variation in child language. *Monographs of the Society for Research in Child Development, 40.*

Boiarsky, C. (1969). Consistency of spelling and pronunciation deviations of Appalachian students. *The Modern Language Journal, 53,* 347–350.

Bond, G. S., & Dykstra, R. (1967). The Cooperative Research Program in first-grade reading instruction. *Reading Research Quarterly, 3,* 5–142.

Bowerman, M. (1976). Semantic factors in the acquisition of rules for word use and sentence construction. In D. M. Morehead, & A. E. Morehead (Eds.), *Normal and deficient child language.* Maryland: University Park Press.

Bowerman, M. (1979). The acquisition of complex sentences. In P. Fletcher, & M. Garman, *Language acquisition.* Cambridge: Cambridge University Press.

Bradley, B. E. (1956). An experimental study of the readiness approach to reading. *Elementary School Journal, 56,* 262–267.

Bradley, L., & Bryant, P. E. (1983). Categorizing sounds and learning to read—A casual connection. *Nature, 301,* 419–421.

Braine, M. S. (1963). The ontogeny of English phrase structures: The first phase. *Language, 39,* 1–13.

Bronfenbrenner, U. (1974). Is early intervention effective? *A report on longitudinal evaluations of preschool programs.* Washington, D.C.: U.S. Department of Health, Education, and Welfare.

Brown, A. (1984). In P. D. Pearson, R. Barr, M. L. Kamil, & P. Mosenthal (Eds.), *Handbook of reading research.* New York: Longman.

Brown, R. (1973). *A first language: The early stages.* Cambridge: Harvard University Press.

Brown, R. (1977). Introduction. In C. E. Snow, & C. A. Ferguson (Eds.), *Talking to children: Language input and acquisition.* Cambridge: Cambridge University Press.

Brown, R., & Bellugi, U. (1964). Three processes in the child's acquisition of syntax. *Harvard Educational Review, 34,* 133–151.

Brown, R., Cazden, C., & Bellugi-Klima, U. (1968). The child's grammar from one to three. In J. P. Hill (Ed.), *Minnesota symposium on child development.* Minneapolis: University of Minnesota.

Brown, R., & Fraser, C. (1964). The acquisition of language. *Monographs for the Society of Research in Child Development, 29,* 43–79.

Brown, R., & Hanlon, C. (1970). Derivational complexity and order of acquisition of child speech. In J. R. Hayes (Ed.), *Cognition and the development of language.* New York: Academic Press.

Bruner, J. (1960). *The process of education.* Cambridge: Harvard University Press.

Bruner, J. (1975). The ontogenesis of speech acts. *Journal of Child Language, 3,* 1–19.

Bruner, J. (1978). From communication to language: A psychological perspective. In J. Markova (Ed.), *The social context of language.* Chicester: Wiley.

Bruner, J. (1983). The acquisition of pragmatic commitments. In Roberta M. Golinkoff (Ed.), *The transition from prelinguistic to linguistic communication.* Hillside, NJ: Erlbaum.

Bruner, J. (1984). Language, mind, and reading. In H. Goelman, A. A. Oberg, & F. Smith (Ed.), *Awakening to literacy.* Exeter, NH: Heinemann.

Burke, S., Pflaum, S. W., & Knafle, J. D. (1982). The influence of black English on diagnosis of reading in learning disabled and normal readers. *Journal of Learning Disabilities, 15,* 19–22.

Butler, D., & Clay, M. (1982). *Reading begins at home: Preparing children for reading before they go to school.* Exeter, NH: Heinemann.

Calfee, R. C., Chapman, R. S., & Venezky, R. L. (1972). How a child needs to think to learn to read. In L. W. Gregg (Ed.), *Cognition in learning and memory.* New York: Wiley.

Calkins, L. M. (1982). *Lessons from a child: On the teaching and learning of writing.* Portsmouth, NH: Heinemann.

Carroll, J. (1960). Language development. In H. Chester (Ed.), *Encyclopedia of Educational Research* (3rd ed.). New York: MacMillan.

Carroll, J. (1970). Words, meaning and concepts. *Harvard Educational Review, 34,* 178–202.

Carrow-Woolfolk, E., & Lynch, J. J. (1982). *An integrative approach to language disorders in children.* New York: Grune & Stratton.

Cazden, C. (1966). Subcultural differences in child language: An interdisciplinary review. *Merrill-Palmer Quarterly, 12,* 185–219.

Cazden, C. (1968). The acquisition of noun and verb inflections. *Child Development, 32,* 433–448.

Cazden, C. (1970). The neglected situations in child language research and education. In F. Williams (Ed.), *Language and poverty: Perspectives on a theme.* Chicago: Markham.

Cazden, C. (1972). *Child language and education.* New York: Holt.

Chall, J. S. (1967). *Learning to read: The great debate.* New York: McGraw-Hill.

Channon, G. (1968). Bulljive: Language teaching in a Harlem school. *Urban Review, 2,* 5–12.

Chicago School Board. (1973). *Survey of pupils whose first language is other than English.*

Chomsky, C. (1969). *The acquisition of syntax in children from five to ten.* Cambridge: The M.I.T. Press.

Chomsky, C. (1972). Stages in language development and reading exposure. *Harvard Educational Review, 42,* 1–33.

Chomsky, C. (1979). Approaching reading through invented spelling. In L. B. Resnick, & P. A. Weaver (Eds.), *Theory and practice of early reading* (Vol. 2). Hillside, NJ: Erlbaum.

Chomsky, N. (1959). Review of Skinner's Verbal Behavior. *Language, 35,* 26–58.

Chomsky, N. (1965). *Aspects of a theory of syntax.* Cambridge: The M.I.T. Press.

Chorvinsky, M. (1982). *Preprimary enrollment 1980.* Washington, D.C.: National Center for Educational Statistics (Cited in Berreuta-Clement et al.).

Clark, E. V. (1973). What's in a word? On the child's acquisition of semantics in his first language. In T. E. Moore (Ed.), *Cognitive development and the acquisition of language.* New York: Academic Press.

Clark, E. V. (1979). Building a vocabulary: Words for objects, actions, and relations. In P. Fletcher & Michael Garman (Eds.), *Language acquisition.* Cambridge: Cambridge University Press.

Clark, M. M. (1976). *Young fluent readers.* London: Heinemann.

Clark, M. M. (1984). Literacy at home and at school. Insights from a study of young fluent readers. In H. Goelman, A. A. Oberg, & F. Smith (Eds.), *Awakening to literacy.* Exeter, NH: Heinemann.

Clay, M. M. (1968). A syntactic analysis of reading errors. *Journal of Verbal Learning and Verbal Behavior, 7,* 434–438.

Clay, M. M. (1969). Reading errors and self-correction behavior. *British Journal of Educational Psychology, 39,* 47–56.

Clay, M. M. (1972). *Reading: The patterning of complex behavior.* London: Heinemann.

Clay, M. M. (1979). *The early detection of reading difficulties: A diagnostic survey with recovery procedures.* Auckland: Heinemann.

Cohen, A. S. (1974–1975). Oral reading errors of first grade children taught by a code emphasis approach. *Reading Research Quarterly, 10,* 616–650.

Coleman, J. S. et al. (1966). *Equality of educational opportunity.* Washington, D.C.: U.S. Government Printing Office.

Cross, T. G. (1977). Mothers' speech adjustments: The contribution of selected child listener variables. In C. E. Snow, & C. A. Ferguson (Eds.), *Talking to children: Language input acquisition.* Cambridge: Cambridge University Press.

Cullinan, B. E., Jaggar, A., & Strickland, D. (1974). Language expansion for black children in the primary grades: A research report. *Young Children, 29,* 98–112.

Cummins, J. (1981). Biliteracy, language proficiency, and educational programs. In J. R. Edwards (Ed.), *The social psychology of reading.* Institute of Modern Languages, Inc., Silver Spring, MD: The Language People.

Dale, P. S. (1976). *Language development: Structure and form* (2nd ed.). New York: Holt, Rinehart and Winston.

Danoff, M. N. (1978). *Evaluation of the impact of ESEA Title VII Spanish/English bilingual education program: Overview of study and findings.* American Institutes for Research. Palo Alto, CA.

Day, K. C. & Day, H. D. (1979). Developmental observations of kindergarten children's understanding in regard to concepts about print and language development. (Cited in Clay, 1979).

DeCecco, J. P. (1967). Introduction. In J. P. DeCecco (Ed.), *The psychology of language, thought and instruction.* New York: Holt, Rinehart and Winston.

Desberg, P., Marsh, G. & Wolff, D. (1976). The relationship between non-standard dialect and academic achievement. ERIC ED 120 779.

Deutsch, C. (1964). Auditory discrimination and learning: Social factors. *Merrill-Palmer Quarterly, 10,* 277–296.

Deutsch, M. (1965). The role of social class in language development and cognition. *American Journal of OrthoPsychiatry, 25,* 75–88.

Deutsch, M., & Brown, B. (1964). Social influences in negro-white intelligence differences. *Journal of Social Issues, 20,* 24–35.

De Valdes, M. E. (1978). Non-English speaking children and literacy. In S. Pflaum (Ed.), *Aspects of reading education.* National Society for the Study of Education. Berkeley, CA: McCutchan.

DISTAR (1968). Chicago: Science Research Associates. (S. Engelmann & E. Bruner, senior authors)

Dixon, S. D., LeVine, R. A., Richman, A., & Brazelton, T. B. (1984). Mother-child interaction around a teaching task: An African-American comparison. *Child Development, 55,* 1252–1264.

Donaldson, M. (1984). Speech and writing and modes of learning. In H. Goelman, A. A. Oberg, & F. Smith (Eds.), *Awakening to literacy.* Exeter, NH: Heinemann.

Donaldson, M. C., & Balfour, G. (1968). Less is more: A study of language comprehension in children. *British Journal of Psychology, 59,* 461–472. Boston: Allyn and Bacon.

Downing, J. (1975). How children think about reading. Paper presented at International Reading Conference, New York.

Downing, J., & Oliver, P. (1973–1974). The child's conception of a word. *Reading Research Quarterly, 9,* 568–582.

Durkin, D. (1966). *Children who read early.* New York: Teachers College Press.

Durkin, D. (1976). *Teaching young children to read* (2nd ed.). Boston: Allyn and Bacon.

Durrell, D. D. (1958). Success in first-grade reading. *Journal of Education, 140,* 1–48.

Ehri, L. C., & Wilce, L. S. (1985). Movement into reading: Is the first stage of printed word learning visual or phonetic? *Reading Research Quarterly, 20,* 163–179.

Engelmann, S. (1970). How to construct effective language programs for the poverty child. In F. Williams (Ed.), *Language and poverty: Perspectives on a theme*. Chicago: Markham.

Engle, P. E. (1975). Language medium in early school years for minority language groups. *Review of Educational Research, 45,* 238–325.

Entwhisle, D. P. (1966). Developmental sociolinguistics: A comparative study in four subcultural settings. *Sociometry, 29,* 67–84.

Entwhisle, D. P. (1970). Semantic systems of children: Some assessments of social class and ethnic differences. In F. Williams (Ed.), *Language and poverty: Perspectives on a theme*. Chicago: Markham.

Ervin, S. (1964). Imitation and structural change in children's language. In E. Lenneberg (Ed.), *New directions in the study of language*. Cambridge: The M.I.T. Press.

Ervin-Tripp, S. (1973). *Language acquisition and communicative choice*. Stanford, CA: Stanford University Press.

Farron, D. C. (1982). Mother-child interaction, language development, and the school performance of poverty children. In L. Feagans, & D. C. Farron (Eds.), *The language of children reared in poverty*. New York: Academic Press.

Feagans, L., & Farron, D. C. (Eds.). (1982). *The language of children reared in poverty*. New York: Academic Press.

Feijo, T. D., & Jaegar, R. M. (1976). Social class and races as concomitants of composite halo in teachers' evaluative ratings of pupils. *American Educational Research Journal, 13,* 1–14.

Ferreiro, E. (1984). The underlying logic of literacy development. In H. Goelman, A. Oberg, & F. Smith (Eds.), *Awakening to literacy*. Exeter, NH: Heinemann.

Ferreiro, E. (forthcoming). The interplay between information and assimilation in beginning literacy. In W. Teale, & E. Sulzby (Eds.), *Emergent literacy: Writing and reading*, Norwood, NJ: Ablex.

Ferreiro, E., & Teberosky, A. (1982). *Literacy before schooling*. Exeter, NH: Heinemann.

Feshbach, S., Adelman, H., & Fuller, W. (1974). Early identification of children with high risk of reading failure. *Journal of Learning Disabilities, 7,* 639–644.

Fletcher, P., & Garman, M. (1979). Introduction. In P. Fletcher, & M. Garman, (Eds.), *Language acquisition*. Cambridge: Cambridge University Press.

Friedlander, B. Z. (1970). Receptive language development in infancy. *Merrill-Palmer Quarterly, 16,* 7–51.

Froese, V. (1984). A comparison of first-graders' ability in three modes of expression: Dictation, independent writing, and story retelling. In J. A. Niles & L. A. Harris (Eds.), *Changing perspectives on research in reading/language processing and instruction*. National Reading Conference.

Fry, E. B., Polk, J. K., & Fountoukidis, D. (1984). *The reading teacher's book of lists*. Engelwood Cliffs, NJ: Prentice-Hall.

Fryburg, E. (1972). The relations among English syntax, methods of instruction, and reading achievement of first grade disadvantaged black children. Unpublished doctoral dissertation. New York University.

Furth, H. (1970). *Piaget for teachers*. Englewood Cliffs, NJ: Prentice-Hall.

Gambrell, L. (1984). How much time do children spend reading during teacher-directed reading instruction? In J. A. Niles, & L. A. Harris (Eds.), *Changing perspectives on research in reading/language processing and instruction*. National Reading Conference.

Gantt, W. N., Wilson, R. M. and Dayton, C. M. (1974–1975). An initial investigation of the relationship between syntactical divergency and the listening comprehension of black children. *Reading Research Quarterly, 10,* 193–211.

Gardner, R. A., & Gardner, B. T. (1969). Teaching sign language to a chimpanzee. *Science, 165,* 664–672.

Garman (1979). In K. E. Nelson (Ed.), *Children's language* (Vol. 1). New York: Gardner Press.

Garvey, C. (1984). *Children's talk.* Cambridge: Harvard University Press.

Garvey, C., & McFarlane, P. (1970). A measure of standard English proficiency of inner-city children. *American Educational Research Journal, 7,* 29–40.

Gates, A. I. (1937). The necessary mental age for beginning reading. *Elementary School Journal, 37,* 497–508.

Gates, A. I., & Bond, G. L. (1935–1936). Reading readiness: A study of factors determining success and failure in beginning reading. *Teachers College Record, 37,* 679–685.

Gates, A. J., & Russell, D. (1938). Types of material, vocabulary builder, word analysis, and other factors in beginning reading. *Elementary School Journal, 39,* 27, 35, 119–128.

Gesell, A. L. (1940). *The first five years of life.* New York: Harper.

Gibson, E., & Levin, H. (1975). *The psychology of reading.* Cambridge: M.I.T. Press.

Giles, H., & Powesland, P. F. (1975). *Speech style and social evaluation.* London: Academic Press.

Goldman, R., Fristoe, M., & Woodcock, R. W. (1970). *Test of auditory discrimination.* Circle Pines, MN: American Guidance.

Golinkoff, R. M. (1983). The preverbal negotiation of failed messages: Insights into the transition period. In R. M. Golinkoff (Ed.), *The transition from prelinguistic to linguistic communication.* Hillside, NJ: Erlbaum.

Golinkoff, R. M., & Gordon, S. (1983). In the beginning was the word: A history of the study of language acquisition. In Roberta M. Golinkoff (Ed.), *The transition from prelinguistic to linguistic communication.* Hillside, NJ: Erlbaum.

Goodman, K. S. (1967). Reading: A psycholinguistic guessing game. *Journal of the Reading Specialist, 7,* 126–135.

Goodman, K. S. (1976). Behind the eye: What happens in reading. In H. Singer, & R. B. Ruddell (Eds.), *Theoretical models and processes of reading* (2nd ed.). Newark, DE: International Reading Association.

Goodman, Y. (1980). The roots of literacy. In M. P. Douglass (Ed.), *Claremont reading conference forty-fourth yearbook.* Claremont, CA: Claremont Graduate School.

Goodman, Y. M. (forthcoming). Children coming to know literacy. In W. Teale, & E. Sulzby (Eds.), *Emergent literacy.* Norwood, NJ: Ablex.

Gordon, I. J., Guinagh, B., & Jester, R. E. (1977). The Florida parent education infant and toddler programs. In M. C. Day, & R. K. Parker (Eds.), *The preschool in action: Exploring early childhood programs* (2nd ed.). Boston: Allyn and Bacon.

Gottlieb, M. (1985). Unpublished doctoral dissertation. University of Illinois at Chicago.

Gough, P. B. (1984). Word recognition. In P. D. Pearson, R. Barr, M. L. Kamil, & P. Mosenthal (Eds.), *Handbook of reading research.* New York: Longman.

Graham, R. T., & Rudorf, E. H. (1971). Dialect and spelling. *Elementary English, 47,* 363–376.

Graves, D. H. (1983). *Writing: Teachers and Children at Work.* Exeter, NH: Heinemann.

Grieve, R., and Hoogenraad, R. (1979). Firstwords. In P. Fletcher, & M. Garmen (Eds.), *Language acquisition: Studies in first language development.* Cambridge: Cambridge University Press.

Griffiths, P. (1979). Speech acts and early sentences. In P. Fletcher and M. Garman (Eds.), *Language acquisition: Studies in first language development.* Cambridge: Cambridge University Press.

Gumperz, (1972). In C. Cazden, V. P. John, & D. Hymes (Eds.), *Functions of language in the classroom.* New York: Teachers College Press.

Hall, M. (1976). *Reading reading as a language experience* (2nd ed.). Columbus, OH: Charles Merrill.

Hall, M., Moretz, S. A., & Statom, J. (1976). Writing before grade one—A study of early writers. *Language Arts, 53,* 582–585.

Halliday, M. A. K. (1975). *Learning how to mean: Exploration in the development of language.* London: Edward Arnold LTD.

Hansen, J. (1984). Readers talk like writers. In J. A. Niles, & L. A. Harris (Eds.), *Changing perspectives on research in reading/language processing and instruction.* National Reading Conference.

Harding, C. G. (1983). Setting the stage for language acquisition. Communication development in the first year. In R. M. Golinkoff (Ed.), *The transition from prelinguistic to linguistic communication.* Hillside, NJ: Erlbaum.

Harrison, M. L. (1936). *Reading readiness.* Boston: Houghton.

The Headway Program: Open Court (1979). LaSalle, IL: Open Court.

Heath, S. B. (1983). *Ways with words: Language, life, and work in communities and classrooms.* Cambridge: Cambridge University Press.

Heath, S. B. (forthcoming). Separating "things of the imagination" from life: Learning to read and write. In W. Teale, & E. Sulzby (Eds.), *Emergent literacy: Writing and reading.* Norwood, NJ: Ablex.

Heath, S. B., & Thomas, C. (1984). The achievement of preschool literacy for mother and child. In H. Goelman, A. A. Oberg, and F. Smith (Eds.), *Awakening to literacy.* Exeter, NH: Heinemann.

Herrick, V. E., & Nerbourg, M. (1964). *Using experience charts with children.* Columbus, OH: Charles Merrill.

Hess, K. M., Maxwell, J. C., & Long, B. K. (1974). *Dialects and dialect learning.* Urbana, IL: NCTE.

Hess, R. D., & Shipman, V. (1965). Early experiences and the socialization of cognitive modes in children. *Child Development, 36,* 869–886.

Hoffman, J. V., & Clements, R. (1983). Reading miscues and teacher verbal feedback. *Elementary School Journal.*

Hoffman, J. V., & Crone, S. (1984). The oral recitation lesson: A research derived strategy for reading in basal texts. Paper at National Reading Conference, St. Petersburg, FL.

Hoffman, J. V., O'Neal, S. F., Kastler, L. A., Clements, R. O., Segel, K. W., & Nash, M. F. (1984). Guided oral reading and miscue focused verbal feedback in second-grade classrooms. *Reading Research Quarterly, 19,* 367–384.

Holt Basic Reading (1980). New York: Holt, Rinehart and Winston. (B. J. Weiss, senior author)

Hudson, R. A. (1980). *Sociolinguistics.* Cambridge: Cambridge University Press.

Huey, E. B. (1908). *The psychology and pedagogy of reading.* New York: MacMillan.

Hunt, K. W. (1970). Syntactic maturity in school children and adults. *Monographs of the Society for the Research in Child Development, 35,* 1–63.

Ilg, F. L., & Ames, L. B. (1965). Developmental trends in reading behavior. *The Journal of Genetic Psychology, 76,* 291–312.

Ingram, D. (1976). Current issues in child phonology. In D. M. Morehead, & A. E. Morehead (Eds.), *Normal and deficient child language.* Baltimore: University Park Press.

Inhelder, B., Bovet, M., Sinclair, H., & Smock, C. D. (1966). On cognitive development. *American Psychologist, 21,* 160–164.

Ives, J. P., Bursak, L. Z., & Ives, S. A. (1979). *Word identification techniques.* Chicago: Rand McNally.

Jaggar, A. M. (1973). The effect of native dialect and written language structure on reading comprehension in negro and white elementary school children. Dissertation. New York University.

Jakobson, R. (1971). The sound laws of child language and their place in general phonology. In A. Bar-Adon, & W. F. Leopold (Eds.), *Child language: A book of readings.* Englewood Cliffs, NJ: Prentice-Hall.

John, V. (1963). The intellectual development of slum children: Some preliminary findings. *American Journal of Orthopsychiatry, 33,* 813–822.

John, V., & Goldstein, L. (1964). The social context of language acquisition. *Merrill-Palmer Quarterly, 10,* 265–275.

Johnson, D. D., & Pearson, P. D. (1978). *Teaching reading vocabulary.* New York: Holt, Rinehart & Winston.

Johnson, L. (1975). Bilingual bicultural education: A two-way street. *The Reading Teacher, 29,* 231–239.

Johnson, P. (1984). Assessment in reading. In P. D. Pearson, R. Barr, M. L. Kamil, & P. Mosenthal (Eds.), *Handbook of reading research.* New York: Longman.

Juel, C. (1984). An evolving model of reading acquisition. In J. A. Niles, & L. A. Harris (Eds.), *Changing perspectives on research in reading/language processing and instruction.* National Reading Conference.

Juel, C., & Roper/Schneider, D. (1985). The influence of basal readers on first grade reading. *Reading Research Quarterly, 20,* 134–152.

Kamii, C., & DeVries, R. (1977). Piaget for early education. In M. C. Day, & R. K. Parker (Eds.), *The preschool in action: Exploring early childhood programs* (2nd ed.). Boston: Allyn and Bacon.

Kessel, F. S. (1970). The role of syntax in children's comprehension from ages six to twelve. *Monographs of the Society for Research in Child Development, 35.*

Kligman, D., & Cronnell, B. (1974). Black English and spelling. ERIC ED 108 234.

Klima, E. S., & Bellugi-Klima, U. (1969). Syntactic regularities in the speech of children. In J. Lyons, & R. Wales (Eds.), *Psycholinguistic papers.* Edinburgh: Edinburgh University Press.

Koppman, P. S., & Lapray, M. H. (1969). Teacher ratings and pupil reading readiness scores. *Reading Teacher, 22,* 603–608.

Kuczaj, S. P., II (1983). *Oral speech and language play.* New York: Springer Verlag.

Kyostio, O. K. (1980). Is learning to read easy in a language in which the grapheme-phoneme correspondences are regular? I. F. Kavanagh, & R. L. Venezky (Eds.), *Orthography, reading, and dyslexia.* Baltimore: University Park Press.

LaBerge, D., & Samuels, S. J. (1974). Toward a theory of automatic information processing in reading. *Cognitive Psychology, 6,* 293–323.

Labov, W. (1966). *The social stratification of English in New York City.* Washington, D. C.: Center for Applied Linguistics.

Labov, W. (1969). Some sources of reading problems for negro speakers of non-standard English. In J. C. Baratz, and R. W. Shuy (Eds.), *Teaching black children to read.* Washington, D. C.: Center for Applied Linguistics.

Labov, W. (1970). The logic of non-standard English. In F. Williams (Ed.), *Language and poverty: Some perspectives on a theme.* Chicago: Markham.

Labov, W. (1972). *Language in the inner city: Studies in the black English vernacular.* Philadelphia: University of Pennsylvania Press.

Labov, W. et al.(1968). *A study of non-standard English of negro and Puerto Rican speakers* in New York City. Report on Cooperative Research Project 3288. New York: Columbia University.

Lacivita, A. F., Kean, J. M., & Yamamoto, K. (1960). Socioeconomic status of children and acquisition of grammar. *Journal of Educational Research, 60,* 71–74.

Laidlaw Reading Program (1980). River Forest, IL: Laidlaw Brothers. (W. B. Eller, & K. B. Hester, senior authors)

Lambert, W. E., Just, M. N., & Segalowitz, N. (1970). Some cognitive consequences of following the curricula of the early school grades in a foreign language. In J. E. Alatis (Ed.), *Twenty-first annual round table: Bilingualism and language contact.* Washington, D. C.: Georgetown University Press.

Landrum, R., & children (1971). *A day dream I had at night and other stories: Teaching children how to make their own readers.* New York: Teachers and Writers Collaborative.

Lazar, J., & Darlington, R. (1982). Lasting effects of early education: A report from the consortium for longitudinal studies. *Monographs of the Society for Research in Child Development, 47,* 1–139.

Leaf, M. (1938). *The story of Ferdinand.* New York: Viking.

Lee, D. M., & Allen, R. V. (1963). *Learning to read through experience.* New York: Appleton.

Lenneberg, E. (1967). *Biological foundations of language.* New York: John Wiley.

Leopold, W. F. (1971). Semantic learning in infant language. In A. Bar-Adon, & W. F. Leopold (Eds.), *Child language: A book of readings.* Englewood Cliffs, NJ: Prentice-Hall.

Levenstein, P. (1977). The mother-child home program. In M. C. Day, & R. K. Parker (Eds.), *The preschool in action: Exploring early childhood programs* (2nd ed.). Boston: Allyn and Bacon.

Liberman, I., Liberman, A. M., Mattingly, I., Shankweiler, D. (1980). Orthography and the beginning reader. In J. F. Kavanagh, & R. L. Venezky (Eds.), *Orthography, reading, and dyslexia.* Baltimore: University Park Press.

Liberman, I. Y., Shankweiler, D., Fischer, F. W., & Carter, B. (1974). Explicit syllables and phoneme segmentation in the young child. *Journal of Experimental Child Psychology, 18,* 201–212.

Lindholm, K. J. (1980). Bilingual Children: Some interpretations of cognitive and linguistic development. In K. E. Nelson (Ed.), *Children's Language* (Vol. 2). New York: Gardner Press.

Loban, W. D. (1963). *The language of elementary school children.* Research Report No. 1. Champaign, IL: National Council of Teachers of English.

Loban, W. (1976). *Language development: Kindergarten through grade twelve.* Urbana: NCTE.

Mason, J. A. (1984). Early reading from a developmental perspective. In P. D. Pearson, R. Barr, M. L. Kamil, & P. Mosenthal, Eds, *Handbook of reading research.* New York: Longman.

Mathews, M. M. (1966). *Teaching to read: Historically considered.* Chicago: University of Chicago Press.

Mazurkiewicz, A. J. (1976). *Teaching about phonics.* New York: St. Martin's. *Encyclopedia of Educational Research.* New York: MacMillan.

McDermott, R. P. (1977). Social relations as contexts for learning in school. *Harvard Educational Review, 47,* 198–213.

McNeil, J. D. (1984). *Reading comprehension: New directions for classroom practice.* Glenview, IL: Scott Foresman.

McNeill, D. (1966). Developmental psycho-linguistics. In F. Smith, & G. A. Miller (Eds.), *The genesis of language: A psycholinguistic approach.* Cambridge: The M.I.T. Press.

McNeill, D. (1970). *The acquisition of language: The study of developmental psycholinguistics.* New York: Harper and Row.

Melmed, P. J. (1970). *Black English phonology: The question of reading interference.* Monographs of language. Behavior Research Laboratory. Berkeley, CA: University of California.

Meltzer, N. S., & Herse, R. (1969). The boundaries of written words as seen by first graders. *Journal of Reading Behavior, 1,* 3–14.

Menyuk, P. (1963). Syntactic structures in the language of children. *Child Development, 34,* 407–422.

Menyuk, P. (1969). *Sentences children use.* Cambridge: The M.I.T. Press.

Menyuk, P. (1977). *Language and maturation.* Cambridge: The M.I.T. Press.

Micucci, P. (1964). Let's NOT teach reading in kindergarten! *Elementary English, 64,* 246–251.

Moffet, J. (1968). *Teaching the universe of discourse.* Boston: Houghton Mifflin.

Morphett, M. V., & Washburne, C. (1931). When should children begin to read? *Elementary School Journal, 21,* 496–503.

National society for the study of education: Twentieth yearbook (Part II). (1920). Report of the society's Committee on Silent Reading. Chicago: National Society for the Study of Education.

Nelson, K. (1973). Structure and strategy in learning to talk. *Monograph for the Society for Research in Child Development, 38,* nos. 1 and 2.

Nelson, K. E. (Ed.)(1980). *Children's language* (Vol. 1). New York: Gardner Press.

Ninio, A. (1980). Picturebook reading in mother-infant dyads belonging to two subgroups in Israel. *Child Development, 51,* 587–590.

Ninio, A., & Bruner, J. (1978). The achievement and antecedents of labelling. *Journal of Child Language, 5,* 1–16.

Nolen, P. S. (1972). Reading non-standard dialect materials: A study at grades two and four. *Child Development, 43,* 1092–1097.

Ochs, E. (1982). Talking to children in western Samoan. *Language in Society, 11,* 77–104.

O'Donnell, R. C., Griffin, W. J. & Norris, R. C. (1969). *Syntax of kindergarten and elementary school children: A transformational analysis.* Research Report Number 8. Champaign, IL: National Council of Teachers of English.

Ogbu, J. U. (1982). Societal forces as a context of ghetto children's school failure. In L. Feagans, and D. C. Farron (Eds.), *The language of children reared in poverty.* New York: Academic Press.

Olson, D. (1984). "See! Jumping!" Some oral language antecedents to literacy. In H. Goelman, A. A. Oberg, & F. Smith (Eds.), *Awakening to literacy.* Exeter, NH: Heinemann.

Palmer, F. H., & Siegel, R. J. (1977). Minimal intervention at ages two and three and subsequent intellective changes. In M. C. Day, and R. K. Parker (Eds.), *The preschool in action: Exploring early childhood programs.* Boston: Allyn and Bacon.

Pascarella, E. T., & Pflaum, S. W. (1981). The interaction of children's attributions and level of control over error correction in reading instruction. *Journal of Educational Psychology, 73,* 533–540.

Patterson, F. G. (1980). Innovative uses of language by a gorilla: A case study. In K. E. Nelson (Ed.), *Children's language* (Vol. 2). New York: Gardner Press.

Peisach, E. C. (1965). Children's comprehension of teacher and peer speech. *Child Development, 36,* 146–180.

Perfetti, C. A. (1984). Reading acquisition and beyond: Decoding includes cognition. *American Journal of Education, 93,* 40–60.

Pflaum, S. W. (1973). Expansion of meaning vocabulary: Strategies for classroom instruction. *Elementary English,* 89–93.

Pflaum, S. (1978). Language and reading acquisition for the English-speaking minority student. In S. Pflaum (Ed.), *Aspects of reading education.* National Society for the Study of Education. Berkeley, CA: McCutchan.

Pflaum, S. W. (1979). Diagnosis in oral reading. *The Reading Teacher, 33,* 278–284.

Pflaum, S. W., & Pascarella, E. T. (1980). Interactive effects of prior reading achievement and training in context of learning-disabled children. *Reading Research Quarterly, 16,* 138–158.

Pflaum, S. W., Pascarella, E. T., Boswick, M., & Auer, C. (1980). The influence of pupil behaviors and pupil status factors in teacher behaviors during oral reading lessons. *Journal of Educational Research, 14,* 99–105.

Pflaum, S. W., Walberg, H. J., Karegianes, M. L., & Rasher, S. P. (1980). Reading instruction: A quantitative analysis. *Educational Researcher, 9,* 12–18.

Piaget, J. (1955). *The language and thought of the child.* New York: Meridian.

Piaget, J., & Inhelder, B. (1969). *The psychology of the child.* New York: Basic Books.

Popp, H. M. (1975). Current practices in the teaching of beginning reading. In J. B. Carroll, & J. Chall (Eds.), *Toward a literate society: The report of the Committee on Reading of the National Academy of Education.* New York: McGraw-Hill.

Ramsey, J. (1972). A comparison of first grade negro dialect and standard English. *Elementary English, 49,* 688–696.

Read, C. (1971). Pre-school children's knowledge of English phonology. *Harvard Educational Review, 41,* 1–34.

Reading Unlimited (1976). Glenview, IL: Scott Foresman.

Rey, H. A. (1941, renewed 1969). *Curious George.* Boston: Houghton Mifflin.

Riske, K. (1982). Unpublished masters paper, University of Illinois at Chicago.

Roberts, L. G. (1973). Observation and analysis of first-graders' oral reading errors and corrections and the accompanying teacher response and teacher pupil interaction. *Dissertation Abstracts, 37,* 4998A.

Rosenshine, B., & Stevens, R. (1984). Classroom instruction in reading. In P. D. Pearson, R. Barr, M. L. Kamil, & P. Mosenthal (Eds.), *Handbook of reading research.* New York: Longman.

Rosenthal, R., & Jacobson, L. (1968). *Pygmalion in the classroom: Teacher expectations and pupils' development.* New York: Holt.

Rystrom, R. C. (1970). Dialect training and reading: A further look. *Reading Research Quarterly, 40,* 581–599.

Sakamoto, T. (1980). Reading of hiragana. In J. F. Kavanagh, & R. L. Venezky (Eds.), *Orthography, reading, and dyslexia.* Baltimore: University Park Press.

Sakamoto, T., & Makita, K. (1973). Japan. In J. Downing (Ed.), *Comparative reading.* New York: Macmillan.

Samuels, S. J. (1971). Success and failure in learning to read: A critique of the research. In F. B. Davis, *Literature of research in reading with emphasis on models.* New Brunswick, NJ: School of Education, Rutgers.

Sanders, T. S. (1981). Three first graders' concept of word and concepts about the language of literacy instruction. In M. L. Kamil (Ed.), *Directions in reading: Research and instruction.* National Reading Conference.

Schacter, F. F. (1979). *Everyday mother talk to toddlers: Early intervention.* New York: Academic Press.

Schell, R. E. (1972). *Letters and sounds: A manual for reading instruction.* Englewood Cliffs, NJ: Prentice-Hall.

Schiefflin, B. B., & Cochran-Smith, M. (1984). Learning to read culturally: Literacy before schooling. In H. Goelman, A. A. Oberg, & F. Smith (Eds.), *Awakening to literacy.* Exeter, NH: Heinemann.

Schiefflin, B. B., & Ochs, E. (1983). A cultural perspective on the transition from prelinguistic to linguistic communication. In Roberta M. Golinkoff (Ed.), *The transition from prelinguistic to linguistic communication.* Hillside, NJ: Lawrence Erlbaum Associates, Publishers.

Sestini, E. (1975). Maternal values and modes of communication. Masters thesis, University of Leeds. (Reported by Tough, 1982)

Shanahan, T. (1984). Nature of the reading-writing relation: An exploratory multivariate analysis. *Journal of Educational Psychology, 76,* 466–477.

Shanahan, T. (unpublished). The reading-writing relationship: Myths and realities. University of Illinois at Chicago.

Shatz, M., & Gelman, R. (1973). The development of communication skills: Modifications in the speech of young children as a function of listener. *Monograph of the Society for Research in Child Development, 38,* 1–36.

Shatz, M., & Gelman, R. (1977). Beyond syntax:The influence of conversational constraints on speech modification. In C. E. Snow, & C. A. Ferguson (Eds.), *Talking to children:Language input and acquisition*. Cambridge: Cambridge University Press.

Shriner, T. H., & Minder, L. (1968). The phonological in the language of disadvantaged children. *Journal of Speech and Hearing Research, 11*, 604–610.

Shuy, R. W. (1971). Untitled paper at Linguistic Society meeting, Minneapolis, MN, University of Minnesota.

Shuy, R. W., Wolfram, W. H., & Riley, W. K. (1966). *Linguistic correlates of social stratification in Detroit speech*. Final report, Washington, D. C.: Office of Education, pp. 1–10.

Simons, H. D., & Johnson, K. R. (1974). Black English syntax and reading interference. *Research in the Teaching of English, 8*, 339–358.

Sinclair-deZwart, H. (1973). Language acquisition and cognitive development. In T. E. Moore (Ed.), *Cognitive development and the acquisition of language*. New York: Academic Press.

Skinner, B. F. (1957). *Verbal behavior*. Boston: Appleton-Century-Crofts, Inc.

Smith, E. B., Goodman, K. S., & Meredith, R. (1970). *Language and thinking in the elementary school*. New York: Holt, Rinehart and Winston.

Smith, F. (1971). *Understanding reading*. New York: Holt, Rinehart and Winston.

Smith, F. (1979). Conflicting approaches to reading research and instruction. In L. B. Resnick, & P. A. Weaver (Eds.), *Theory and practice of early reading* (Vol. 2). Hillside, NJ: Erlbaum.

Smith, F. (1984). The creative achievement of literacy. In H. Goelman, A. A. Oberg, & F. Smith (Eds.), *Awakening to literacy*. Exeter, NH: Heinemann.

Snow, C. E. (1977). Mothers' speech research: From input to interaction. In C. E. Snow, & C. A. Ferguson (Eds.), *Talking to children: Language input and acquisition*. Cambridge: Cambridge University Press.

Snow, C. E. (1982). Knowledge and the use of language. In L. Feagans & D. C. Farron (Eds.), *The language of children reared in poverty*. New York: Academic Press.

Snow, C. E. (1983). Literacy and language: Relationships during the preschool years. *Harvard Educational Review, 53*, 165–189.

Snow, C. E., Dubben, C., & DeBlariw, A. (1982). Routines in mother-child interaction. In L. Feagans, & D. C. Farron (Eds.), *The language of children reared in poverty*. New York: Academic Press.

Snow, C., & Goldfield, B. (1982). Building stories: The emergence of information structures from conversation. In D. Tannen (Ed.), *Analyzing discourse: Text and talk*. Washington: Georgetown University Press.

Snow, C. E., & Ninio, A. (forthcoming). The contracts of literacy: What children learn from learning to read books. In W. Teale, & E. Sulzby (Eds.), *Emergent literacy: Writing and reading*. Norwood, NJ: Ablex.

Soar, R. S. (1973). *Follow-through classroom process measurement and pupil growth (1970–1971): Final report*. Gainesville: University of Florida. (Cited by Rosenshrine and Stevens, 1984.)

Spache, G. D. (1963/1972). *Diagnostic reading scales*. Monterey, CA: CTB/McGraw-Hill.

Spache, G. D. et al. (1966). A longitudinal first-grade reading readiness program. *Reading Teacher, 19*, 580–584.

Stallard, C. (1977). Effect of selected prereading skills and subsequent first grade achievement. Paper at Illinois Reading Council.

Stauffer, R. C. (1970). *The language experience approach to the teaching of reading.* New York: Harper.

Stein, M. L. (1985). Phonics instruction in beginning programs. Paper presented at American Educational Research Association, Chicago.

Stein, N. L., & Glenn, C. G. (1979). An analysis of story comprehension in elementary school children. In R. O. Freedle (Ed.), *Advances in discourse processing* (Vol. 2). Norwood, NJ: Ablex.

Sternberg, D. D., and Yamada, J. (1978). Are whole word Kanji easier to learn than syllable Kana? *Reading Research Quarterly, 14,* 88–99.

Sternhell, C. (1984). Bellow's typewriters and other tics of the trade. *New York Times Book Review,* September 2.

Steward, M., & Steward, D. (1973). The observation of Anglo-Mexican and Chinese-American mothers teaching their young sons. *Child Development, 44,* 329–337.

Stewart, W. A. (1970). Toward a history of American negro dialect. In F. Williams (Ed.), *Language and poverty: Perspectives on a theme.* Chicago: Markham.

Sulzby, E. (1981). Kindergarteners begin to read their own compositions: Beginning readers' developing knowledge about written languages project. Final Report to the Research Committee of the National Council of Teachers of English.

Sulzby, E. (forthcoming). Writing and reading: Signs of oral and written language organization in the young child. In W. Teale, & E. Sulzby (Eds.), *Emergent literacy: Writing and reading.* Norwood, NJ: Ablex.

Sulzby, E. (in press). Children's emergent reading of favorite storybooks: A developmental study. *Reading Research Quarterly.*

Tavris, C. (1976). Compensatory education: The glass is half full. *Psychology Today, 10,* 63–74.

Taylor, D. (forthcoming). Creating a family story. In W. Teale, and E. Sulzby (Eds.), *Emergent literacy: Writing and reading.* Norwood, NJ: Ablex.

Taylor, M., & Ortony, A. (1981). *Figurative devices in black language: Some psycholinguistic observations.* Center for the Study of Reading. University of Illinois at Urbana-Champaign.

Teale, W. H. (forthcoming). Home background and young children's literacy development. In W. H. Teale, & E. Sulzby (Eds.), *Emergent literacy: Writing and reading.* Norwood, NJ: Ablex.

Teale, W. H. (1984). Reading to young children: Its significance for literacy development. In H. Goelman, A. A. Oberg, & F. Smith (Eds.), *Awakening to literacy.* Exeter, NH: Heinemann.

Temple, C. A., Nathan, R. G., & Burris, N. A. (1982). *The beginnings of writing.* Boston: Allyn and Bacon.

Thorndike, E. L. (1973). *Reading comprehension education in fifteen countries: An empirical study.* New York: Wiley.

Torrey, J. W. (1973). Learning to read without a teacher: A case study. In F. Smith (Ed.), *Psycholinguistics and reading.* New York: Holt, Rinehart and Winston.

Tough, J. (1973). *Focus on meaning. Talking to some purpose with young children.* London: George Allen and Unwin.

Tough, J. (1982). Language, poverty, and disadvantage in school. In L. Feagans, and D. C. Farron (Eds.), *The language of children reared in poverty.* New York: Academic Press.

Van Lawick-Goodall, J. (1971). *In the shadow of man.* Boston: Houghton Mifflin.

Vellutino, F. R. (1977). Alternative conceptualizations of dyslexia. Evidence in support of a verbal-deficit hypothesis. *Harvard Education Review, 47,* 334–354.

Velten, H. (1943). The growth of phonemic and lexical patterns in infant language. *Language, 19,* 281–292.

Venezky, R. L. (1978). Two approaches to reading assessment: A comparison of apples and oranges. In S. W. Pflaum (Ed.), *Aspects of reading education.* National Society for the Study of Education. Berkeley, CA: McCutchan.

Venezky, R. L. (1981). Non-standard language and reading—Ten years later. In J. R. Edwards (Ed.), *The social psychology of reading.* Institute of Modern Languages. Silver Spring, MD: The Language People.

Vygotsky, L. S. (1962). *Thought and language* (Edited and translated by E. Haufman, & G. Vakas.). Cambridge: The M.I.T. Press.

Vygotsky, L. S. (1978). *Mind in society* (Edited by M. Cole, V. John-Steiner, S. Scribner, & E. Souberman.). Cambridge: Harvard University Press.

Walberg, H. K. (1984). Improving the productivity of America's schools. *Educational Leadership, 41,* 19–30.

Weber, R. M. (1970a). A linguistic analysis of first-grade reading errors. *Reading Research Quarterly, 3,* 429–451.

Weber, R. M. (1970b). First-graders use of grammatical context in reading. In H. Levin, & H. P. Williams (Eds.), *Basic studies in reading.* New York: Basic Books.

Weener, P. D. (1969). Social dialect difference and the recall of verbal messages. *Journal of Educational Psychology, 60,* 194–199.

Weir, R. (1962). *Language in the crib.* The Hague: Morton.

Wells, G. (1981). *Learning through interaction: The study of language development.* Cambridge: Cambridge University Press.

Williams, F. (1970). Psychological correlates of speech characteristics on sounding "disadvantaged." *Journal of Speech and Hearing Research, 13,* 472–488.

Williams, F., Whitehead, J. L., & Miller, L. M. (1971). Ethnic stereotyping and judgements of children's speech. *Speech Monographs, 38,* 166–170.

Williams, F., Whitehead, J. L., & Miller, L. M. (1972). Relations between language attitudes and teacher expectancy. *American Educational Research Journal, 9,* 263–275.

Wolfram, W. (1970). Sociolinguistic alternatives in teaching reading to non-standard speakers. *Reading Research Quarterly, 6,* 9–33.

Wolfram, W., & Whiteman, M. (1971). The role of dialect interference in composition. *The Florida FL Reporter, 9,* 34–39, 59.

Woods, M., & Moe, A. (1981). *Analytical reading inventory* (3rd ed.). Columbus: Charles Merrill.

Woodward, A. (1985). A historical study of reading textbook teachers guides. Paper presented at American Educational Research Association, Chicago.

Zutell, J. (1981). Cognitive development, metalinguistic ability and invented spellings: Comparison and correlations. In M. L. Kamil (Ed.), *Research and instruction.* National Reading Conference.

Index

The Author

Susanna Pflaum received her bachelor's degree from Radcliffe College, her master's from Harvard Graduate School of Education, and her doctorate from Florida State University. She taught elementary school in Newton, Massachusetts, and San German, Puerto Rico. Formerly a Professor of Education and Dean of the Honors College at the University of Illinois at Chicago, Dr. Pflaum is currently professor and dean of the School of Education, Queens College, City University of New York. In addition to *The Development of Language and Literacy in Young Children*, Dr. Pflaum has edited the book *Aspects of Reading Education* and has authored or coauthored a number of papers in education research journals.